THEY FIGHT LIKE SOLDIERS,
THEY DIE LIKE CHILDREN

ALSO BY ROMÉO DALLAIRE

Shake Hands With the Devil

THEY FIGHT LIKE SOLDIERS, THEY DIE LIKE CHILDREN

ROMEO DALLAIRE

Hutchinson
London

Published by Hutchinson 2010

2 4 6 8 10 9 7 5 3 1

Copyright © Roméo A. Dallaire, LGen (ret) Inc.

First published in Great Britain in 2010 by
Hutchinson
Random House, 20 Vauxhall Bridge Road,
London SW1V 2SA

www.rbooks.co.uk

Addresses for companies within The Random House Group Limited can be
found at: www.randomhouse.co.uk/offices.htm

The Random House Group Limited Reg. No. 954009

A CIP catalogue record for this book
is available from the British Library

Trade Paperback ISBN 9780091796327
Hardback ISBN 9780091796310

The Random House Group Limited supports The Forest Stewardship
Council (FSC), the leading international forest certification organisation. All
our titles that are printed on Greenpeace approved FSC certified paper carry
the FSC logo. Our paper procurement policy can be found at:
www.rbooks.co.uk/environment

Mixed Sources
Product group from well-managed
forests and other controlled sources
www.fsc.org Cert no. TT-COC-2139
© 1996 Forest Stewardship Council
FSC

Printed and bound in Great Britain by
CPI Mackays, Chatham, ME5 8TD

The child, face and hands caked in red earth, wearing a dirty, ill-fitting bush uniform with a cross dangling from a chain around his neck, furtively aimed a machine gun at me. As bullets started to spew from the barrel, the child's eyes flared in hate. Where is that child today?

CONTENTS

FOREWORD
by Ishmael Beah

I AM SIMULTANEOUSLY GRATEFUL and deeply troubled to be writing a foreword for this very important work that aims to shed new light on how to end the use of children in war. Grateful that I am alive and was lucky enough to survive the civil war in my country, Sierra Leone, where I fought as a child soldier at the age of thirteen. My survival has allowed me to put a human face to this experience. I am also grateful for the fact that some measures have been taken on the international front to remove children from war, hence the possibility of my writing at this moment in time.

However, I am also deeply troubled because the usage of children in war continues and international and national mechanisms to prevent this appalling phenomenon—and to hold accountable those responsible for such acts—remain weak. Troubled, because what happened to my childhood and continues to destroy lives of children and their childhoods can be prevented and yet nothing concrete has been done to date.

As you read this, there is a child as young as eight, nine, ten and up to seventeen years of age in Latin America, Asia, Africa and the Middle East, who is at the brink of losing his or her childhood to war, who is starting on the path of believing that violence is an acceptable part of life. I have yet to meet a parent who would like such a life for their child. So why should the world turn a blind eye on such a paramount problem, one that will undoubtedly destroy the moral and ethical foundations of a majority of the next generation? I do not have any explanation for this blindness to the countless lives of children that have been lost, that have been amputated, the countless children who have become traumatized and lost entire families. What I do know is that there is interest in the issue and that over the years much has been learned about children who are caught up in war. As a result, a greater awareness has come about and support to create international standards to deal with this issue has grown exponentially. But this growth in awareness and the push for international legal and non-legal standards, though admirable, has yielded far too little or no impact on the ground in places of conflict and in the lives of the children who are at risk of entering conflict.

Vigorous work to bring international attention to the issue of children in conflict began in 1996, punctuated by Graça Machel's report *The Impact of Armed Conflict on Children*. Since then, international instruments such as the Optional Protocol to the Convention on the Rights of the Child on the involvement of children in armed conflict and United Nations (UN) Security Council resolutions 1612 and 1882 (enacted to report and monitor the use of child soldiers and to hold recruiters accountable) have come into existence. In addition, there are various declarations and principles at regional and sub-regional levels to support and further expand on the existing international instruments. Unfortunately, in my view there are no workable mechanisms with direct influence in the field in place to implement these instruments. As the enforcement mechanisms continue to be ineffective, the possibility of more children finding themselves in the theatre of war increases.

As someone who knows first-hand the impact of war on children, I am constantly in search of new ideas of how to end this scourge. I strongly believe that the Child Soldiers Initiative (CSI), developed and led by Lieutenant-General the Hon. Roméo A. Dallaire (Ret'd) in association with the Centre for Foreign Policy Studies, Dalhousie University, is an innovative project that goes at the root of the problem. It gathers all sectors and stakeholders involved in dealing with children in armed conflict to not only put an end to their use and recruitment but to eradicate the very concept of "child soldier" and to generate a strong global political will that is presently lacking.

It is my hope that through the pages of this remarkable book, you will discover groundbreaking thoughts on building partnerships and networks to enhance the global movement to end child soldiering; you will gain new and holistic insights on what constitutes a child soldier; you will learn more about girl soldiers, who have not been fully considered in the discussion of this issue; you will discover methods on how to influence national policies and the training of security forces; and you will find practical steps that will foster better coordination between security forces and humanitarian efforts.

I challenge you to read this important and timely work and discover that we as human beings, as nations, as the international community, have the capacity to end the use of children in war. We must not waste another minute as the task is clearly outlined in these pages.

Ishmael Beah,
author of A *Long Way Gone: Memoirs of a Boy Soldier*

INTRODUCTION

*The blue sky glittered like a new-honed knife . . . The purity of the sky
upset me. Give me a good black storm in which the enemy is plainly
visible. I can measure its extent and prepare myself for its attack.*
—ANTOINE DE SAINT-EXUPÉRY, WIND, SAND AND STARS

MAGINE YOURSELF ON A HILLSIDE in the chaotic throes of
war, with a sea of innocents behind you whom you are tasked
by duty, honour, mandate and ethics to protect. Your weapon
is drawn, and you are prepared for the attack. Over the hilltop,
right in front of you, comes a troop of marauding rebel soldiers
with rifles and machetes. You raise your own weapon and peer
through the magnifying gunsight at the leader.

Shock hits as you realize this soldier is not a man nor a professional—not your equal in age, strength, training, understanding.
This soldier is a child, in the tattered remnants of a military
uniform, with dozens more children behind him.

As you stare at him, you picture yourself in a flash, aged ten,
playing war games in the woods. For a split second, you are
transported to the world of childhood, with its make-believe, its
wonder, its potential. And in that split second, you must decide
your own fate, the fate of the villagers under your protection, and
of these children in front of you. Do you treat this person aiming

his weapon at you as a soldier or a child? If you do nothing, dozens will be slaughtered and you put your own life at risk. If you fire to frighten or disarm, you begin a doomed and bloody shootout. Fire back to kill, as you would at an adult, and you will save a village, but at what cost?

I was a soldier. A peacekeeper. A general. Years have now passed since I stood among the corpses of a human destruction that rivalled anything Dante could have imagined. The smells, the sights, the terrible sounds of the dying in Rwanda have been damped down in my psyche to a dull roar through constant therapy and an unrelenting regimen of medication.

But no similar intervention has liberated me from the ethical dilemma that spat in my face far too often during that catastrophic period of inhumanity in Rwanda, one hundred days in 1994 that saw 800,000 human beings slaughtered in a genocide no one in the international community could muster the will to stop.

Was that rebel coming over the hill a soldier or a child? Was that rebel acting of his or her own free will or because he or she was coerced and indoctrinated? Is a child still a child when pressing the barrel of a gun to your chest? Those child soldiers' eyes were wide and brilliant, screaming of pain and anguish and fear and hatred; what had they seen and what effect had it had on their souls?

"Civil" is ironically what we call a war where civilians are the primary target, and power over them is the principal gain—a war where combatants mingle with civilians and use them as shields, as camouflage, as bait and as recruits for the "cause." In the failed states and war-plagued regions of the globe, young recruits exist in unlimited numbers, available at will.

It may seem unimaginable to you that child soldiers exist. It seemed impossible to me when I first encountered them that anyone would abuse the state of childhood so ruthlessly. And yet the reality for many rebel and gang leaders, and even state governments, is that there is no more complete end-to-end weapon system in the inventory of war machines than the child soldier. Its negligible technology, simple sustainment requirements, unlimited versatility in all possible facets of low-intensity conflict, and capacity for barbarism has made the child soldier the weapon of choice in over thirty conflicts around the world, for governments and non-state actors alike. Man has created the ultimate cheap, expendable, yet sophisticated human weapon, at the expense of humanity's own future: its children.

Thanks to a worldwide proliferation of light weapons and ammunition, combined with the limitless resource of children as a result of the overpopulation in developing countries in conflict, such as we see in so many cases in Africa, there is no more readily available, cost-effective and renewable weapon system in existence today. Desperate children, boys *and* girls, are cheap to sustain, have no real sense of fear, and are limitless in the perverse directions they can be manipulated through drugs and indoctrination since they have not yet developed a concept of justice and have been ripped away from their families to fend in the new perverted family of armed force.

Children are vulnerable and easy to catch, just like minnows in a pond, especially in places where families are being destroyed by famine, epidemic, AIDS, warring factions. Children are faceless and they are considered expendable. The guns are light enough for children to carry, and they are plentiful. There are illicit arms traders in the dozens who (for blood diamonds, especially) are most accommodating. The children dig up the diamonds and sustain the weaponry, and they are the expendable platform to conduct the killing. Girls are an even greater asset, as they can do everything that boys can do, and so much more. They set up bivouacs, prepare the food, control the younger children and are used as sex slaves and bush wives.

Children are excellent as combatants, as bait for ambushes, as cannon fodder. They are light to transport but still heavy enough to explode land mines so adults can move safely in their wake.

Young children are walking the earth right now with no sense of youth, of imaginary worlds, of joy, of love, of human warmth. They are not truly children in any definition except biological. But of course they are still children, are they not? Have conflict, abject poverty and abandonment mutated them into some other type of being that is neither child nor adult? A category of their own that does not fit any description of what civilizations over the millennia have called a child?

What has humanity created? What have we permitted to be created? Alive and breathing in the hundreds of thousands in not-so-far-off lands are beings who have the physical form of children, yet who have been robbed of the spirit, the innocence, the essence of childhood.

It is hard for me to believe that in the twenty-first century, after hundreds of years of renaissance, of enlightenment, of modernity and human rights, we are faced with child soldiers in their hundreds of thousands. Where do we go from here?

As I will describe later in the book, my first encounter with child soldiers came in 1993 in Rwanda, where I was serving as the UN force commander of UNAMIR (United Nations Assistance Mission for Rwanda). It was not meant to be a hot spot of an assignment. I was sent with minimal troops to help ensure that all parties adhered to the peace agreement that had been brokered between the government and the Rwandan Patriotic Front (RPF), a rebel army composed mainly of second-generation refugee Tutsis who had won significant military victories against the regime. I was also to help prepare the way for democratic elections that were designed to enshrine power-sharing between the Hutu majority and the Tutsi minority. While in Rwanda I bore witness to preparations for what ultimately became a genocide designed to annihilate an entire ethnic group, the Tutsis, along with moderate Hutus and opposition politicians. Despite my increasingly desperate pleas and the presentation of overwhelming evidence, the international community insisted that I not, under any circumstances, interfere in these preparations, raid arms caches or otherwise take action. I was commanding a peacekeeping mission, not fighting a war.

A hundred days. Eight hundred thousand innocent people slaughtered.

I stayed at my post throughout the genocide that began on April 6, 1994, along with a small contingent of Canadian and African—mostly Ghanaian—soldiers who decided to stay with me, doing what we could, which was nowhere near enough.

Even now, a sensation, especially a smell, can send me back to scenes from that slaughter. I hear a sticky, tacky sound, and then flash to decaying bodies slithering like fish in the net of an open mass grave, and I am briefly unable to extricate myself from this quicksand of memory.

Despite the increased responsibilities and the more and more senior appointments I took on after I got back to Canada in September 1994, I spent the next six years intensely reliving the Rwandan genocide—in my mind, at podiums around the world, and at the International Criminal Tribunal for Rwanda. I made no progress in healing. Rather, I maintained a pace designed to drive myself to the self-destruction I felt I owed the people of Rwanda as retribution for my part in the failure of the international community to come to their aid.

Then, in April 2000, I was given a medical release from the Canadian Forces and asked to clear out my office at National Defence Headquarters. April, of course, is the anniversary of the beginning of the genocide, and is a difficult month for anyone with ties to those horrible events. Though I understood that I was no longer able to cope with my job as assistant deputy minister (human resources—military) at National Defence, I could not imagine being cut loose from military life, which had been my first love through my childhood as the son of a non-commissioned officer (NCO) in the Canadian Army and my own reality for thirty-six years. Since I also had absolutely no idea of what I would (or could) do in civilian life, I entered a period of ever more turbulent days and nights that no amount of medication could ease. I could not imagine being "retired," with nothing but therapy to break the hamster wheel of regret, self-doubt and self-flagellation that left me relentlessly rethinking every action I'd taken, every order I'd given, through every moment of my time in Kigali.

One morning during the exit process from the forces, I received a standard briefing from the group public affairs officer, and he happened to mention that his wife was heavily involved at Foreign Affairs with a large international conference on war-affected children, which was to be held that September in Winnipeg. She and I soon spoke, and we agreed that I should present a paper. To my surprise, her boss endorsed her recommendation.

I had given hundreds of speeches and written thousands of words on Rwanda, but there had always been one reality of the genocide that I hadn't allowed myself to fully explore. It was one thing to remind people of the children who had been orphaned, maimed or murdered, and another thing to remember them myself. The usual mental image conjured by the phrase "war-affected children" is of the child victims of conflict, and I had encountered many vivid, heartbreaking examples.

But what about the other kind of war-affected child, the one compelled to pick up the machete or the gun, the one who becomes a crucial part of the killing machine? I had also met many such children in Rwanda and had witnessed the consequences of their work: they inhabited my nightmares.

As a military commander I'd been forced to deal with the fact that children were foot soldiers of both the genocide and the resistance in Rwanda—much as I still wanted to write them off as an aberration, a one-time-only historical phenomenon. I'd blocked the knowledge out of my mind: there were so many horrors, so many unthinkable things. Now I decided I was finally going to talk about the children. All of them.

What I couldn't know when I agreed to prepare a paper and participate on a panel of "experts" on war-affected children was that I was about to find a vocation to replace my long commitment to the military—a calling to act on behalf of children affected by war, children drawn into the arena of war as child soldiers. To this day, this commitment is the driving force of my humanitarian work, and of this book.

By 2000, humanitarians, non-governmental organizations (NGOs) and governments had made great strides at identifying the scope of the crisis facing our children and in putting the issue of child soldiers on the world agenda. The UN achieved its landmark Convention on the Rights of the Child in 1989. The most significant work since then had been done by Graça Machel, the widow of the Mozambican president Samora Machel (killed in a plane crash in South Africa in 1986), who was appointed by the UN to lead a study focused sharply on the dangers to children who found themselves in the midst of war, as victims or as victimized perpetrators. Her report, "The Impact of Armed Conflict on Children," presented to the UN General Assembly in 1996, called on the international community not just to note these harsh realities but to respond. And to some extent it did, appointing a UN special representative on children and armed conflict and (around the time I was being retired from the Canadian Forces) adopting an optional protocol to the Convention on the Rights of the Child that pledged its signatories to limit the military use of children.

The Canadian government was actively involved in the diplomatic and UN action on the issue, riding a wave of optimism over its ability to play a leadership role on humanitarian and human security issues. More than optimism, in fact, since the Ottawa Treaty to ban land mines was proof that Canada could in fact lead global change. Lloyd Axworthy, then the minister of foreign affairs, and Maria Minna, the minister in charge of the Canadian International Development Agency (CIDA), had now dedicated themselves to drawing attention to the gaps in the international efforts to protect children affected by war. The conference at which I'd just been invited to speak turned out to be the first global ministerial-level conference on the issue, drawing delegations from 132 countries and 126 NGOs, as well as representatives from the UN, the corporate sector and academia, and fifty youth delegates who were to bring the voices of child soldiers and child victims into the discussion during two days of dedicated talks.

We convened in Winnipeg on September 10, 2000, and I spoke on the second day of the section of the conference devoted to hearing from those in the know. The relatively small room where we met was packed to the rafters with attendees and media. Since this was my first foray into the spotlight out of uniform, I suspected that most of the journalists were interested in my command of the Rwandan mission, and questions during the scrum before the session proved me right. That was fine in a way, as it provided me with an initiation into speaking my mind without previous guidance from government officials on what to say or avoid saying.

My fellow panellists spoke of war-affected children as victims of circumstance, describing various parts of the world where failing states were unable to stop massive crimes against humanity, including the abduction and abuse of children by the belligerents. When it was my turn to speak, I remember squeezing the microphone as I described how youths in Rwanda had been indoctrinated by extremist ideologues, had been captured by the mass hysteria of racism and hatred, and had literally chopped their way across a nation in a rampage of human destruction encouraged and energized by adult leaders and racist radio broadcasts. In Rwanda some children had been abducted by one force or another and others were victims and innocents, but many were disenfranchised youths enticed by power, by the machismo of weapons, by the idea of belonging to an organization that was feared by all. At the end of my twenty minutes or so, I was sweating—literally burning with the desire that people understand how inconceivable it was for children to be used in this fashion. I don't remember much about the question period after the panel, but I do remember the absolute silence in the room when it was my turn to respond, as if the audience was expecting me to take them somewhere they did not want to imagine. To my own chagrin, I delivered on that expectation with vivid scenes from the genocide. But my point was that we had to stop extremist adults from turning children into killing machines.

Maria Minna had attended the session, and later that night offered to make me a member of Canada's official delegation to the conference so that I could participate in the resolution-framing part of the exercise. At the closing news conference, the minister announced that she had made me a special advisor on war-affected children to CIDA, reporting to her, the first position of its kind. I could not have asked for a better place from which to address the moral, ethical and legal dilemmas of using children, arming them and employing them as the principal weapon in conflict. I now had the chance to influence the actions of my own country through the minister, to help make war-affected children and child soldiers a *cause célèbre*.

As the minister's special advisor, I took my first trip back to Africa since I'd come home from Rwanda, travelling to Sierra Leone and Guinea in 2001 to gather information on what was happening to African children, attempt to advance the demobilization process that was already launched, and bring their stories and some ideas for long-term solutions back with me. As I was operating outside the regular bureaucratic stream, and because I had been a general not a humanitarian groomed inside the UN or on the board of an NGO, I soon found that I came at the issues from a different place than most.

I met with the UN political leaders and military commanders, and talked to peacekeepers at all levels, right down to the young corporal guarding a demobilization site. They spoke of frictions and difficulties in coordinating with their civilian colleagues from the political and humanitarian realms and how complex it was to gain their confidence and support in security matters. Because I was retired from the military, those same NGO workers so often leery of people in uniform briefed me equally candidly, though I think the old hands in the world of humanitarian work probably viewed me as more odd than useful. As for the leaders of the armed groups and the child soldiers themselves, my rank gave me access to their world view in a way that wasn't offered to either the aid workers or the UN troops. I came away thinking that maybe I really would be able to dig into the nature of this beast from a different angle than my civilian colleagues.

What stood out starkly for me then was the continued influence that the child soldier leaders had on their peers—and even on the adults delivering the demobilization, rehabilitation and reintegration programmes. These were fourteen-year-olds who were going on twenty-five, who were still very much in charge and who were not going to buy into any simplistic Dick-and-Jane rehab programme delivered by adults, no matter how well-meaning. They were seeking much more than just a short-term return programme to social normality. They could influence and they could command, and they demanded recognition of the power, the potential and the respect they had earned over years in the bush. They could spell the success or failure of any programme; to work effectively with them, the adults needed to realize who they were dealing with, and figure out how to help these youths find a path away from brutal addiction to power, toward using their powers of leadership to beneficial ends.

Later I travelled to Brazil to meet children who'd been hauled into the gang wars that raged in the *favelas* of places like Rio de Janeiro, and it struck me that the drug lords found children useful for the same reasons that combatants in Africa did: they were easily recruited, cheap to maintain, they could fire a light submachine gun as well as any adult, and occasionally the fact that they were children could disconcert an opponent for a crucial moment.

—

At the same time as my involvement in the subject of child soldiers deepened, I was also at last working on my account of the genocide, *Shake Hands with the Devil,* published in Canada in the fall of 2003. Needless to say, the act of disinterring memories and researching every step and misstep was both gruelling and gruesomely clarifying. I was able to travel back to Kigali for the tenth anniversary commemoration of the genocide in April 2004 with a certain amount of strength drawn from my close examination of events, and pay tribute to the lost, to the mourners, to the survivors, without being completely hijacked by shame. For a time, the attention paid to the book threw me full-time into the work of genocide prevention, and when I was offered a fellowship for the academic year of 2004–2005 at the Carr Center for Human Rights Policy, which is part of the John F. Kennedy School of Government at Harvard University, I believed that my academic and research work would focus on conflict resolution, and the new role of peacekeepers actively attempting to make peace, not just enforce it, in the planet's numerous barbaric wars in failing states.

But in the end, the children kept drawing me onward. Since the Machel report had been released in 1996, there had been some research done on the recruitment of children—mostly anecdotal—and on the disarmament, demobilization, rehabilitation and reintegration of child soldiers, but there was almost no analysis of the child's own experience during conflict and even less on the recruiters and the commanders using them. Absolutely no one was looking at the tactical advantage of using children in war, and no cohesive or concrete results were coming forth as to why they were being recruited in the first place let alone what made them so valuable to commanders. After some cursory research, I discovered that no country had developed tactical responses to this issue from the military or even the policing point of view. No doctrine existed to deal with child soldiers in the field, even though soldiers and police were facing them daily. This new weapon of war had snuck into the inventory of conflicts around the world and—despite the diplomatic conventions and protocols we were passing and signing and ratifying—we were acting as if it wasn't there. Much money and effort were being spent, are still being spent, on picking up the pieces in post-conflict settings. Children were being cared for in the aftermath of war, but no one was thinking of ways to neutralize this weapon, nor successfully preventing child recruitment in the first place.

My experience in Rwanda taught me that soldiers—be they rebels, armed thugs or conscripts—respond to soldiers: it turned out that I could use my military rank and my operational credentials as a bridge to negotiate even with the bloodied youth leaders of the Interahamwe, whose machetes had hacked their neighbours to death. No matter what force you fight there is an unspoken respect for rank that could be taken advantage of. Rebel leaders who relied on child soldiers had been bombarded with attention from the NGOs, which would of course never discuss the actual tactical and strategic value of the use of children with them, but they had never been approached by a former senior operational commander in a humanitarian role. No one seemed to be speaking the language the rebel leaders were using when it came to their primary operational forces, these child soldiers. No one was making the argument that the inexhaustible availability of child soldiers as well as the proliferation of small arms were actually fuelling conflict and keeping wars going.

Quickly my research began to focus on children being used as weapons of war. *Tools* used by adults to wage war. Much like a soldier would use his gun or grenade, the child had become another weapon in their repertoire. The thesis of my research became clear: in these conflicts around the world, and especially on the African continent, children had become a weapon of choice for commanders. Indispensable. My very keen and adroit research team was soon deep in the exploration of what exactly made this weapon system so attractive to commanders. Beyond the ubiquity of children, what made them a military weapon of choice?

I was amazed to find that my new military or operational vocabulary shocked people working in the field. But out of it came my mission and the mission of this book. If it is possible to use a child as a weapon system, it should be possible to decommission or neutralize that weapon system: to eradicate the use of child soldiers. Not to eradicate the child, but to eradicate the use of that child in war.

This book explores how I am attempting to decommission a weapon system that is itself a crime against humanity yet is used extensively in the ongoing conflicts around the globe. On the battlefield, how does one render such a weapon ineffective—even turn it into an impediment? How does one prevent such a choice weapon from being used in the first place? How does one change these human weapons into plowshares after demobilization?

Child soldiers are not weathered warriors who have consciously, willingly and wholeheartedly committed their adult life to the use of force against others and are prepared to pay the price of the same against them. We are not speaking of Sparta and Athens in ancient times, where young boys (and only boys) were selected by competition and breeding to be indoctrinated into the warrior caste through years of education in the knowledge of war, of training to hone weapon-handling skills, of experience through deliberate apprenticeships mentored by seniors, of bathing in the stories of exploits of great fighters and of being led by wise and astute generals once they were of age. Nor are they combatants in countries that consider the use of force as limited exclusively for protection and self-interest, and use it under strict rules and codes, whereby civilian leaders issue mandates to those who are professionals in the art of war and conduct themselves within an honourable ethos. These children fight and die where there seem to be no rules except self-preservation—basic survival.

There are now international and national laws against the use of children under the age of eighteen in armed combat. Couldn't we eradicate the use of child soldiers by applying those laws to the adults who recruit children to fight their wars? Couldn't we simply arrest the culprits at every opportunity and have them thrown in jail *ad vitam aeternam*? Can't we stop this impunity?

We immediately run up against the question of who will apply these laws and international arrest warrants. What political will or capital would be expended by foreign governments to go into a sovereign nation in conflict and conduct operations to arrest the adult leaders, be they from the government forces or the rebels, on the basis that either side or both sides are using children as weapons of war? And what tactics do you use to secure an arrest when these adult leaders are surrounded by drug-induced "brain-dead" child fanatics?

The 2007 Paris Principles—a culminating point in a decade of activism and legislation guided by Graça Machel, in particular— vigorously argue that the long-term impact on child soldiers is so horrifying that the international community needs to assume the responsibility for enforcing its own laws. But the response has been slow, barely noticed, uneven and often overshadowed by more pressing concerns in the search for ceasefires, truces, peace agreements and permanent freedom for the people afflicted by the conflicts.

What if, rather than waiting for the great powers of the world to rise up in unison and come crashing down on these sovereign yet imploding and chaotic states, we were able to create another solution? What if we were able to bring to the field a sort of tool kit of actions that could be taken by a variety of players and institutions attempting to solve the conflict in the first place?

What if we addressed the problem of this new low-technology weapon system by confronting it directly, on the ground and in the bush where it hides and preys on its victims? Leave to others the complex socio-economic quagmires that have created the conflict in the first place. Leave to those already well versed in these things, the demobilization, rehabilitation and reintegration of those children who have escaped, been abandoned or rounded up.

What if we actually went after the weapon system itself? What if we directly attempted to neutralize its effectiveness in the field and in the conduct of its evil crimes? What if we introduced a set of tools that would eradicate this weapon system from ever being employed or even created ever again? What if?

Today more than ever, on distant and disparate battle zones, we find the professional soldier, buoyed by years of experience and tradition in the most modern of technological instruments of war, coming face to face with the absolute opposite. It would be nearly impossible to invent a more complete antithesis to the modern, mature warrior-cum-peacekeeper than the child rebel, the child fighter, the child soldier. And what response can there be when the child combatants fire the murderous weapons in their hands? Do you kill children who kill? Do you use force to prevent their continued use of the guns they carry?

Can we actually eradicate from the minds of evil adults the very idea of using children as weapons of war? Is there room for innovative research and training to counter and prevent their use? Is there a way by which we free citizens can engage with political leaders to stop the massive abuses of children in conflict-riddled and imploding nations where poverty drives desperately corrupt and ill-begotten power?

This book is my best effort to show some of the ways in which we can answer yes to these questions. It is also an attempt, drawing on my own experience and the research I've undertaken over fifteen years, to understand the exact nature of the crime against humanity that is involved when a child is used and destroyed in this manner. A small warning to readers: I've done my best to come at these questions imaginatively as well as through facts and argument, and in three of the chapters of this book, I have created a fictional narrative involving the abduction of a child, the indoctrination of that child as a child soldier, and the moment in which that child and a UN peacekeeper meet in combat. I tell the story from the child's point of view in chapters three and four: "Kidom" and "Kidom Lost." Then in chapter eight, "The Moment: Killing a Child," I switch to the vantage point of the peacekeeper.

I believe that because this material is so painful, and because many of these children live in places many of us have never travelled, we create barriers in our own minds that prevent us from recognizing and feeling the damage that is being done to the fabric of humanity by allowing our children to be abused in conflict zones around the globe. Just as this book is a plea to protect the imaginative growth of children everywhere, it is also me putting my money where my mouth is by trying to use the power of my imagination to help the reader to connect to the reality of child soldiers. In my humble way, and with no comparison implied, I took my inspiration in this attempt from *The Little Prince*, Antoine de Saint-Exupéry's classic. I believe that none of us will hesitate to act if we at last connect to these children through the child that survives within ourselves.

Imagine yourself on a hillside.

1.

WARRIOR BOY

WHEN I WAS A CHILD, my father set out to build a cabin in the bush in the Laurentian Mountains in Quebec. The site was on a small cliff overlooking a violin-shaped lake, with virgin bush for tens of kilometres in nearly all directions around it. In the late fall and winter, the local farmers would go into the woods with their enormous horses and chains and tackles and sleighs to cut and then haul out spruce and cedar, and even the odd oak, to the provincial road where the logs would be piled sky-high until spring. I would marvel at these weather-beaten and muscle-bound farmers and their sons, who seemed to effortlessly wield enormous axes and bucksaws a hundred feet long.

My father was a staff-sergeant serving in the Canadian Army, with three children and a wife to support and no money to spare on any kind of a dream cabin. And so he brought down some of the huge trees around the site (he'd been a lumberjack before he joined the army in 1928), had them sawn into lumber at the village sawmill, and over the course of several years scrounged the rest of what he needed to complete what we not-so-affectionately dubbed the Slave Camp. Nothing really fit, be it window, plumbing or stairs. The dock regularly went astray, as the battle between man and beast (the beavers) kept the water levels in constant flux. A trip to the cabin meant steady work.

Beyond the need to constantly tweak the make-do materials of our shelter in the woods, there were other reasons for the unending labour. Dad was a huge man with a very powerful chest, heavily tattooed arms, and hands that could smother a pineapple. He was a veteran of the Second World War, and like many veterans was haunted by that experience, sometimes to the point of allowing that destructive world to invade our home life. When the brain injury we now call post-traumatic stress disorder (PTSD) took hold of him, he was reliving, not remembering, the carnage he had witnessed, and perhaps caused. Sometimes he could damp down the horrors with alcohol, but often that didn't work. The cottage turned into a therapeutic instrument that provided him with a healthier outlet for his demons. He essentially lived for the summer weekends and the two weeks of vacation each year when he could escape to the bush and work on "his" cabin.

Dad really needed to keep busy, and he expected his only son to act as his gofer. How I despised that job. Go get this, and that, and the other, for hours on end when the lake was beckoning me to swim, to fish. But no, that was play and there was no time for that when he was at the lake.

I lived for the summer days when Dad had to be in town, leaving my mother, my two sisters and me at the cabin. Although he'd pile enough chores on me to keep two men busy all week, I now had the lake to swim in without having to guiltily avoid him, and the nearby sandpits to disappear into, where I built grand fortresses and fought the greatest battles of all time on its plains using small plastic soldiers and Dinky Toy tanks. And I had the endless bush to discover.

The forest was dense and totally enveloping. I would roam at will, stopping often to idle, to listen for birdsong and animal rustling, and to dream in unadulterated freedom. I forded creeks and swamps, and climbed high cliffs to bask on large exposed rocks where the sun would soon cover me with sweat. Alone in my humanity, I shed all constraints, rules, hypocrisy, pain and sorrow, escaping from that intense childhood stress of living according to other people's demands.

At a swamp's edge between small lakes, birds fluttered, ducks and wild geese swam, and bugs skated on the surface of the water. There was abundance for all and no sign of calamity or friction. Life buzzed along in a sort of symphony of small sounds that soothed rather than worried or excited me.

I would daydream in the stillness, experiencing pure joy. I would tear my T-shirt into two pieces, mark it up with crayon and dirt, then string the pieces, front and back, like a loincloth. In that moment I had transformed into a Huron, an Iroquois, a Cree, a Montagnais. I was a warrior. I was a brave, skilled in the ways of the forest and free to move by instinct, by need.

The forest protected me. The canopy far above shaded me from rain and wind, and the soft forest floor cushioned my steps. I learned how to run swiftly and stealthily, without the rustle of a branch or the snap of a twig.

Among the trees I had no boundaries except what I could see and smell and touch and sense. I was alive and I was without limits. I would observe the chipmunks and marvel at the speed and adroitness of their skirmishing, neither hurting their opponent nor injuring themselves in their leaps and bounds from the forest floor to the ends of hanging limbs. I would listen to birds and wonder at so many disparate songs and screeches, and their mastery of communication. The rare deer I spotted would remain motionless to blend into the brush, but its big eyes would always give it away, for they sparkled. With a wave of its tail, it would eventually relax and move on, nibbling at vegetation as it went.

And then there were the bugs and bugs and more bugs: scurrying around old fallen dead trees and in the trunks still standing, or scuttling away from me in the mud when I lifted a mat of fallen leaves, or gliding on the surfaces and diving in the depths of the little streams. The rat-a-tat-tat of the occasional woodpecker punching holes in rotting trees and feasting on their tiny but abundant prey led me to imagine how it must have been for soldiers at the front facing murderous machine-gun fire. It seemed an unfair match.

The ants were busy and impatient, as were bumblebees, whereas friendly ladybugs would stop for a rest on my arm and look up as if to say something important before flying away. Butterflies were like that, too. They seemed to take the time to show off their magnificent wings, as if they were gracing me with a visit rather than working to survive.

One majestic insect stood out from all the others. The dragonfly did not seem particularly interested in me; it remained aloof even when lighting briefly on my arm, as if it didn't matter that I was watching. By name alone, the dragonfly evoked images of a place that existed within and beyond my childish imagination: a magic world of castles and wizards, knights and fair damsels, dark forests and the evil that lurked therein. The other insects had their own exciting roles to fill. I was fascinated with their passion for survival. My forest friends, without exception, were obsessed with building, carrying, protecting. Their lives were perfect examples of Thomas Hobbes's view of existence in the state of nature — "nasty, brutish and short" — and yet I saw a magic in their existence that I did not see in my own.

To me, the dragonfly was the leader of the insect world, superior in strength, beauty and skills but, I imagined, compassionate also. The dragonfly led me into a world I created for myself, far away from civilization with its pain and hardships. I built that world not from fantasies, but from the realities of my life. I would play out an experience that had frustrated me with my cast of insect characters, reworking it to my satisfaction. In my forest world, I could correct injustices and stand up for myself and other small, weak and young creatures. In this world of freedom and play, I was unconsciously creating my character as a human, and becoming a man.

At the end of a day of such play, when I stumbled back to civilization, with all its harsh realities and limitations, I carried my imaginary world in the recesses of my mind. It was there whenever I needed to escape. It was my refuge, my place to enjoy and learn, my place to settle my emotions and work out my inner battles to understand the confusing and difficult adult world around me.

No matter how I clung to it, however, I could never use it to resolve the anxious pain in my stomach I felt when I had to emerge from the freedom of the forest and return to the confines of the adult world with its clothes, chores and rules. At times, of course, the real world contained people who offered me genuine love and respect, but they were few and far between. I felt as if the adult world was a place where there was no time to play, too much work, and zillions of restrictions on how and why to do things designed to mould me to its will. This indoctrination was conducted without consent on the part of the child. *Au contraire*, it was done "for your own good."

How I would come to dread the appearance of the long shadows made by the enormous maples of the forest, announcing that the day was coming to an end. As the sun made a fast getaway behind the hills, I would be plunged into semi-darkness. It often caught me by surprise, this darkness that brought me back to the adult world each night.

And, as the summer drew to a close, the shadows signalled a complete return to the adult world over the long winter months, without the respite of the forest.

With the hangover from the Labour Day weekend's grand fete resolved with a last swim, we joined the great procession of city dwellers heading back home—into lives of opulence for some and into urban swamps for others. We lived in one of the swamps: east-end Montreal. I dreaded the stench of the petrochemical plants around which the government had built cheap and "temporary" wartime housing for veterans and their families.

You could smell my part of town from the other side of the city if the wind was blowing in the right direction. You could see my part of town from space due to the large flames from the oil refineries and petrochemical plants. You could hear my part of town for miles, as the massive mosaic of intertwining refinery pipes spewed gas and steam from their pressure valves. The air was too toxic for us to play outside for long. We never cut the grass, as it could not grow. There were no leaves to rake in the fall because they all fell, withered, by the third week of June.

But as my dad would say, over and over, the roof doesn't leak, the furnace has fuel, the inside of the house and our clothes are clean, and there is enough food for three meals a day: what more do you want? You can survive the bad air for a few months.

And so, in the absence of a Laurentian forest in my backyard, I attempted to create a world of make-believe indoors. Grand battles with brave commanders played out on the large, reddish, living-room rug. By day, I was a student, a Cub Scout, an altar boy, a folk dancer, a flag carrier in the band and, later, an army cadet. But at night, with playing cards, plastic soldiers and metal Dinky trucks and tanks, I guarded fortresses and conducted great flanking manoeuvres in the semi-darkness of the living room. It was not unusual for my parents to find me asleep on the battlefield after three or four hours of intense activity in my own world, where soldiering was never eternally fatal: we always rose again to fight another day.

As the years passed, our family atmosphere became more tense, and increasingly I became isolated from my sisters, my harassed mother, and my strict and troubled father. School life was burdened by the ever-present Brothers of St. Gabriel, and the increasing French-Catholic/English-Protestant tension in the parish.

The ethnic and cultural mix in our part of town was dominated by French-Canadians, with a smattering of Anglos here and there.

When I hit school age, I was sent to a French-Catholic school while our English neighbour's daughter, the same age as me, was off to her English-Protestant school. From then on our daily schedules were different, our days off from school were not often the same, and I spent more time at school and in church than with the Anglo friends I had played with on the block. No adult explained why we were forced into these two camps or attempted to moderate the effects.

Disquieting ideas started to creep into our conversations at school, influenced by some of the older kids, who probably heard things from their parents. Negative intent, ill will, ignorance of the other, isolationism, disdain and, at times, envy. Nastiness soon festered in the alleyways, on the way to school and in the school-yard, but only later in any overt way in the classroom. Gradually Anglo-Protestants became the historical and constant adversary, and despite my confusion I knew I had to adopt this new perspective on my neighbours, or else.

The small fields that survived around the wartime housing development, the alleyways behind each block, the skating rinks in the small asphalt playgrounds a few streets over, the sheds behind family homes: all these zones became confrontational terrain upon which hatred, anger, fear and even at times blood was spilt in the name of something we absolutely could not understand: they were the Anglos (*les têtes carrées*) and we were the French (frogs) and we had to be antagonists without question.

Blindly we learned to dislike, mistrust, hate, despise and ultimately denigrate old friends, to treat them as not as human as we were. Though I was often caught in the middle because I had gone to Cub Scouts where we spoke English, I never lost the desire to be on both sides and neither side of the cultural and linguistic divide.

We were kids being influenced by a world run by adults and orchestrated by their beliefs, disappointments, ambitions and fears. Our kid world was simply buried by the attitudes of the bigoted, by perceived and real inequalities, by historical and long-festering adult frustrations. That adult truth made our preschool world just "kid stuff." And we forgot that once upon a time, we simply played with other kids, whoever they were, from wherever they came.

By the age of about twelve, I was wondering how I could escape from the looming, oppressive realities of home, of school, of street corner. There was the lake, which I could escape to, but which had the drawback of the constant toil for my father. When I went to high school, I was obliged to join the army cadet corps and take part in weekly drill parades. As the end of the school year approached, I volunteered and was chosen for army cadet summer camp. I had lived my entire life under the thumb of a firm disciplinarian who was a stickler for eating on time and being home by curfew. I was used to uniforms and shining boots. It was like I would be going from one institution to another, except for a major difference. Within the confines of the huge army camp, and among a couple of thousand other boys, I would be my own person. It seemed like a chance for a bit of adventure, a chance to fulfill my fantasies of being a gallant, noble and fearless warrior.

But I soon learned that many of the boys and young men at cadet camp were not there for summer fun, freedom and adventure. The older boys in positions of authority were playing for keeps and for the attention of the instructors. They were already aware of the criteria for advancement and privileges in the military, and had their eye on future opportunities in the escalating chain of command. They already fit into the regimented mindset of pride in the uniform, the team, the platoon. They could smell the prize of winning the commander's weekly pennant and the prestige it would give them among the other junior leaders and lower camp dwellers.

They compelled the young campers to fit, as best we could, into uniforms tailored for the adult men of the last great war. They ensured we kept our quarters, our kit and our spit-polished boots as per the specifications laid out in the bivouac guide. They were always looking for ways to improve our platoon and company surroundings. As ravenous as beavers, they would send us out into the woods after supper to cut birch and poplar branches to bring back to our tented lines so that we could build fences with various geometric designs and an elaborate, yet fragile, archway to the orderly room, the centre of the company. The fences and the arch required near-constant repair, but the effort was designed to foster team spirit, to nurture pride and self-discipline.

And then there were the rocks. We were sent scurrying over the fields and into the woods looking for rocks to mark the boundaries of the walkways. We painted them all white. Where the paint came from remains a mystery to me, as the quartermaster's stores were always out of everything and out of bounds. We ended up with white rocks all over the place in neat lines. We raked the sand and dirt of the paths inside these lines as if we were apprentice Japanese gardeners. And heaven help the cadet who walked beyond the rocks; his Saturday was immediately volunteered to freshen the yards for the Sunday church parade. Yes, we had church parades. Christian values were strong among the veterans who ran the camp, who had seen the worst that humanity could offer.

Like my peers, I was anxious to please and to avoid punishment. We were children in a very adult business, offering very small gestures to express our loyalty to our platoon, our company. Doing things better than the other groups of boys around us fostered esprit de corps: a sense of belonging that rested on excelling at activities and not on some specious air of superiority. Our cohesion had nothing to do with the evil expressions of ethnicity and culture that created so much hate back on my city streets, and everything to do with the positive sense of worth we were gaining in this very structured organization. Amazingly, the fact that we were learning warlike skills with weapons that were taller than us never really registered. None of our commanders pointed out that these weapons were made to kill other humans. They were purely for target practice on paper bull's eyes at six hundred yards, conducted under the close supervision of qualified instructors.

The relatively few adults at the camp were either real soldiers and veterans of the wars overseas or officers of the reserve, many of whom were teachers during the school year. Some of them were members of the religious orders who ran the cadet corps in the Catholic schools and community centres across the province. Those Catholic brothers and fathers, some Jesuits, felt no hesitation at donning the khaki uniform and easily fit into the military life with its organized way of going about things. Were they the descendants of the monkish knights of medieval times who fought the infidels in the Middle East? Hardly, but they certainly were at ease with military discipline and order. And, in my observation, they liked to throw their weight around.

Maybe I would have become a good brother or priest. I liked the distinction of wearing a uniform that displayed who I was on its shoulders and breast. I was used to never having any money but still getting by. I was at ease in an organization that knew what it had to do and how to go about doing it. I could be me within an organization that created uniformity. I could wear the uniform but still be free inside this structured life that was clear, unambiguous and overt. The army was big and powerful and yet also welcoming and very human indeed.

In the vastness of the tented camp, among thousands of other boys, in the all-encompassing way of life, in a real expression of belonging, of supporting others and being counted on and supported by others, too, I found my soul. Unabashedly and generously offered such richness by the army—the institution, its ethos and its people—I responded with zeal. I found my vocation there: that world of the army cadet linked seamlessly—astonishingly— with the imaginary world of my childhood.

The vets gave the summer cadets the sense of being part of something much bigger, steeped in history and traditions, sacrifice and glory. They made and applied the thousand-and-one rules around the camps that ensured we remembered we were in the army now and not somewhere in upstate New York bunking down with a bunch of bored rich kids. Rain or shine, they never seemed to either sleep or waver in the maintenance of the "standard" of perfect order and good discipline, and heaven forbid if you dropped a candy-bar wrapper on the grounds. That wrapper went into the garbage pail, but not just *any* pail, as some were there just for show and were spotless inside and out.

Although all the veterans smoked like chimneys off duty, they had a particular aversion to finding cigarette butts dropped even on the grass. We wanted to learn to smoke in order to emulate these old sweats. We would roll our cigarettes individually with varying levels of success—I ended up smoking more paper than tobacco for the longest time. We would try to talk and do odd jobs with the cigarette in the corner of our mouths and the longest possible ash still attached. But either the smoke got into our eyes and nearly blinded us or the ash fell on our clean boots and made a mess. We were very careful where we dropped our cigarette butts.

Still, for the longest time, we were allowed to remain kids playing at a grown-up game. I was a *boy* soldier, an apprentice at some of the skills, but I had not yet acquired the ethic of the warrior class in our democratic and peaceful society. We were playing at soldiers. We never really believed we were preparing for war. We never really thought it could happen. The closest we ever got to a battlefield was the odd evening war story from a veteran, although as a rule they tended to be quite tight-lipped about their war experiences. But boy, did we love the stories they told, stories edited to stress the valour and not the horror.

We also loved Saturday movie night: black-and-white Hollywood epics featuring great First or Second World War battles were shown in the huge drill hall, with all of us sitting on the floor downing the only Coke and chocolate bar we were allowed to purchase each week. The echoing drill hall amplified the sound of the guns and screams on the soundtrack, and the brave words of the combatants. When the lights came up, we would be marched back to our tents, high on sugar and often still dazed by the scenes on the screen.

Dreams came easily once we'd quieted down and closed our eyes. On my favourite nights for sleeping, light summer rains beat on the canvas of our large, canopied tent. Some of the canvas walls bore graffiti from others who had slept on the top bunk, close to the roof, like I did. Were they soldiers of the war or were they last summer's cadets? I never could read the faded scribbles, but this did not stop me from thinking about them each night as I entered my own secret, special, boy world.

Yes, my world. That totally imaginative place that was everywhere and nowhere would come to life when I closed my eyes against the reality around me, night or day. At times I would be reprimanded for daydreaming in the most unexpected places, such as when standing to attention during inspection parades, or on the rifle range firing point (waiting with my relay for the order to lay down and pick up five rounds of .303 calibre Second World War munitions), or walking in a column through the dark forest as we practised night orienteering.

In the poorly lit classroom tents where only an occasional breeze reduced the heat and humidity, I was an ace at escaping into my world. I amazed myself at being able to walk in file surrounded by comrades or to lay cold and shivering under my poncho in the wet grass at first light, and still cross into my world. With a flicker of thought, I would be back in the forests of the Laurentians and I would be free and wild and so very much alive.

By the time I was into my eighteenth year, I had been back to cadet camp several times and had achieved considerable success in leadership roles. During my last summer camp, the die was truly cast: I received my acceptance to military college. Attending the Collège militaire royal de Saint-Jean for five years and then the Royal Military College in Kingston, Ontario, were my first steps to becoming a career officer and a university-educated citizen.

—

I passed from childhood and became a man—a soldier, an officer, a general—but the boy never really disappeared. My imaginative world remained alive, if often dormant, inside that evolving, professionally trained military commander who manoeuvred in the adult world. Marriage and kids of my own did not reduce my longing to escape at times into my own universe. And I tried to foster a similar imaginative space in the psyches of my children, or at least to help them realize that their life's ambition was not simply to become an adult, but to become themselves, masters of their internal realm of freedom and imagination first and foremost. I believe that children must have room to protect that place in their brains that makes them different and unique for their short lives on this planet and for the eternal lives of their souls.

The adult soldier goes about the business of mastering the craft of controlled violence, of living and staying alive in far-off lands for causes that are seldom clear or even tangible. Keeping peace, upholding freedom, defending human rights, protecting the moderates and the innocents caught in the crossfire of conflict, creating the buffer zones of fairness and security—these are definitions of a soldier's role that have evolved over centuries in which hundreds of thousands of people have suffered, paying the price for change, for reform, for a better way of life. The gallant old soldiers who taught me as a boy created a learning atmosphere that was serious yet very considerate, very human, inculcating lofty ideals and noble-warrior dreams in their charges.

The contrast between my path as a youth and the path of so many youths and children in war zones and failing states today is stark. We cadets knew all this military stuff would be over in so many days that we could strike off on the calendar. The child soldiers under the gun of inhuman adults see no end in sight. My teachers took care of us and understood we were only boys, but the men and women leading their contingents of child soldiers destroy the children and youth they indoctrinate, literally and spiritually—sacrificing them at the whim of their ambitions and perverse needs.

The world of the child soldier was not portrayed in any of the doctrine and tactics books that had been my soldier bibles before I arrived in Africa in 2003. I was completely unprepared to come in contact with an enemy who wore the trappings of childhood so familiar to me, but who was so different from the soldier I had become. I was so unprepared that for a long time I was blind to the implications of what I was seeing.

2.

LITTLE SOLDIERS, LITTLE KILLERS

I WAS FIRST CONFRONTED WITH CHILD SOLDIERS in the Rwandan civil war. I saw them, heard them, faced them down, and eventually confronted them in the midst of a carnage that swallowed their youth and my professional warrior ethic. They, the once-children in unknown villages on the tops of the thousand hills of Rwanda, were real, determined, deadly, and in some strange way quite adept at camouflaging the incredible fear they must have been experiencing in the presence of professional and adult soldiers.

At first they seemed to be children just like I had been, dressed up and playing adult games. But I soon realized that these were not students falling into line and listening obediently to teachers who spoke to them of discipline. They were not cadets at summer camp toying with military practices on parade squares and with compasses and maps on field exercises. These were not children sent off willingly by nervous parents to live a few weeks under canvas and be fed heavy meals and bunked in dry sheets changed every fifth day.

No, these were soldiers. Little soldiers with big guns often grasped in both hands or resting heavily on the shoulder, wearing ill-fitting uniforms and parading before visitors in hidden lairs to show the strength of purpose and of military force.

The helicopter, shuddering vigorously, was nearly out of control. The Rwandan army pilot was pulling harder and harder on the control stick to slow down enough to avoid crashing into a small ledge near the top of a high hill, among so many other high hills, in the middle of the rebel-held zone in northern Rwanda.

The air is thin at this altitude and the temperature was just hot enough to exacerbate an already tenuous situation for flying. We hit the ground with such force that I didn't really know whether we had landed or crashed.

It was August of 1993, and I was on a reconnaissance mission to the region in advance of deploying a UN peacekeeping force. On this leg, I was touring the rebel side of the demilitarized zone (DMZ) established to keep the RPF and the Rwandese Government Forces (RGF) apart. We'd landed at a rebel battalion headquarters in the western part of the DMZ, and from the looks of things (confirmed on the tourist map scrunched in my hand) it was very isolated from the rest of the world. There were no roads, only foot-paths, and no electricity or repeater stations to permit any mobile communications. Even in the helicopter, radio communication was iffy at best because of all the hills. I needed as much informa-tion as I could get in those hectic few days, to confirm the rebel army's claims about its force structure, and also assess what I would need in terms of troops and equipment to monitor and observe the ceasefire and the implementation of the Arusha Peace Agreement, brokered between the rebel army and the mainly Hutu regime, which ended the civil war and established the goals necessary to creating a democratic government in Rwanda.

My legs were still wobbly from the landing when I was sur-rounded by a squad of keen, smartly dressed young soldiers in high rubber boots, and uniform jackets and caps that looked familiar. On closer inspection, I realized they were wearing a version of East German Army summer-camouflage combat dress, and I wondered briefly how the RPF had got hold of the uniforms. But with the end of the Cold War and the reunification of Germany, huge quantities of military material and hardware had recently become available at rock-bottom prices on the arms market; the offer of U.S. dollars in those days would get you what you needed from most Eastern European nations without too many questions asked.

Although at the ready, these young soldiers did not seem trigger-happy or overexcited. They seemed efficient and disciplined, and were totally devoid of any expression other than determination. An older chap with no visible rank on his shoulders, but with the air of an NCO, led the way toward a group of huts slightly hidden in the bush, clearly the command post. A tall, slim officer was standing there waiting for me with his staff. After a very smart salute, he smiled and extended his hand in a gesture of warm welcome, greeting me in English with an accent that was decidedly North American. He commented wryly that if my helicopter had kissed the ground a little more amorously it would have been a long walk back to Kigali.

This commanding officer was *au fait* with what had happened at the peace talks a few weeks earlier. He knew what the agreement entailed for his side and for the Rwandan government, too, and he responded promptly to the few questions I had as to his unit's boundaries and tasks on this rear flank of rebel-held territory.

I wanted to walk over the tactical deployment of his forces — whose territory contained several hilltops as well as a massive volcano that loomed over us where we stood—and his defensive positions. And so he led me on a short tour of the main bivouac area and then farther west of his area of responsibility to show me a spot where the DMZ was so narrow and the opposing forces so close that his troops could throw rocks at them. As we walked, I learned that the commander had been trained in Warsaw Pact countries and had fought in the Ugandan civil war under Yoweri Museveni, the current president. There was no doubt that he was a professional and that he had a number of equally experienced subordinate leaders and staff officers in various posts in his command.

The bivouacs were impeccably laid out for the comfort of the troops, protected from prevailing winds and with good drainage, and within a strong defensive posture for immediate reaction to any surprise attack. Even though they were young, his NCOs had the demeanour and command presence of soldiers trained by the Brits or by British-trained colonial instructors: I felt as if I was in a British camp like the one I had visited in northern Germany in the 1970s.

The soldiers themselves, both at headquarters and at the forward defensive positions, were lean but in top physical condition. I saw no layabouts, sick-parade ill, or injured personnel. There were several sections doing squad-level drill to the sound of the soldiers' own singing. We walked by a platoon listening to a lecture on terrain features and movement, and the use of dead ground (natural features such as gullies) to protect them from being seen or from coming under fire from the enemy as they advanced. Another group was conducting open field formations, and still others were sitting in a circle cleaning their personal weapons as an NCO gave them pointers on the best way to render their guns more effective, as well as relentlessly reminding them never to be caught without their weapons. On a small stretch of open ground, soldiers were playing soccer with a ragged ball that had clearly had its original markings kicked right off it, "skins" against "shirts." The shirts wore impeccably clean white T-shirts, but all the players were barefoot on a pitch that had more small stones than grass.

Morale seemed high among the troops, who also seemed ready to respond at any time to a threat from an enemy. I was impressed that this force—months into a ceasefire and with a recent peace agreement supposedly easing tensions—was still at such a high state of operational readiness. I would have expected a laxer standard in a force that had been sitting still for six to nine months.

But as I admiringly studied these young soldiers and junior NCOs, it finally dawned on me that I was looking not at young men but at teenagers: a good number seemed well under eighteen. These were, in effect, companies of kids or youths being used as front-line troops. It was clear that they were very well trained and indoctrinated: they were there to fight, if necessary, as they had done rather effectively for the last three years. The other thing that struck me as unusual was that there were absolutely no women or girls in sight. The RPF soldiers had left their families in the refugee camps in southern Uganda.

If I subtracted three years from eighteen, I came up with a disturbing answer. Had this civil war between the RPF and the RGF been fought by youths, by children, led by adult officers and NCOs? The answer came in part from the commander, who told me without hesitation that up to 75 per cent of his troops were already veterans who had been battle-tested at various times during the last three years of civil war. Most of his officers and NCOs also had previous experience fighting in the civil war that brought Museveni to power in Uganda nearly a decade earlier.

When my reconnaissance was over, and as my unsure helicopter pilot attempted to get us off the ground, I could not come to grips with the fact that these young soldiers, these youth combatants, might have been as young as fourteen when they first entered the fray in 1990. They were veterans and yet had not even reached adulthood. They had fought and seen action against some determined professional soldiers from Belgium and France, who had come to the aid of the RGF, and by all accounts they had held their own. They had killed, and some of them had been killed and wounded in return, and they were not yet men.

While serving in Germany I had wandered through row upon row of tombstones in military cemeteries in northern Europe marking the graves of young Canadian soldiers who had died in action far from home and for a less intimate cause than the one for which these young rebels were fighting. Far too often the birth and death dates would strike me, and I'd do the math, and feel repelled, even guilty, at the loss of a soldier as young as seventeen; once, when my father was with me in Holland where he had fought, we came across the grave of a sixteen-year-old. My father had been a thirty-seven-year-old, experienced NCO in that war; a sixteen-year-old enlisted man was an aberration, he said, but later admitted that he had felt almost like a grandfather to some of the troops, many of whom enrolled before their eighteenth birthday.

But being a sixteen-year-old on that hill in Rwanda made you not an aberration but a seasoned veteran. These were combat-ready and experienced boy soldiers with competent adult leaders who were fully aware of the underage state of their charges. Barely eight months later, these child soldiers would be crossing through the DMZ just south of this position to conduct assault after assault on the RGF and its own youth militias in the civil war and geno-cide that would rock their homeland. One of the most horrific slaughters that one nation suffered in the last century would be played out by so many youths serving under one flag or the other, as adults manoeuvred for power and supremacy.

And what of the youths those well-trained young RPF soldiers would soon face?

In the months leading up to the outbreak of the genocide on April 6, youth militias from Rwanda's major political parties regularly demonstrated their bravado and disdain for authority, especially the authority of my small force of foreign blue berets. The disturbances and friction that the youth wings of the Coalition pour la défense de la république (CDR) and Mouvement révolu-tionnaire national pour le développement (MRND)—respectively, the Hutu extremist and the president's political parties—created not only in the capital, Kigali, on Sundays after mass but through-out the country in every little mountain-top village was emblem-atic of the aggressive gang violence that was to come. These were not youths out for a good time at the expense of innocent bystand-ers. They were dressed distinctively in a sort of multicoloured clown suit and cap. They seemed well led by handlers who instilled in the boys through song, dance and the blowing of horns and whistles, as well as illegal enticements and aggressive behaviour, a feeling of omnipotence.

Before the genocide began, I received inside information that these kids, youngish teenagers, were being taken to the south of the country, to the large forests, and trained with weapons and military tactics by extremist elements of the Rwandan political parties who were supposedly supporting the peace process.

Many of the Hutu youths who obeyed the siren call of the mili-tias were disenfranchised, spending their days and nights standing around street corners and in open-air drinking spots, doing nothing but discussing the inequalities in their society, their need for a fair chance to study, to find decent work, to have a good time of course and to get married and have children. Such cries of social injus-tice were normal—completely to be expected in a poverty-stricken nation state that was dependent on foreign aid for food due to the overpopulation. But these were also ideal recruits whom adult manipulators could whip into a state of frenzy every night and then leave alone the next day to muse on the no-win situation they found themselves in. These youths had been cut free from tradi-tional family structures because they could not be housed or fed from the family plot, and so they gravitated to market squares and urban areas where they became the ripest of candidates for recruit-ment into any ruthless organization that wanted to lure them to the dark side—but also for any NGO or national government body that could gainfully employ and train them. They stood on the cutting edge between a life of destruction and crime and a life of reasonable fulfillment and honest but difficult work by which they could support families of their own.

What choice did many young Hutus make? No NGO or legiti-mate organization had a reach, an allure, to equal the growing

campaign of disinformation provided on the street corners by pro-
vocateurs, over the airwaves by an extremist radio station and at
large rallies held before and after soccer games in stadiums on
Sundays. The Hutu extremists were interested in these youths,
wanted to train them, were happy to give them beer, to arm them,
even to provide them with a rough and ready uniform so they could
truly identify with something. And so Hutu youths swarmed to the
militias. Their new cause, their aim in life, became to seek out and
destroy this other troublesome ethnic group, the Tutsis, people who
were deemed by the extremists to not be people at all, even though
Hutus and Tutsis were so intertwined in the villages and cities of
Rwanda, in the church congregations and marketplaces, that no
one could really tell them apart. But the extremists bent on preventing the peace process had embarked on a campaign to dehumanize
the Tutsis, to turn them into vermin, into cockroaches that needed
to be exterminated for the good of all. The campaign spread twisted
facts of history against the Tutsis, claiming that they had subjugated
past generations of Hutus, and were on the verge of stealing their
futures through a peace agreement that, the extremists said, simply
weakened the majority Hutus, and whose enactment would signal
the annihilation of the Hutus by the RPF.

At a time when my mission was trying to aid in the implementation of the Arusha Peace Agreement, the major and most vocal
anti-Tutsi party in the Rwandan political landscape was inciting
riots, training a youth wing called the Interahamwe and turning
it into a militia. I knew this was happening, and alerted the chain
of command at the UN and the international community, and
was ordered not to conduct any offensive action against them,
their arms distribution or their training areas. I was only given
authority to submit formal observations and information to
President Habyarimana, the minister of defence, the RGF chief
of staff, and political party officials, and also to pass such information to selected international representatives in residence
in Rwanda.

So the training and arms distribution continued and when the president's plane was shot down at 2032 hours on April 6, 1994, they were ready. These same previously disenfranchised youths, intoxicated by overwhelming power over their fellow civilians, were let loose with orders to exterminate the Tutsi insects. They were sustained by the hysteria spewing from the hate radio station (which became known as "genocide radio"), by quantities of alcohol and drugs, by the material gain of what they could plunder from their victims. But most of all they were sustained by the constant support and encouragement of their elders to find ever more effective ways to rape, mutilate and slaughter as many Tutsis as possible every day, of all ages, including the unborn.

Soon checkpoints were set up along every road, trail and track throughout the government-controlled areas, manned by a rabble of street kids—children and youth armed with machetes and other agricultural instruments, overseen by older youths and a few adults. Some wore parts of police or military uniforms and all were deadly serious about the business they were engaged in: culling Tutsis from the long lines of people hoping to escape the city and gain the relative safety of the hills, and not only killing them but ensuring that they died with the maximum possible suffering and humiliation.

Mere days before, Kigali was a rather comfortable, westernized city, home to a population of 350,000 souls; now it was chaos at every corner. Endless so-called self-defence barriers against the feared rebel infiltration were established by the militia and political youth every 100 to 150 metres along the roads and pathways through the thousand hills and valleys. Swarms of fanatical and drug-influenced young people and kids, mostly boys, decided who would be pulled out of the line and hacked to death or drowned in nearby latrines and sewers. Those who survived one roadblock would have to go through the same traumatic ritual at the next one until they reached the forests and borders. The city emptied to less than thirty thousand souls, but since most of the country's roads converged on Kigali from all directions, hundreds of thousands of displaced persons from other parts of the country ran the gauntlet of its main arteries.

And as long processions of Rwandans passed through the culling checkpoints of the city, constant fighting between the two opposing forces flared from one hill to another, shells landing in the valleys and the city slums. The indiscriminate use of mortars and artillery kept everyone on edge. There seemed to be no pattern to the targets they were after. The RPF rebels did not yet want to engage in set-piece open combat due to their inferior number of troops, so they employed the tactic of harassing fire throughout the city that, at times, caused injuries and casualties among my forces and among the thirty thousand Hutu moderates and Tutsi refugees we were harbouring in the city's main stadium, as well as at the two major hospitals where thousands of wounded waited for whatever treatment the few doctors could provide.

During this battle for the capital, the presence of young men—teenagers and boys—was ubiquitous; they were at every check-point I saw in the city, and throughout most of the countryside during all of the war. And for the hundred days until the RPF was able to assert control over the capital, and then for years after in refugee camps in neighbouring countries, the work of these youths and boys carried on—killing and maiming anyone remotely sus-pected of being a Tutsi, and even those among their own people who were less than enthusiastic about the cause of Hutu Power.

High school kids, junior high too, boys and some girls. They wore the blood that spattered all over them with pride. They hacked, mutilated, all the while smiling at the faces of fear and horror they created. Adults looked on and encouraged them, even proposing new methods of using the grossest of weapons, the machete, on pregnant women and little children to see the effects of different strokes and twists.

They were the same ages as my kids back home. They were

children in body but they had lost their child's soul to an adult world that had distorted their minds to the point of destroying their consciences, their compassion, their capacity for empathy. Their eyes did not see the human beings they were destroying with such zeal and gusto. They saw insects, evil and parasitical ones, that had to be crushed for their own protection.

And as these thousands upon thousands of young boys and teens were being turned by adults into monstrous killing and mutilating machines, a civil war raged: the standard-bearers of the rebel army were also youths.

There was a country to win over and a government to establish and power to gain and money to be had. There had to be a winner on the battlefield, even though the real human tragedy was being meted out behind the government lines, mostly by the youth of the Interahamwe.

Beyond the checkpoints, the government forces directly employed a number of these young militiamen to reconnoitre the places they knew best, the villages and districts where they'd grown up. They made excellent messengers, as they could move through the roadblocks much faster than RGF soldiers, who were prey to internal divisions between the moderate Hutu officers, even some surviving Tutsis, and the hardline proponents of Hutu Power. In the capital, for example, the Interahamwe also provided rear-area security and ran wild in parts of the city that the army controlled, and as such continued the extermination of innocent survivors, both moderate Hutus and Tutsis, at every opportunity, all in the name of security.

Facing them across the ill-defined no man's land were the RPF forces, constantly probing at night, harassing with snipers and indirect fire during the day, thrusting often at first light into specific sectors of town to continue to close the noose around those government forces still inside.

In numerous trips through the lines to negotiate ceasefires, the release and transfer of people from our swelling numbers in

protected sites, and to permit the very slow arrival of some humanitarian supplies, I encountered among the RPF the same type of
young boy soldiers as I'd met before the war. They were fighting
and dying in the thick of the battle for the city. They were also in
the rear areas to the east that had already been conquered by the
rebel army. They were in the security forces mopping up isolated
pockets of government resistance. And they were controlling the
flow of what little population was left behind in the territory they
had won.

I saw them being tended to in their field medical stations, their
young bodies ripped apart by fragments of artillery shells. They
would die far from home, from family, from the warmth of a last
hug or kiss from their parents. Alone and often conscious that
they were about to die, some would cry, not in pain but in sorrow,
in loneliness, in despair. Their last conscious thoughts most likely
were of loss and abandonment as their wounds silently stole the
life force from their young bodies that had barely started to live.
They fought like soldiers, like warriors for a cause they and their
families believed in, but in their torn and bloodied soldiers' uniforms, they died like children.

Throughout the hundred days of war and slaughter that was the
Rwandan genocide, and for the month that followed the end of hostilities, during which I remained in command of the UN mission
(marginally reinforced by eleven Canadian officers deployed with
only a few days' notice from other missions in Africa or from their
home bases in Canada), child soldiers continued to play a significant role. Having won the war, the RPF rebels were consolidating
their grip on the whole of the country except for the Humanitarian
Protection Zone, which had been established by a Franco-African
coalition intervention force called Opération Turquoise and into
which approximately two million frightened Hutus had fled.

During the campaign, the rebel forces had put a call out for rein-
forcements and many youths from the Tutsi expatriate community

around the world, as well as some from neighbouring countries such as Uganda, joined late in the fight. These youths were green in the ways of a disciplined military force. They did not demonstrate the same restraint and diligence that the young veterans generally maintained. These new members of the rebel force were also kids, young teenagers who had hastily volunteered for the cause and were outfitted in a slightly different uniform and seemingly equipped with a chip on their shoulder that was not often held in check. They were cocky, gun-happy and arrogant, throwing their weight around and causing enormous amounts of friction and near-catastrophic encounters with the newly arrived UN forces—who, in turn, were both mandated and quite prepared to use force against these punks in uniform. The sooner the RPF got rid of these new recruits and brought back the iron discipline of the original young veterans still in service, the sooner the transition to nation building could commence. But throughout this tense post-conflict period, it was young boys who held the local power. Yes, they were often supervised by adults, but more often they were overseen by more senior boys.

And what of the young militiamen, the Interahamwe, during this same post-conflict period? Had they resigned themselves to the defeat their military masters were being subjected to, the total humiliation of their army by the rebels? Did some outside body or organization come to dissuade and disarm them, to try to rehabilitate them back to a semblance of societal normality?

Not really. The young militia slipped away either through the Humanitarian Protection Zone into Bukavu, in the Democratic Republic of the Congo (DRC), or with the refugees on the move from Rwanda into the closest possible facsimile of Dante's Inferno—the town of Goma, also in the DRC, at the foot of an active and ash-spewing volcano. There the human masses fell into the hell of refugee camps set up on black and unforgiving volcanic rock, where thousands would die of dysentery and other hygiene-related diseases. As they crossed the zone, the defeated Hutu soldiers and the Interahamwe on the run wiped out the last pockets of Tutsi civilians on the western border, right under the noses of the French humanitarian protection forces, hundreds of emergency NGO workers and the cameras of media from around the world. This second phase of the massive destruction of human lives gained enormous notoriety but did absolutely nothing to quell the conflict—now spread to the region—and the confinement of millions of black Africans in self-destructive refugee encampments.

At Bisesero, an enclave of a few very small villages on the top of a couple of nondescript hills in Kibuye province, a mass grave now honours a unique group of Tutsis who had defended their families and lands from extremist assaults for years before the genocide, and who successfully resisted the génocidaires for close to a hundred days. With bows and arrows and stones, hiding under the rotting bodies of those who had already fallen, in order to surprise and ambush the militiamen, eating leaves and grass and drinking the morning dew to survive, they fought off wave after wave of Interahamwe and RGF troops until the French soldiers finally arrived. Nearly twelve thousand were still alive when they were persuaded by a French patrol that the genocide was over and they could safely come out of hiding. The French soldiers subsequently withdrew to get more personnel and vehicles to evacuate them as well as bring humanitarian relief supplies, without leaving any security behind. The Interahamwe, monitoring all this, then moved in for the *coup de grâce*, slaughtering these surviving heroes in their thousands. Scant few scrambled back up the hills and survived to tell this tale of mass slaughter.

Even though these Hutu youth militia members realized that their cause was lost, that the war was essentially over, and that some day they would have to enter into a period of reconciliation and reconstruction, they did not hesitate to use their machetes on the near-skeletal survivors.

By the time the French returned to Bisesero the next day, the militia members were making their way across the lake into the

DRC. There, they would continue to slaughter their own brethren in the refugee camps, and at times even returned to kill more in Rwanda. To this day a number of these original militia members still run amok in the northern Kivou area, searching out and killing Tutsis and "collaborators." They are men now, with new youth recruits, and they have indoctrinated those youths with their disdain for life and humanity, for people different from them. They continue to prey upon the weak and will do so until the day they themselves are rendered *hors de combat*.

How many times did I bully, threaten, negotiate or simply ram my way under fire through roadblocks put up by these young militias and their supporters and adult leaders? But I could never reconcile my sense of their youth and potential with the hatred, the guile, the blatant evil in the eyes of these teenagers: boys, and yes, even girls. Their faces, so many of them, still appear in a sort of composite form in front of me, even as I write.

We owe it to these youths, as much as to the children we consider more "innocent," to eradicate the idea that children can be used this way.

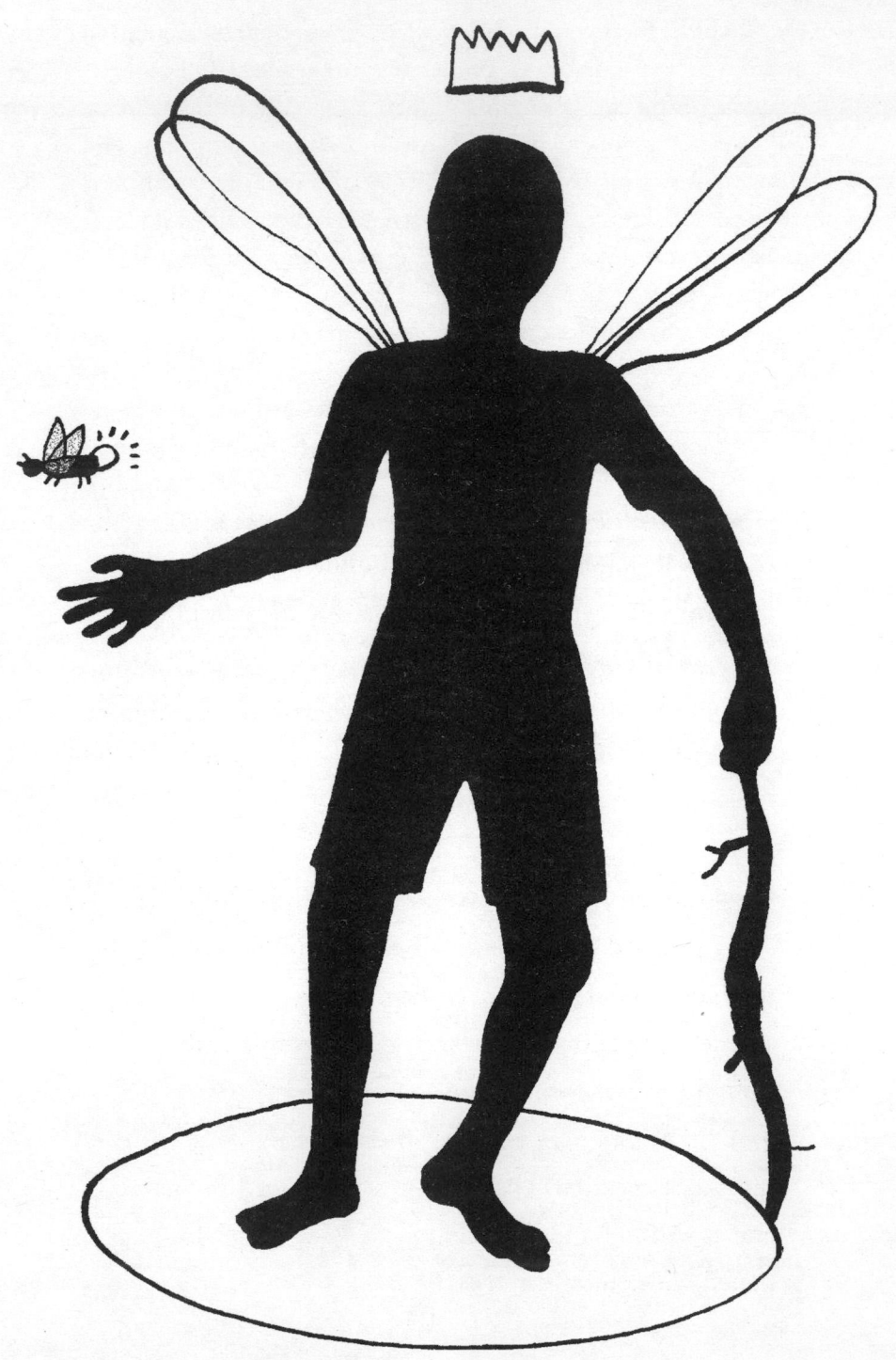

3.

Kidom

1

A dragonfly is born in the mud, a clumsy bug. With hundreds of its kind, it struggles toward the bushes, the trees and walls that will take it to the sky. It crawls and then it rests, and the warmth of the sun dries its shell to a delicate golden brown.

We sat and watched, my sister and I, basking like baby dragonflies in the hot midday sun.

When the moment finally came, a special silence filled our ears and made them ache. All the little necks split open and the dragonflies began to unfold, shimmering red or shocking blue, putting the rose and the sky to shame. Stretching, spreading, growing impossibly big from their tiny, crispy shells.

A slight touch, even a too-strong breeze, could stunt the transformation. Disturb one before it is fully grown and it will fall and be swarmed by predators. This happened once, and we couldn't watch.

We named the survivors, and cheered them when they finally took flight. To celebrate, Kesi dragged a stick around us in the earth, tracing a circle.

"We are the rulers of the dragonflies! And this," she said, "is *our* world. This is *Kidom*."

We passed through the circle together, Queen Kesi and I. When she approached her ride—a shimmering dragonfly with golden antennae—I helped her mount, and she leaned forward to whisper directions to her winged steed for our victory ride. But I did not need a mount, only to unfurl my purple wings, so large I could wrap myself in them like robes. And all the insects of the forest and the bush began to gather about us to honour Queen Kesi and me for the safe birth of the dragonflies.

We have had many such adventures. Last week, the honeybees needed us to lead them from hive to flower, and afterwards, when the nectar was gathered, we celebrated with a dance. Not long ago we fought and won a battle against a ruthless aardvark, and saved a hill and thousands of ants.

On that occasion, the ants made us a feast. We slipped down the tiny entrance hole into their nest and through a web of tunnels. Past one, two, three cooking fires, and seven rooms filled with dozens of mothers and their young, wearing hats of new spring leaves.

As Kesi lingered to admire the babies in their pretty hats, I wandered down the endless corridors, peeking into room after room. The halls were shiny green from the algae smoothed over their earthen sides. Each doorway opened onto a new delight: some rooms so surprisingly bright and airy they seemed like private gardens, others snug and cozy with ember fires glowing and colourful weavings lining the walls.

One door led me into a moist, dripping cavern filled with towering trees with thick flat leaves and giant orange and red flowers that cascaded down onto the benches of crystal that sat beneath them. The floor was dewy with moss. An old ant, with scraggly mandibles sticking out from his long beard, was scooping water from a rock pool.

"Is this your garden?" I asked in admiration.

"I am the gardener."

I paused. "But does it belong to you?"

He blinked. "This is the colony's garden. It belongs to everyone."

"It is all so beautiful, but what is it for? Can you eat anything in here?"

He smiled at me but didn't answer. He hefted his pail and hobbled a few steps to a cloud of tiny sprouts over which he carefully dripped the water. As he wouldn't talk any more with me, I left him to wander along the twisty paths, sniffing blossoms, stroking palm trunks and tracing the patterns of dew on the crystal benches. The air was sharp and clean. I plucked a silky petal off a rose, and as I rubbed it against my cheek, I understood. It was simply a beautiful place, made more beautiful by the gardener's work, which was his gift to everyone.

Back in the tunnel, I wasn't entirely sure which direction would take me back to Kesi. But then a long parade of little silver creepers scurried past me, tinkling, each one covered in tiny carved wooden bells hanging from grassy threads. They danced past my feet as if I wasn't even there, and I stood very still so I wouldn't step on anyone. An elder creeper also cloaked in silver but without bells, carrying a golden staff, brought up the rear.

"Hello, Madame," I greeted her.

"Hello, dear one," she replied, as if she already knew who I was. "Please excuse this silly lot. They are so excited about the feast I can't bear to be harsh with them. They work as furiously as they play."

And so I followed them to find Queen Kesi already in the main hall, which was an enormous cavern lit by sunlight that flowed like water through a hundred hair-thin tunnels to the outside world. The walls were decked with spiders' silk and painted with berry juice. And every creature there raised a cheer for Queen Kesi and me, toasting us with cups filled with morning dew.

The battle with the aardvark had been swift and ferocious, but the victory feast was loose and free. We laughed and sang and played through the rest of that day and into the evening, when duty called us back to our other life, our ordinary life, as children of the village.

My mother and father say Kesi and I spend too much time lost in our own world, and not enough time attending to our chores. But I told my parents it was our teacher, Baingana, who told us to observe the dragonflies.

"What purpose is there in staring at the ground?" Daddy growled.

"How can you bear to look at all those wriggly things so closely?" Momma asked, giving a shudder. She would rather squash a beetle than cup it in her hands and feel it tickle her palms.

I loved tiny things. I loved them best of all because they were secret from the grown-ups. It seemed like only the inhabitants of Kidom really understood them.

But I kept these thoughts mostly to myself—I rarely challenged my parents' rules in our home. Besides, I *did* my chores. I was proud to prepare the fire for the tea, and I did that every single morning, even when I had that terrible earache. And I pulled the weeds from around my avocado tree (always careful to check for caterpillars), *and* I had done all of this since I was seven years old.

Kesi was still only six, and it was true, she'd rather play than do her chores any day of the week, but she didn't get reprimanded as much as me because she could make our parents laugh. Her teeth were crooked, and when she smiled her nose wrinkled up like a rabbit's. Because she liked it so much, she always wore her bright pink school wrapper around her waist, even over her regular clothes, and our mother let her get away with it. The pink was so bright you could see her even in the dark, or from very far away.

Our brothers were older than us. Mashaka thought he was cool, like a rapper. He used to be a lot more fun before he became so cool. He used to be home all the time and never minded playing with us, but he had a big fight with Daddy and now was gone a lot of the time. He was the one who actually invented Kidom: he said all you had to do was trace a circle around yourself with a magic branch, and you would leave Momma and Daddy and school and the village behind you and enter the tiny world of insects. There we were giants, kings and queens.

We used to spend hours with him in Kidom. We would sit together in a circle on the bush floor, a mist of green surrounding us like mosquito netting but softer, shimmering with dew and magic. And Mashaka would describe the elaborate kingdoms inside the trees and under the ground, where we were able to wander in robes of spiders' silk. And as he talked, I would feel myself leaving my body, like flying in a dream. Everything did become tiny—whole worlds could fit on the tip of my finger.

But when he was home these days, Mashaka was sullen and quiet. Always off on his own, with no time for us. At first, Momma said it was because he was growing up, and that growing pains are difficult. When I grow up, I told her, I won't forget everything important. But she didn't make excuses for him anymore. Sometimes when he was away he sent short messages through confusing chains of people to Momma, but they only seemed to make her sad.

My oldest brother, Mosi, had no such growing pains. He was beautiful—everyone said so. We all wished we looked like Mosi. His eyes were like my eyes with thick black lashes, and his mouth was like Mashaka's, full and soft. His laugh was like Kesi's and they both had ears that were close to their heads, not like mine that stuck out. Each of us had pieces of Mosi, but on him it all came together in a way that made everyone admire him and want to be near him.

Sometimes a truck with soldiers drove through the village, scattering chickens and honking its horn. All of us would run to see the men in their uniforms with their guns bound with rags. Whenever they drove past, they always stared at Mosi.

One time, a truck stopped and the man in the front seat spoke to him. The man was smoking a thick cigarette and the white smoke streamed from his mouth and nose like he was a dragon. I was afraid that if the smoke touched Mosi's face, he would get swallowed up.

I snapped a dry branch from a bush, and Kesi and I flew toward our brother. He reached out a hand to each of us, and we backed away from the dragon soldier. As we went,

I tried to draw a constant circle to protect us from the dragon watching our every step. Mosi's hand was damp in mine. I looked up at him, and the sun behind his head made his hair glow orange. It grew and grew until he became a giant moth with massive golden wings, and Kesi was a little pink beetle, buzzing around him. My ears stretched into antennae, and I waved them warily, sensing danger from the dragon.

3.

After dinner, I went outside by myself. I walked beyond the circle of firelight, past my avocado tree and even further, to the long grass by the baobab. I lay down on my belly in the soft dust, with my chin cupped in my palms, and watched a little sandfly struggle over the uneven ground. Why was he walking? If I had wings, I'd always fly.

The sun sank behind the hills and the blazing light was replaced in moments by a curtain of blackness. I often tried to notice the exact second this happened, but no matter how steadily I stared, it always seemed to happen when I blinked. I stayed where I was, allowing my ears to pick up where my eyes left off. I heard the murmur of my father talking, ants rustling and the occasional faraway bird calling or child squealing, so vivid now that the darkness had come. The black air lapped over me like water, and I turned lazily onto my back.

I looked up at the stars, humming softly, listening to the rustle of the grasshoppers in the dust and high grass. The sky was pulsing with a scatter of stars so low that they danced in the treetops and cascaded down to the horizon. It was like the Kidom circle had come to life—a twinkling curtain drawn close around me—and through it I could see both worlds.

The stars danced like clouds of fireflies. I tried to look directly at one, but it faded away. When I looked sideways at it, there it was again, bright and clear. I picked another star that was much bigger, one I could look deeply into. I stared and stared, until all the other stars disappeared into the darkness. It felt like someone on that star was staring hard at me, and all at once we were rushing toward each other, about to crash like antelopes jousting with their horns. I pulled my eyes away quickly, just in case.

I waved my hands softly in the air. In the darkness they seemed to separate from me, each long finger transforming into a silver wing, almost invisible in the night sky. Dragonflies, dragons with wings. The king and queen of insects, with their army of fireflies behind them, filling the sky.

I drew a line with my finger, connecting the silver dots on that vast blackboard, like drawing with chalk on my slate. I drew a drum and a locust. I drew a hand holding a stick or a ladle. I shook my head, making the lines disappear. Then I drew an ancient warrior mounted on a giant butterfly. This was harder, because there were not enough stars for the left wing. I closed my eyes. The warrior had a giant boulder in a sling over one arm, and a long spear like Tinochika's, the elder who had given me bitter tea to cure my aching ear. Muscles bulged on his arms, and his hands were so huge they could pluck a baobab like a blade of grass.

I felt myself slipping slowly into sleep, remembering that night in Tinochika's hut as I drifted. My ear throbbing, Tinochika in his long white robe, mixing the foul-smelling herbs, shaking a fetish of black chicken feathers. The frightening sound of his chanting, and behind him a wall hung with pictures of Jesus covered in blood from spikes around his head and tortured people hanging naked over fiery pits. Above me the skies rumbled as the warrior raced across the sky to battle . . . to battle . . . and night erupted in cries of clashing metal. I woke up to a waterfall on the metal roof of our house. Rivers of water were already running wild over the ground right up to the door. Rain and rain and more rain. And yet by morning all was dry and even dusty again, as the earth's thirst is seldom quenched.

4.

Morning is the most beautiful time of day in my village. The thick mist in the valleys makes the green peaks of the hills seem to float free of the earth, and the only way from one to another is to fly.

I walked with Kesi to school, kicking up the dirt with my bare feet. Mornings were the only time when my little sister was quiet — I think she was still sleeping inside. I was the one chattering, more to myself than to her. "We'd need an extra big stick — as long as a tree trunk — to circle the whole hilltop. Then we'd always be in Kidom, and we could fly to school."

As we joined the main path, Kesi skipped away to be with her friends who were kicking a ball of wadded-up banana leaves. I met my friend Jacob by the mango tree behind the schoolhouse, and we took turns hoisting each other up to try to reach the lowest fruit. There was nothing that tasted so sweet in the morning.

Jacob's home was the closest to ours, and every Sunday I would follow the path to his place. We would run through the trees to the river. It was too shallow for swimming, but we would splash around, tossing rocks, watching tiny fish and water bugs.

Jacob loved to play warrior. Not like the soldiers who passed through the village nor the dressed-up big leaders with shiny buttons on their jackets and large leather straps around their waists and across their shoulders. Jacob loved the true warriors of our people, the warriors who dressed in leopard skins and wore their braids flowing down their backs. The ancient warriors of stories, songs and dances — the courageous, proud protectors of the tribe. Jacob would spend ages searching for just the right branch to use as a spear for the day and would meet me with his pockets bulging with bottle caps, feathers and plastic scraps. He would adorn himself and put on the face of a fearless warrior, standing there as if the wind could never blow him down. I would start to clap a rhythm and he would dance, my beat twisting and turning him so that his arms and legs flew as if about to break from his body. He would lift his feet and stomp the ground, sending a message of thunder. But he couldn't keep dancing as long as I could clap, and he'd eventually collapse, covered in sweat. I'd flop down beside him and we'd talk about the old days. Did warriors have to go to school like we did?

This morning, we couldn't reach high enough to grab a mango, so Jacob picked a branch off the ground and proceeded to launch it into the tree to try to knock down the fruit. After the third time the stick came crashing down — still with no mangos — we felt a large shadow loom over us.

"All you are doing is hurting the tree." Baingana's deep voice.

Baingana was our teacher and a village elder. Our parents gave us chores and told us how to behave, but it was Baingana who made us want to obey. Something about his calm ways, his words, his very long fingers and bushy beard, made us feel safe. Baingana put things into our heads that we had never heard of or seen. We had no books, but he had no need for them — his mind was filled with knowledge. He explained how to grow an avocado tree, how to find France on a map, when to use an adjective, what astronauts do, and why our water tasted better when we gathered it higher up the hillsides.

But he also spoke of the roots of our traditions, how our ways of doing things in the village came about and why we must understand and follow these ways to be respected and succeed in life. He showed us the marvels of the creatures and plants that lived all around us and how to commune with them to stay honest and attentive and fair. I felt I was on the right path if I put my feet where Baingana stepped.

"Ooooh, you are in big trouble!" I whispered to Jacob, as Baingana led the way into school.

"Me!" Jacob teased. "If you hadn't been screeching like a monkey he wouldn't have even noticed us."

Squabble, squabble, until we reached the doorway. This was our daily routine. Annoying. Comforting.

"In your seats, please." Baingana's deep voice rumbled.

We all scrambled to our wooden desks, the little ones in the front rows, and the oldest in the back. I settled into my place beside Jacob in the fourth row, and made my silent daily plea to my Kidom guardians to help me pass into the next level so that I could at last have a seat by the window.

5.

Our school was one room, cool and comfortable, our benches lined up to face clean blackboards. All of the children from the village and nearby farms came here every day. The rains could fail to come, but we never failed to arrive on time, dressed in our crisp white shirts. Home could be wanting, the roads muddy or dusty or frightening, but school was secure.

I sat up very straight, hoping to be chosen as the day's helper. Each morning, Baingana chose one of us to fetch water for the schoolroom, beat the chalk out of the erasers and perform other equally important tasks throughout the day. It was a position of honour, especially, Baingana said, for those old enough to appreciate the privilege and young enough to be willing to help.

Before he spoke to us again, Baingana gave us his warm smile. But when he opened his mouth, BANG! A loud noise outside sent us older children scrambling to the window.

I could see nothing, but another BANG! came, followed by the pitiful bleating of goats, and we all began to cry out.

"Calm down!" Baingana boomed, striding to the doorway and blocking it with his huge frame.

I craned my neck but could see only a glimpse of blue sky above the crowd of heads in front of me.

Then the oldest kids began to point. "Hey, neat! Check it out!" "Oh yeah!" "Look at that one!" "It's Danno!"

Danno was a film from America about a strong man with guns who shot people in the jungle. I had never seen it, but I knew this much: soldiers were out there.

I moved away from the window to find my little sister where she still sat in the second row.

"Come on," I whispered, and we made our way to stand behind our teacher.

He was still blocking the doorway, but he was silent as he stared into the front yard. Most of the other boys and girls came to crowd behind us at the door, pushing and shoving and trying to poke their heads around our teacher's waist or through his legs so they could see. I edged my head around him and looked up to see his face. It wasn't the usual face of Baingana. It was still, yes, but not calm. His mouth was wide open, his eyes bulging.

I turned my eyes to look where he was staring. The soldiers outside the school were shorter and skinnier than any I had seen before. Their movements were quick, not lazy and leaning like those of the dragon man. They were carrying guns in their hands, and some of the guns seemed as big as they were. Then I got it: they were kids. It was weird, ridiculous. They were dressed like real soldiers but in miniature. They were our ages but their faces looked as if they were wearing angry masks held in place by dirty bandanas and skullcaps. Where did they come from and why were they here? But as we watched them spreading out from the truck with their guns pointing in all directions as if they were going to shoot or at least scare everybody else, questions disappeared from my head. My stomach clenched and I pulled Kesi closer.

Five or six of them were crowded around an old goat herder, who towered over them. He was shouting at them and pointing to his goat flopping on the ground—it had blood on its face and was bleating more softly now.

One tall child raised his gun like a stick and swung it at the herder. We all gasped as the thick part of the gun smashed into his old, thin face and made his head snap around. We gasped again as he fell to the ground and these children—were they really children?—laughed. This was unbelievable. It was not possible. What child would strike an elder? I began to shake so hard my teeth were clacking together.

Far along the path behind them I could see Mosi running toward the school. My heart was pounding and I couldn't breathe properly. I gulped and swallowed at air full of the children's shouts and the cries of the goat herder, the sound of their feet kicking him.

Mosi was coming for me and Kesi. I pulled my head inside and led her to the bench at my desk, where we huddled to wait for him.

It was quiet inside the schoolhouse now. Breathless. We could hear the crunching of those children's steps on the ground outside, their shouts to each other. Baingana backed up from the doorway, shooing the children away. "Students, I want you to sit under your desks. NOW."

He turned and went back to the doorway, as the shouts outside got closer.

He aimed his big voice into the schoolyard, at the horrible miniature soldiers with their guns. "My children, God bless y—"

There was a bang, and Baingana fell back inside the classroom, crashing onto the floor, where he lay still, his head gushing blood.

Those evil children in their dark-green uniforms burst in, shouting, flailing their guns, jumping over and around Baingana—no, these were not children, not like Jacob, Kesi or me. Scars on their arms and legs stood out shiny, as if they were wet. The veins in their necks were tense and bulging, and their eyes were large, red and wild. One had a black feather fetish like Tinochika's tied around his forehead. It frightened me more now than it had in that terrible voodoo ceremony. It made the boy look like an evil bird, a black and green woodpecker out to find and swallow the sweet insects hidden under the tree bark.

Some of the girls were screaming now. BANG! BANG! Then came more crashes. These boys with guns were overturning the desks, grabbing the smaller children and pulling them outside. Others were pointing their guns at the older students, shouting at them and shoving them toward a corner.

Our fear was choking the air from the room.

I covered Kesi with my body and we started crawling toward the window, along the line of desks. I whispered into her ear, "I'll push you up and out, okay? Then I will jump through and we will find Mosi."

Kesi was whimpering, and I could feel her wet tears on my hands as we crawled.

"Shhh, shhh, don't worry. I'll draw the circle, shhh, shhh." I stopped for a moment, hugging her close, and traced a circle around us.

"We're in Kidom, okay? Getting little, tiny. We're turning into tiny little purple dragonflies, okay?" My voice was shaking. "Now let's go. Together we can fly out the window—we are practically invisible. Kesi? Come on now, come with me. We'll fly far away, up up up. We'll be safe."

We made it to the wall and crouched behind an overturned desk, slowly raising ourselves to peer out the window. Behind us was a thrashing mass of horrible monsters. But we were free, flying above, through, away.

There were more soldier spiders outside, but they weren't near the school. They were on the path, wriggling in a pile.

"Mosi!" Kesi cried, spotting our big and brave brother, and we were flying toward him. Mosi was struggling, his giant wings trapped, fighting against an enormous sticky web.

But before we reached him, Kesi and I were grabbed. She screamed and wriggled, and I kicked out, struggling to wrench free, but the children soon pinned us down. Both of us froze when we felt the guns poking at us. We were so scared that no sounds came out of our mouths, we just watched the destruction through the stench and sting and blur of smoke. These kids were black spiders but also vile green mantises with long metal limbs that smoked out dull explosions.

Two small trucks drove up and more soldiers, older ones, jumped out. They picked up Mosi, Kesi, me and some others and tied our hands together with twisted plastic rope and threw us into the back. Then they tossed three goats into the truck bed too, and the animals stumbled and righted themselves before cringing away from us.

Mosi's face was shining with sweat, and a blob of something thick and red sat over his left eye. Kesi wriggled away from me to snuggle next to him.

"Mosi, this isn't Kidom at all," she whispered.

"No, little one, no, this is something else. Just be quiet and good and we'll get home soon."

The road was bumpy and we were unable to hold ourselves up as the truck bounced, swinging violently, along the uneven bush road from our village. I was sure I would fall off the truck and lose Kesi and Mosi forever. The rope around my wrists was too tight but the more I struggled to get free, the more the rope rubbed and burned my skin. Kesi was right. This was not Kidom, and it was nothing like our home world either. So there was another world, filled with loud noise, with scary, scary things, with horrible smells and smoke and strange, bad people who carried weapons.

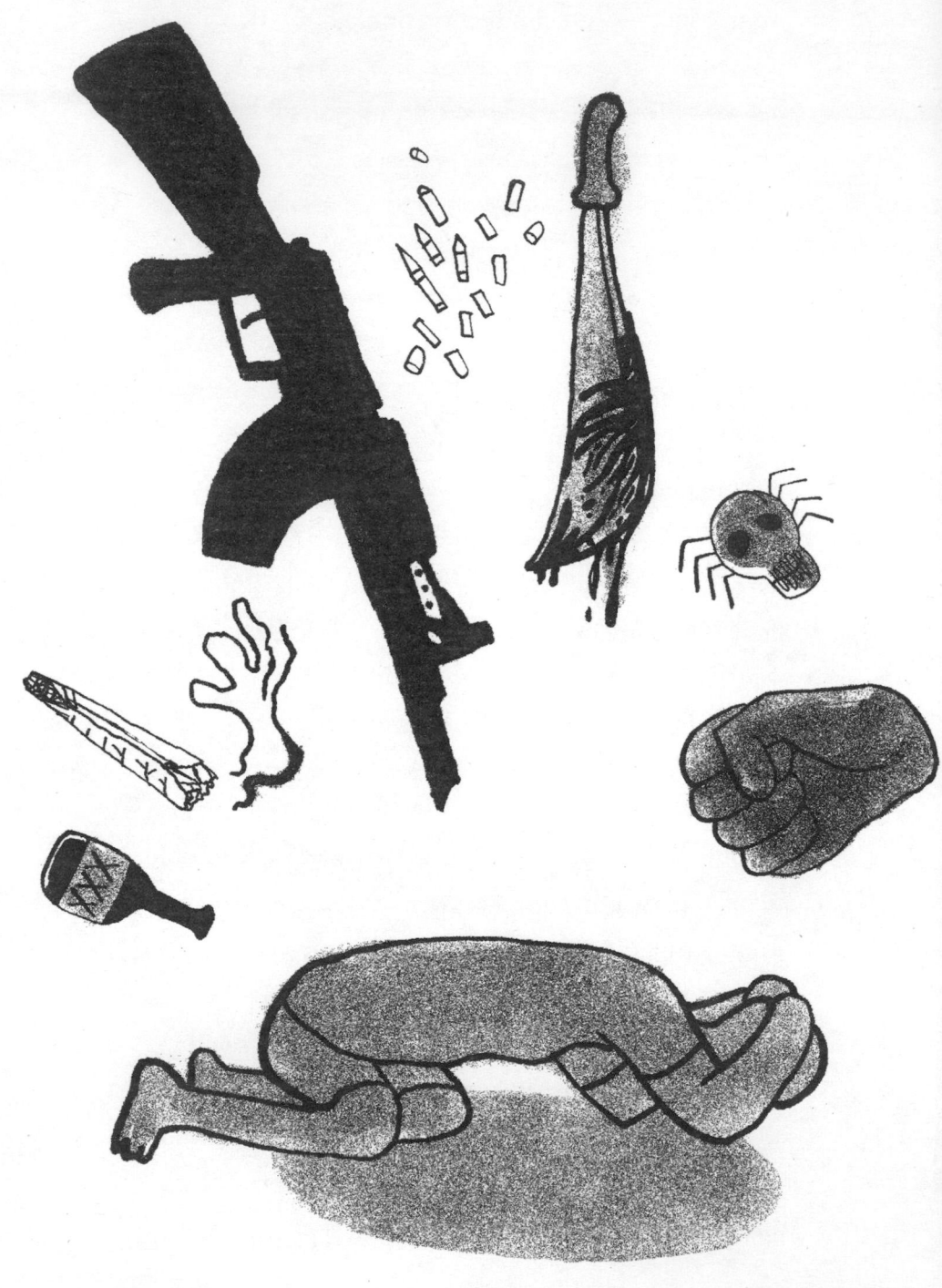

4.

Kidom Lost

6.

We arrived at a camp with several large lean-tos, more trucks and many more people. We were unloaded and left to stand in the dust, guarded by one of the older children. The sunlight felt hazy and unreal. Everything was strange, like we'd been dropped in a ghost forest, with demons lurking beneath rotting brush. The air was sour, metallic, and there were dragons everywhere, breathing smoke and fire.

Mosi was watching something intently, squinting against the sun. I followed his eyes to a loud group of dragon soldiers who were shoving each other and laughing. Some were sitting on the ground but most were standing, leaning on sticks, guns and machetes. They were all green except for a blue one in the centre. It was Mashaka, my brother. He was laughing too and never glanced our way no matter how hard we stared. Someone handed him a cigarette and as he held it to his mouth, his skin began to buckle, forming scales. By the time he had exhaled the grey smoke from his nose, he was a dragon too.

Hours passed and no one brought us anything to eat or drink, but the entire time two or three dragons with guns half-watched us. I became desperate to pee. When I stood up and gestured to the guard to try to show him what I needed, he glared at me and waved with his gun for me to sit down again. I sat. I was afraid and sick to my stomach from lack of food and fear all mixed up inside and in the end I peed where I sat. I could not look at anybody.

Mosi spent the time trying to soothe Kesi, but he could not talk above a whisper or the dragons would come and kick him. She just cried and cried. There was no hushing her or stopping her even when there were no tears left.

I shuffled away from where I had wet the ground and slumped over to lie with my cheek in the dust. I watched the ants. Funny how they never seemed to stop working. Sometimes I blew some air at one to force him to change his path. He would tumble over with all his legs waving wildly, then right himself and find his way back to the trail. I fell asleep trying to picture myself following them to their home, slipping into their hole and down, down into their kitchen. Sipping tea with their king and telling him how industrious and determined his subjects were.

The dragons left us there all night. When I woke the sky was as black as the ink in the little bottle on Baingana's desk and I could see nothing at all, just feel Kesi still shuddering, hear Mosi still murmuring. I struggled to sit up, and then wiggled close to them, hoping to share our warmth.

7.

The next day we were put into a truck and driven back to our village. We were all exhausted from broken sleep and weak from no food or water. My clothes were stiff and smelled sour from my accident. But as bad as I felt, our village looked a thousand times worse, blackened and burned and in places still smoking. Clothes and cooking utensils were strewn everywhere, but I didn't see any people. They'd hurt Baingana, but maybe they just scared the rest away.

The soldiers let us out of the truck and didn't seem to care if we wandered around—our hands were still tied. Mosi, Kesi and I ran awkwardly to our hut, but it had been burned to the ground. Our parents were not there.

My soul and the souls of my ancestors in me lurched in agony to see the faint pattern of what had been my mother's garden, the clever design of beans and corn that her grandmother had passed down to her. This little plot of land—our garden, our hut—on which generations of our family had lived, died, been buried and born, had been alive. Now it was dead, and we had nothing.

Kesi began to cry again, but I felt as though I was floating away from her and from Mosi. I twisted to snap a twig off my charred avocado tree and tucked it in my waistband.

Some soldiers appeared and herded us back to the village centre, prodding us along with their guns. A swirl of sound and smells assaulted us there, and I felt like I'd gone blind. My head was spinning and I fell to the ground, a sharp, terrible smell of metal and salt in the air.

More soldiers were coming from the direction of the schoolhouse, shoving several adults in front of them. A woman fell, and several of the soldiers stopped to kick her, then hauled her up and pushed her toward us.

BANG! Everyone jumped and screamed, and looked around with the whites of their eyes showing. A tall man, a gun in his hand, was climbing out of the cab of another truck as several children jumped off the back to follow him.

"You see?" the man shouted at us. "These stupid people thought they would ambush you! Shoot and kill you! These are the enemies of the struggle. They are traitors, they are cockroaches, and they must be exterminated!"

Most of the adults were weeping, pleading. One woman sobbed and said, "We were protecting and supporting you," but a young boy soldier pushed her and kicked her in the stomach as she fell, causing the others to laugh.

Mosi gasped, and we all saw Daddy. He saw us at the same moment and jerked forward, shouting our names.

The leader flew toward us like a giant wasp, his voice a buzzing drone. "If you are to join us, it is essential that you understand the importance of our fight and prove your loyalty. These traitors, they must be punished for starting this war, for turning against their people. They are nothing but infected dogs, they are dirty insects and must be destroyed before they infect more minds and pollute our cause of freedom."

I stared at the ground, shaking, as Mosi raised himself up, his arms still tied behind his back.

"This is my father," he said in a loud, clear voice. "These are all our people, and we will not allow them to be harmed." A hideous scream, a terrible, terrible sound, punctuated Mosi's words.

I raised my eyes to the squirming, writhing mass of our elders in front of us and saw flashes of blue, of red. And then my eyes focused on Mashaka, a soldier's bandana around his head. He was holding a bloody machete in one hand and our father's head in the other. He was grasping Daddy's hair, tilting his face to the sky, his exposed neck split open like a goat's. Mashaka was yelling and dancing and jerking in all directions. His eyes were wide and wild and seemed to pierce everything he looked at.

Mosi and I lunged forward, screaming, and everything exploded. Some of the soldiers began shooting and hacking at the elders, as others grabbed us children by the necks and pushed us to the ground. In the chaos I lost track of my sister, could not see the flash of pink anywhere.

Mosi was next to me, with a fat soldier's knee in his back and a gun in his face.

"Where's Kesi?" I choked out, my voice cracking.

Mosi began kicking, hard.

Then we heard her scream and both of our heads craned to find her under the mango tree in the school-yard. The air turned thick between us as her tiny body was torn free of her brilliant pink wrapper. Giant black arms pulled her limbs, pushed her little skinny legs apart. She was screaming out of fear and pain, and Mosi attempted to fight his way up from the ground only to be hit in the head with a rifle butt and collapse face down in the dirt. Everyone around me went quiet then, all of us listening to the noises the soldiers were making over my sister. I did not look up until those noises stopped. The last man was doing up his belt as the rest of them moved away, and Kesi was lying still and quiet. I struggled to my feet and took an unsteady step toward her but then a massive blow to the back of my head knocked me to the ground, and all went black.

8.

I woke in a blind panic, my heart pounding. My arms were free. I pushed myself to my feet and found myself in a grassy clearing, with low huts scattered here and there, and rows of lean-tos around it. It hurt to walk, and my head throbbed with every step, but I wanted to find Mosi.

There were soldiers everywhere, huddled in groups or carrying piles of wood and metal. Some were in army greens, others in blue jeans and long-sleeved shirts, still others were dressed like me, only dirtier.

Mosi wasn't anywhere that I could see. The camp itself had a cluttered, messy feel to it. I could smell the uncertainty and chaos, I could feel it on my skin.

I looked down at my hands, which seemed far away and not a part of me. The wrists were raw and the palms were red. Red. My heart started to pound again and my eyes welled with tears, remembering. I pressed the tail of my shirt against my eyes hard, so colours swirled and flashed. My clothes were dirty and torn. No, I would not think.

Mosi was nowhere to be seen. I was all alone.

I felt something poking my back and reached into my waistband to find the charred avocado twig. Crying hard now, I snapped it in half, into quarters, destroying it like the rest of my world. Gone gone gone. Kidom destroyed as much as my home world.

An older boy walked straight toward me, thin and dressed in green camouflage. He gestured to me to sit down, and then he hunkered next to me and handed me a drink. I took the cup from him and drank the bitter liquid till the cup was empty, feeling both grateful and ashamed for taking anything from these people. But I had not eaten or drunk for two days.

The boy took the empty cup back without a word and patted me on the shoulder. My mouth was full of the nasty taste of the drink and I longed for some clear water.

I couldn't help thinking about Kesi, and tears started to leak from my eyes when suddenly my brain seemed to leap to the side. Whoosh! Then it was normal again. Then whoosh, whoosh. I tried to raise my gaze from the ground but it followed me. Everything was swirling, and I could feel my sadness easing as the world transformed into giant grains of sand and huge monster blades of grass.

An ant crawled onto my hand and looked me in the eye. He waved his little front leg hello.

"Welcome," he said. "You are finally here!"

I turned my head and body around slowly. I was in Kidom! It wasn't destroyed and it wasn't make-believe.

I was about to reply to the ant, when his pincers began to grow bigger and bigger. His face was growing cruel, and I was getting smaller and smaller.

More ants were coming toward me, crawling over me, nipping my flesh. I struggled to get away but my body was filled with wet sand. Then wasps and mosquitoes were filling the air around my head, moving in slow motion. Coming to get me. I fell back into the darkness, alone.

9

As the next day passed, I began to notice the comings and goings of these children in uniform. The only adults hung out under a shelter at the far end of the camp, sitting around wooden tables and talking long into the night, sometimes laughing loudly. Older boys led groups of littler children out into the bush around us, and sometimes I could hear the bang of guns. I could walk a little more easily, but my headache was unrelenting and they mostly left me to myself. I wanted to find Mosi and I wanted to get away from this terrible place. I needed a plan. Since I missed my family so much, surely these young soldiers must miss theirs too. Why did they all stay? There were no fences around the camp, but the bush was thick and I just did not know in what direction to go. My village was gone, my father and little sister were dead. I didn't know what happened to my mother, or where Mosi was, and Mashaka . . . he was dead to me now.

The older boy who had given me the awful drink came to find me a couple times and talked to me a bit. One suppertime he brought me a bowl of beans, and as I ate he told me a little about himself.

"I was selected years ago," he said, "and became a good fighter. Then one day a fancy white truck drove into our camp and some white people in clean shirts took me and the other boys away. We went to a tall building in the city, and were told we were no longer soldiers. I was given money—they called it a trust fund. I took the money and bought jeans and sneakers. Then I had nothing else to do and no one to talk to, and in that city there was no place to sleep except in an alley. So I came back."

"Why didn't you try to find your family?"

He just looked at me as though I was stupid.

After that, he offered me more of the bitter drink, and instead of saying no I reached for the cup again.

10.

Even though it didn't seem like anyone was paying attention to me, when my head stopped hurting, they showed me a lean-to built of large branches from banana trees and said that this was where I would sleep. They put me to work collecting firewood with the other new recruits. Tired, thirsty, dirty, discouraged and lost, we were jumpy and raw. When I gathered firewood at home, I would often dawdle, playing in Kidom. Here, I was under guard, trapped in this world, the only release the bitter drink. But rather than making the world brighter and bigger, the drink closed things in so that I could cower inside it. If I asked for it, though, Christian (this was the older boy's name) would laugh and walk away. For some reason, it had to be offered.

As we searched for wood and dried roots that would

burn, we sometimes roamed as far as a training place cleared in the bush, where very young children and some my age, carrying sticks and knives, were barked at by the older soldiers. These children were not wearing uniforms, but I knew that now they were soldiers too.

One time when I approached, a group of them was sitting and listening to a commander give instructions. I moved close to a boy about my age at the end of a line and sat down near him, greeting him quietly. He raised his eyes briefly and glanced away from me, toward his commander, who wasn't looking in our direction. I didn't know how to ask the questions jumbled in my mind, so I just blurted them out, one by one.

"What are you doing?"

. . .

"How long have you been here?

. . .

"Is any of your family with you?"

. . .

"Have you ever tried to leave?"

. . .

The long pauses after my whispered questions were filled with silence from the boy, except for the last one, to which he finally mumbled, "Leave? Where would I go?"

He glanced again at his commander, whose attention was still elsewhere, then whispered, "Papa knew the soldiers were coming. He and Mama argued about it.

I didn't understand why until they came for me. They embraced Papa and shook his hand. They left him a parcel and took me with them. No one said a word, and my mother was crying and wouldn't look at me as the truck pulled away. I called out for her but my father blocked her view and then I was gone.

"When I asked what was happening, one of the soldiers laughed and told me that my father had traded me to the soldiers and made a poor bargain of it. If I went home, he would just send me back.

"So now I do what the commander wants and stay out of the way of the older boys, and try not to be scared when we go to fight the enemy. I do not want to die like the others who were here with me when I arrived."

I shivered and did not know what to say to this boy.

11.

The next day a whole troop of children was sent out on foot, leading a convoy of trucks crammed with older boys and girls. I picked my moment and asked a grown-up soldier where they were going.

He stared down at me, picking then sucking his teeth, as if he was deciding whether I was worth an answer. Then he said, "The cockroaches bury anti-personnel and anti-tank mines on the roads and larger trails. We send new kids like you in first to clear the way because it's better for the cause that you step on the mines—we don't want to lose a soldier with more experience."

He stared at me some more, as if daring me to argue with his logic, then said, "It makes sense. We also send you inexperienced ones ahead to attract enemy fire and use up most of their ammo—we know they don't have much. If you survive your first battle then you might be worth really training."

It seemed to me that the young ones were going to suffer a lot more than the older ones, but this whole world was upside down. I gathered my courage and asked him if he had any of the bitter drink. He laughed and gave me some sticky brown gum and told me to try it instead.

When the soldiers came back late that night, I stood at the opening of the lean-to and watched. I could not tell if any of the youngest ones were missing, though some of them were injured. The rest were either very happy, dancing and singing, or very quiet. I reached inside my waistband to find the last little bit of sticky gum, popped it in my mouth, went back inside and fell asleep.

12.

Outside the commander's lean-to, which stood out from all the rest because it was where smells of delicious food came from, a girl my age was sitting and weaving long grasses into a bracelet.

She smiled at me when I walked by and asked me to sit with her.

She told me that she was the commander's best wife, and that because of this she always got the best food and drinks. She then offered me a piece of meat and some sliced cassava from her bowl, which I gobbled down greedily. Remembering my manners, I thanked her. I asked her why she was here, why she didn't escape or try to go home.

She looked at me with a tilted head, then lowered her voice. "This must be my home now. Some of the girls were sent away from here because they were sick or pregnant, but one of them came back, begging to stay here. She told me that when she tried to go home to her village, she was shamed and turned away. Her own relatives threatened her. She works here now.

"And for me it would be worse. When they came to our hut, two soldiers tied up my father and brothers and took me in front of them. No, no, no. I cannot return.

"At first, I wished very much to escape—even just to disappear in the bush. Each night a different soldier would come and sleep with me. I was ashamed and wished to die.

"But then I was lucky. I was chosen by the commander to be one of his wives. Now I am protected from the other soldiers, I live in a hut, I eat nice food, I am in charge of much in the camp. I have a better life here than most girls."

Sadly, silently, I nodded, and chewed another piece of my brown gum. I now knew that it was called hashish.

13.

The next day, after a breakfast of beans and goat's milk, one of the lieutenants pulled me aside.

I don't know what he was seeing on my face, but he explained to me that going back to the life I had before I was captured was not an option for me anymore.

"You and your pretty brother now belong to us, and you can be proud—you will soon be fighting this war too, for the good side, the side of freedom!" I didn't know what he meant by this "freedom" because I was a prisoner here. Was there something that he and the others were doing that would make life better than it was when I was in my village and with my family? But all the leaders here said things like this over and over, during the days and the long evenings by the fires, and they said it like they were really convinced it was true.

I wanted so much to belong to something or someone so that I was not so alone and afraid all the time. I had not seen Mosi for days. I missed my mother and my father and my sister. I wanted to scream and run away no matter what. I couldn't help myself and shouted at him, "My father was murdered! My sister . . ."

"It is terrible." He was calm, his voice almost kind. "Your brother Mashaka was a bad young man—he was a traitor, you see. He had joined the opposing side and was acting as a spy. We have taken care of him, my friend. You are now safe. You and Mosi are with us now and we will avenge the terrible slaughter of your family."

He stared at me so hard after he stopped talking I was confused. I tried to think back to that day, but it was a blur of strangers and chaos and blood.

My brother. Mashaka. He was gone too. Tears filled my eyes and I looked away to follow a pair of dragonflies soaring past me, into the sky. At least my father died trying to protect us, to defend our lives. My brother, he was dead only for war.

I followed the lieutenant to a field where they were teaching the newest children how to use guns. He picked one up and handed it to me and pointed to the others so that I knew I was to join in the training. He said I was going to learn to shoot people who were bad and needed to be punished. We were going to save our country. We were going to be the warriors who protect those who are oppressed in the struggle for freedom. Again he used the word freedom, but what did it really mean? I was not free, nor were any of the other children. How do we create freedom if we are not free?

The gun smelled of oil and was a little slippery and when I dropped it, the leader hit me with his stick. "Never drop your rifle because it is precious and it is your best friend from now on. You will clean it and sleep with it and carry it all the time. Your lieutenant will tell you when to put bullets in it, but for now we will teach you how to aim at targets. The first time you hit a target I promise you will find it very exciting, and you'll be proud to see it burst into pieces."

14.

There were seven of us who slept on the dirt floor of the lean-to. It was too small for this many people, but in the loneliness of night it was somewhat comforting to be close, even to strangers.

All night, every night, I heard soft whimpers and muffled sobs from the other children. It seemed that we could say things to the black night that we couldn't say to each other's eyes in the day. Fragments of thoughts and unconnected words would float through the air above us, hovering, seeking a safe place to land.

"Mommy!"

"I had to."

"No!"

"They made me."

"I'm sorry."

Hideous images were conjured on that ceiling: Flesh splitting under knife blades. Brothers butchered like animals. Sisters raped then tossed in latrine pits. Babies snatched from their mothers' breasts and dashed to the ground with milk still spilling from their lips. People reduced to meat wrapped in cloth.

During the day I was so tired from the night, that I could not stop trying to cry. But I had no tears left. It just hurt and my eyes would get blurry and I would choke a little and feel my heart pounding. I was so homesick yet I had no more home.

"Training" consisted of waking before the sun. We would have to fill sacks with heavy rocks and then carry them on our backs as we ran around the compound in the dark or went for long marches in the darkest places in the bush. Where the night had once drawn safely around me like a curtain, it now frightened me. Everything—low bushes like enemies crouching, the rustle of insects like crunching boots on gravel—was potentially alive and dangerous. And yet, on those long night drills, my mind would sometimes still be lulled by the thick, soft darkness back to my home, my world, my child world, my Kidom.

If we faltered, the commanders chased us with thick sticks, hitting us on the backs of our knees. They would push us to the ground, shout in our ears and scream orders again and again. Before the sun was even at its peak, we were exhausted.

Then, often without being allowed to remove the sacks from our backs, we would practise shooting. The guns were not as heavy as they looked, though they were too long for some of the children to hold steady and straight. Those kids were sent back to do chores in the camp or to carry food and water and ammunition for the rest of the soldiers. I was scared the first time the leader put a bullet in my rifle and told me to shoot a big melon a little ways away. The rifle had come to life and it was now a dangerous thing. There were at least twenty of us training that day, and we were told to line up and shoot one after another. When it was my turn, I held the gun up and steadied it to see through the sights and find the melon. When the leader yelled "Fire!" I pulled the trigger and the gun made such a loud noise and hit my shoulder so hard I nearly dropped it. I do not know where my bullet went.

Even after all the kids fired, the melon was still there. The leader was very mad and yelled at us for wasting very valuable ammunition. He warned us that we had better try harder the next time. And there were so many next times until we could hit the melon.

Every so often, a gun would spit fire and hot metal pieces as the cartridge shattered at the breech instead of firing normally, and the child holding it would be burned on his face and arms, or be cut and bloody, or even blinded. Crying and screams were so common, though, that I got used to them and stopped noticing after a while.

Explosions from hand grenades and bullets were terrifying. The older soldiers fired near us so that we would get used to the sounds of battle. I was always scared that one of them would aim too close or too poorly. Dirt would shower us with each explosion. Our tears and sweat caked the dirt, and our clothes and skin were torn from running in the bush.

Each day, one or two children were pulled aside, usually after they had inflicted some degree of torment on someone smaller than themselves. The next day they'd turn up with a camouflage bandana, a bunch of feathers, an army vest—a reward from the commander.

This one afternoon when the sun was at its hottest, we were lined up as usual at long rickety tables and instructed to tend to the weapons. We piled ammunition, and then stripped, oiled and reassembled our guns. The leaders made us repeat these drills for hours so we could do them with our eyes closed, just as we would have to do when we went for a long night march to battle and had to clean our weapons before the attack. I soon got very good at this, and the lieutenant noticed that the kids near me would ask me for help with theirs. I actually was proud of my new skills, and I became attached to my own AK-47 and did my best to keep it clean and oiled.

A young girl I had seen before came up to me this day as I was putting my gun back together. She winked at me and held out her fists. I stuck out my palms, and into one hand she placed a piece of candied fruit. And into the other, a pretty pink beetle shell that looked like a jewel, it was so shiny and smooth.

I longed to speak to her, but the lieutenant shouted for me to get back to work.

I put the fruit in my mouth, and the shell in my pocket, gently. As the sweetness melted on my tongue, the shiny pink of the shell misted my sight, and I was back with Kesi, flying through Kidom.

Later that day, after a shooting practice and an interminable hike with heavy sacks, I went to seek out the girl. It was quite dark already, and I didn't know which shelter she was in. I peeked into several to see youths playing cards and smoking. I checked the area around the cooking fire where many of the girls congregated, watching over some of the younger children who were doing chores, but she was not there.

The camp at night was poorly lit with small fires, and there were many shadows and sounds of exaggerated laughter, submissive moaning and the odd shriek. Several of the children were sick and uncared for, or, having been beaten, they were suffering from wounds. At night, the hell of day turned into a black hole where devils were even more evident: living ghosts.

As I passed by the commander's tent, I thought I would ask his best wife if she knew the girl. I heard a commotion coming from behind the tent and crept carefully to peer around the corner. The commander and two of his lieutenants were standing around a girl who was lying on the ground. The commander's wife was holding her shoulders down. As the girl writhed back and forth, I could see it was my friend.

She was naked, and one at a time the men lay on top of her, grunting and groaning. The leaders often did that to young girls but also to some of the most delicate of the young boys too. It was so evil and it hurt us so much. This was torture and punishment, but with luck you might avoid it by being a very good and obedient foot soldier.

I went back to my dirty hut and sat on the floor facing the wall, chewing the last of my hashish. I pulled the delicate beetle shell from my pocket and crushed it in my fist.

15.

For days, Gamba, the lieutenant assigned to my group, had been preparing us for a supplies raid.

The youngest children in our group had gravitated to me, and they followed me with more and more devotion each day. Sometimes I told them stories of Kidom, or played with them the quieter games that I had played with Kesi, games that Mosi had also played with me. But other times I didn't feel like it. I would tell them to be quiet and listen to Gamba so that I could be alone.

We spent a lot of time listening to Gamba talk and talk and talk, but it was so difficult to understand what he was really saying. It was even harder to measure what he kept telling us against what I had seen and what had happened over these last weeks. The more he spoke, the more confused I became. The hashish, the lack of food, the nightmares that woke me every time I tried to sleep: all these things were mixing me up.

Some of the young soldiers had told me stories of being forced to kill people with machetes. They would chop up the bodies, and blood would splatter all over their hands and arms and legs and uniform. The leaders wanted to teach people a lesson by making them suffer, but other times they used the machetes because they did not have any bullets left. But Gamba insisted that we were in the right to do these things, that the evils being perpetrated against us were what we were fighting about. I shook my head to clear it but the horror scenes were always there. This madness was being forced into our heads day in and day out. It was like a sickness in my brain that would not leave except when I could get some of the drugs, and then all would become cloudy again and I was numb and nothing hurt me for some hours. It was an escape I wanted more and more.

One afternoon I set the little ones up with some hard nuts we had collected so they could play a game of marbles, and I went off on my own. Gamba came after me. He told me in confidence that I was crucial to the success of my group, that I was not only the tallest but also the smartest and understood better than anyone the importance of our work. I did not tell him how little I understood. I never questioned his reasons for selecting me. I was just relieved to be noticed without reprimand.

We were standing on a dusty patch behind my lean-to. I told him that I was ready to be in charge of the younger ones and I would do what I could to protect them, but I wasn't sure I could go into battle. "What if someone fought back? I am still afraid that I could kill someone for real. Mosi would never do such a thing."

"Bah, Mosi." Gamba rolled his eyes, but wouldn't explain himself, or answer any of my questions about my brother, who I'd only seen once at a distance, carrying a load of firewood. "Don't be stupid," Gamba said. "Do you feel bad when you swat flies? Or pluck blades of grass? These people are nothing—insects standing in our way. Besides, we don't kill everyone. I have the power to pick and choose. The best, like you, we take."

Swatting flies. My mind leapt back to me and Kesi sitting on her mat, perfectly still, the circle drawn around us, willing the pretty green flies to settle on our out-stretched arms, which we had smeared with honey. If we charmed enough flies to cling to our arms, maybe we could fly too. We begged them to come to us, treasured those that landed, sang to them.

I tried not to share this memory with Gamba, but it

came out anyway. He laughed loudly, and then pulled black feathers out of his pocket, which he twisted into my hair, like Tinochika's horrible fetish. He told me he could grant me flight and that I never had to crawl with vermin again.

For three days he spent all his spare time with me. We would sit and chew hashish or smoke marijuana and I would fly and fly. He discussed our higher purpose of freedom with me as if I was an adult. All those words were still difficult for me to grasp or feel. But I had gotten used to the repetition of the argument and was not so confused when he talked about the cause. He pushed on me the reasons for the cruelty, the reasons for the horrors, why it was so important to fight back and even kill people. He pushed me: could I do it? I couldn't answer and that annoyed Gamba, but he would continue to talk and gave me the drugs that I needed to create the numbness I craved. Constant and repetitious words driven into our ears and minds, drills and drugs day in and day out, following orders because of the drugs and to get more drugs. We were like machines most of the time as long as we had enough drugs. And I realized that I had become a child soldier like the older ones and that my small group would surely be tested soon. With people, not melons, at the end of my gun.

———

On the evening of that third day, Gamba took me for a walk. He had two machetes with him, which he gave me to carry, along with hashish, and a sharp mix of cocaine and gunpowder, which I sniffed up my nose. He laughed as my eyes grew big and my lips stretched in a grin. I felt the back of my neck tingling and my shell breaking open. I felt the unfolding of my wings, stretching bigger and wider.

Then we were in a clearing, and I was spinning in the star-filled sky, swinging my long sharp claws, laughing crazily. I was a giant, I was ruler of everything. Gamba was cheering me, shouting at me to "squash it—smash the dirty thing."

I saw a stupid fly, dirty and useless, wriggling on the ground, and my control was perfect and total. I swung my arm with its long silver blade and severed the fly in two. I tore its wings off and jumped back to watch it writhe and buzz uselessly, and then stop.

Many other young soldiers swooped in close to me, jumping and dancing and shooting their guns. Sparks and flashes and noise were everywhere. Gamba loomed near and offered me more of the gunpowder cocaine, and I sniffed it straight into my brain and it all went wild and stayed wild for some time.

I was dancing too, dripping with sweat. My clothes felt sticky on me and my head was full of loud sounds and bright sights and I was not seeing very well at all. After what seemed like hours, I was so tired that I stumbled and fell, and the others picked me up and shoved me into the middle of a circle of grinning faces and white-rimmed eyes. The world started to slow to near paralysis and I looked down at the broken fly in the centre of the circle and saw Mosi's beautiful face staring up at me, his eyes surprised, frozen. I staggered toward him, but Gamba pushed me away and down the path that led back to camp.

"I think I killed him," I shouted, and I began sobbing and could not catch my breath as tears gushed out of my eyes like blood. "No, no, no, no . . ." Gasping, choking, my face aching, I struggled to breathe through my cries. Gamba walked beside me, a hand on my back. Every time my tears would stop, my brain would force Mosi's face, his eyes, into my mind. That beautiful, gentle face.

"No, I couldn't have," I sobbed.

And Gamba began to sing softly, "Life is a circle; there is no need to cry." He put one strong arm around my shoulders and held me up and told me that I had acted like a courageous soldier committed to the cause. I had passed the test and was now a young leader, and he seemed so proud of me. I felt sick and disoriented and could not stop crying, but I never wanted him to take his arm away.

At last we stepped out of the shadows into the circle of fires at the camp. At last my tears dried up as I felt myself enter another, familiar world. Not my own, but at least not that one where I had just been. Maybe it hadn't really happened.

Then my machete, which I was dragging behind me, hit a rock. The thump reminded me, and I saw Mosi's eyes again. My stomach lurched. The blade was heavy and burning in my hand and I dropped it, letting go of what seemed like a thousand pounds. I would never carry a machete again, I swore. I was dirty and wet. The smell of drying blood on my arms and face sickened me. Now I was a monster just like them, these soldier leaders, and they were happy for me.

Gamba walked me to my lean-to, to my comrades. No one asked me anything, and someone handed me a beer. It was wet and delicious on my sore throat.

One of the other adult leaders ducked into our shelter and dropped the bloody machete in front of us and laughed as we all stared at it. One of my comrades picked up the bloody weapon and slapped me on the back, and carried it away to a corner where he cleaned it as we had been taught to do, then sharpened it with a stone, the rhythm of his strokes the only sound in the hut. There was some sympathy in the faces around me, and at last one of the older ones said, "The first is the hardest. You want the ground to open up and swallow you afterwards. You do not want to go on. The second time, you wait to feel that bad again, but you do not, and you hate yourself for that. By the third time, you are curious to see what happens."

I could not ask if the first person he had killed was his own brother.

We smoked marijuana late into the night, and I thought, for me there is no home world, there is no Kidom. All I have now is this. Kill or be killed. Teach the others to become just like me, so I won't be the only one.

17.

Over the next two weeks, I was officially put in charge of a small group of children. I was to train them to use the weapons and ensure that they were made strong. A few of the others in the camp also came to me after their initiation with helpless, defeated eyes, often with the blood of the dead dried on their lips.

I understood that these initiations were important to prepare good soldiers, but I still felt . . . well, I still felt. But not very much.

Then one morning Gamba told us we needed to prepare for a raid.

"Go through the village like you are shopping at a market," he said. "Take anything we can use—things, people."

Please, please, please, please, please, no machetes, I thought. Just my AK-47. How much easier just to shoot and never see the people up close, or look into their eyes.

Just stand back and pull the trigger. No slice, no thump, just BANG! I shook my head, shook out my thoughts and reached into my pocket for some hashish to chew.

Gamba stared at me for a moment, and then handed me some knotted grey rags to wrap all around the full length of my barrel. These rags turned my AK invisible in my hands, not a gun anymore but a power stick to bring death, the work of the devil. I was a rebel leader now, and my lieutenant had faith in me. I straightened my shoulders and looked around for my assigned followers.

We headed out, several groups of kids, each with its own leader, along with Gamba and two other lieutenants. My soldiers trusted me totally now, especially because of Gamba's constant acknowledgement of my fitness to lead them. I walked at the head of them all. I was the smartest and the strongest. I am the leader, I thought, and they are my army, behind me.

The sun's heat made the thick green leaves in the valley shimmer as we passed. We marched and marched, singing loudly and boldly, shouting slogans the commander and the lieutenants had taught us.

We marched for a very long time, checking the position of the sun for direction, but soon it was directly overhead—of no help at all.

"So," called Gamba, "now we sleep. We will march the rest of the way in the cool of the night, and you will make your attack in the morning."

18.

That night the sky was beautiful and the moon ever-present. This made it much easier to lead the way along the small tracks through the dense bamboo forest, but it also made me and the others nervous that our movement might be seen from the hillsides around us. We had slept most of the afternoon, but the sleep had not been restful. So much was wildly bouncing around inside my head.

Gamba had told us to expect an exciting day. By attacking this village, we were going to teach all of the people that they had better remain loyal to us and our cause or they would be exterminated.

After hours on the trail we stopped to rest by a small creek. I was called with the other junior leaders to receive our final orders, repeated several times so they would sink in. We were to attack from the wooded side of the village at dawn with the sun at our backs so we could see the targets clearly but the villagers would have a hard time seeing us. We would attack as they awoke for morning chores and we would catch them totally by surprise. This was good because it would mean less chance of any of my group being injured or killed. Back at the camp during the long nights, I had heard how so many others had been abandoned during attacks or later, along the trail, to be prey for animals, insects or the surviving villagers, or to die slowly, and alone.

Just as Gamba finished talking, a crash of thunder followed by lightning shocked us all. Then came the torrential rain that we always expected in this season, but which had held off until now. As I stumbled through the downpour toward my group, I looked back at Gamba and he was beaming.

"It is a perfect cover for our approach," he called after us. "They won't be able to see or hear us through the rain."

I found my eleven boys and girls, all armed and in their ill-fitting uniforms, huddled together under large banana leaves, trying to stay dry. They gathered around me, and I spoke as quietly as I could over the roar of the rain on the trees and splashing puddles all around us, giving them their orders.

We got the signal to move forward at first light, the rain still pouring down. At the edge of the trees, I ordered my comrades to spread out at arm's length from each other. Despite the training and everyone's confidence in me, my palms were sweating. This was a critical moment for our surprise attack but also for me. The commander was ruthless with leaders who failed to live up to what was expected of them. I also knew that if I showed any fear to my small band of young soldiers, we would be lost. So I went to each one of them in turn as they crouched in the wet, tall grass at the edge of the bush and asked if they were okay. There were sets of eyes that were fierce and angry, who wanted to go in fast and furious. There were other sets of eyes that were blurred by drugs but were at least pointed in the right direction, their guns ready. And then there were eyes on the edge of shock and fear that looked straight ahead, hoping that they would not see any people or have to shoot their guns at them. I gave them as much encouragement as I could, then crept into the grass ahead of them and waited for the signal from the lieutenant.

Our weapons were ready and loaded. I cocked my weapon and listened to the snap of safeties being released on guns behind me. I had put so much oil on my AK-47 that the rain was making bubbles on any part of the barrel that was bare of the rag coverings. I was sure it would fire if I pulled the trigger and that gave me some security.

Gamba finally blew the whistle around his neck. On and on it sounded, and as though powered by some hidden spring, I jumped up and ran forward from the line of trees through the tall grass and corn patches between us and the first huts. I was yelling and pulling the trigger, shooting from the hip toward the huts. As I rushed forward I could feel my comrades following me, firing and running, firing and running. Large bangs from rocket launchers and hand grenades boomed extra loud in the rain and low clouds, but I kept us moving toward the edge of the village. I concentrated on the circular, mud-brick house ahead of me, shooting at the windows, and then angling left to cut between it and the other huts. My heart pounded and my dry throat made it hard to yell at the others as well as frighten the villagers, but I kept acting out the plan according to my training, and the fear and apprehension of only moments before totally dissolved, and I was suddenly as high as I'd been on the gunpowder cocaine.

Like ants scurrying out of their hill, people began to spill from the huts, screaming and running in all directions. A grenade hit the hut I'd been shooting at, and it burst into flames. No one was putting up a fight—they were just trying to get away from us. I was sure it would be over soon. I finally reached the gap between the burning hut and the house beside it. As I had been trained, I continued firing my machine gun as I ran between the huts, prepared to shoot blindly inside the door the minute I was in front of the building.

Suddenly, the sound of gunfire greatly intensified and became massive in my ears. There was a lot of shouting from the centre of the village, and many more weapons seemed to join in. But I was already so focused on my next move that these sounds barely registered.

I could sense my group of young warriors behind me, moving at the same reckless speed as I was. Some had already opened fire toward the next row of huts and the open spaces in between. A couple steps more and I was in front of the hut, firing without ceasing, ready to kick in the door. Not twenty feet in front of me was a tall grown-up soldier wearing a blue helmet so bright against the dull colours of the bush and the rest of his uniform that it shocked me so much I nearly stopped. He had his rifle pointed right at me.

My eyes were burning and my mind was overloaded with conflicting instructions and emotions. I felt as much wild excitement as fear. In this moment, we were two warriors—he with his gun, me with mine—and I was still pulling hard and long on the trigger.

I could see my bullets chewing at the bricks, creating small explosions of dried mud as they went. The soldier in the blue helmet moved away from the wall and I saw the tiny flash from his weapon.

I was slammed by what seemed like a big stick right across my chest. The overwhelming force and instant pain tumbled me over backwards so fast I lost all sense of direction and strength. Suddenly, I was on my back in the mud with the rain still falling on me but so gently I could barely feel it. My chest burned as if it was on fire, but I couldn't put it out.

I did not seem to be able to move. I tasted blood in my mouth and my breathing became difficult, like I was underwater and not able to get any new air in my lungs. It came to my mind simply and clearly: I have been shot by the blue helmet and I am going to die.

My mind began to race so fast that I felt lost in it all, searching, grappling for something familiar, something to protect me. Kesi, Mosi, Momma, Daddy, Jacob, Mashaka, Baingana, the creatures of Kidom—these made me hurt even more, from a different place, from my stomach, from my inside. I had suffered so many nights and days of being lonesome for my family, my friends, my home, my world, and now I was going to lose them forever. A wave of lonely pain and fear spread deeper through me, dumping me into blackness.

19.

I can see him beside me now. This soldier. I can make out as if through a haze his pale face and big eyes staring down at me in surprise. I too am surprised. He is enormous, but still. His khaki uniform is dark but his helmet is light blue with the letters "UN" written on it. I know what this means. It is the sign of peace, of the peace-keepers, of protection. But what is he doing here? Why did Gamba not tell us that peacekeepers were protecting this village? This was wrong—we were not supposed to be fighting the peacekeepers and they were not supposed to be fighting us. The commander told us that all of us were working for security, for victory, and we had to punish this village so that it would stop the fighting and the war.

My mind is thick and jumbled but I can make out the shadow of his leg beside my hand, and I reach out to clutch the cloth of his trousers. His bullets have hit me and I am hurting so, but I see his white face, his shocked eyes. My bullets did not hit him and I am not supposed to miss. Why did I miss and why did his bullets crash through me?

The pain in my chest is suffocating me. Where is my mother and brothers, my little sister, my father, where is Baingana, my teacher, whose words were so full of wisdom? I reach out my other hand to try to draw a circle around me, because this is not for real, just as Kidom was not for real. But I want to go there. I want it back.

My chest still hurts, but I feel lighter and the silence around me is like it was at night when I used to create Kidom with my stick under the dark sky with so many bright stars above me.

I do not feel alone now. I might even let Kesi enter my circle again if she is quiet. I am not angry or mad or sad or lonely. I am not a soldier or a warrior, either. I am free to be me. I am free now. I have been freed by this pain in my chest and I am me again.

I am flying, gripping the wings of a dragonfly. I am no more, I am nowhere. I was a warrior and now I am a child again.

5

HOW A CHILD SOLDIER IS MADE

T HE CHILD SOLDIER WHO DIED at the end of the last chapter at the hands of a UN peacekeeper is fictional, but the circumstances are all too real. There are estimated to be more than a quarter of a million child combatants in wars around the globe; in the last decades of the last century, many adults in many countries undergoing various levels of social breakdown and civil war, in South America, Africa, the Middle East and Asia, have made the tactical decision to recruit and deploy children to fight their battles for them. (In case readers in stable democracies think this weapon system is only deployed in countries with serious social unrest, they should remember the growing number of children used in many of the same ways by street gangs in the drug trade.)

We live in a time when human rights have been championed at the international level in an unprecedented way in human history, spurred by reaction to the Holocaust and the invention of the global governance body, the United Nations. Yet at the same time as international humanitarian and diplomatic efforts have focused on codifying and protecting the basic rights of all human beings, including security of the person, humankind has been inventing a new weapon system, now widespread, that abuses the most vulnerable, the most hope-filled among us, and uses humanity's future in order to destroy humanity's present.

The limited use of children in the military as porters, drummers, cooks, and in other non-combatant roles in garrison locations is a long-standing tradition dating back to ancient times. But through all those centuries, deploying children (especially those under the age of sixteen) in active combat was generally viewed as abominable. So how exactly did this tragic recent reversal in thinking come about?

In short: when states fail, when leaders go mad, when the chaos of violence takes over souls, the time is ripe for such terrible ideas to enter the minds of human beings and be acted out. This practice is not limited to Africa: consider the systematic creation and exploitation of vulnerable children as mass murderers during the reign of the Khmer Rouge. But because of my personal experience and because it is estimated that over half of the world's child soldiers are in Africa, I will use select countries of the Great Lakes Region (particularly Burundi, the DRC, Rwanda and Uganda) as exemplars of the larger global problem.

What struck me when first arriving in the region in 1993 was the lushness of it, a far cry from the parched images of Africa I had been led to expect. I felt that I had truly entered an Eden of rolling green hills, brilliant tropical flowers and birds, rich mists hanging heavily in dewy valleys.

Each of the Great Lakes countries enjoys a moderate climate, rich soil, plentiful minerals (principally in the Congo) and substantial water supplies; given these blessings, they should be some of the more prosperous countries in the world. Instead, they are among the world's poorest and most devastated. Centuries of

Euro-Western interference and exploitation through slavery, colonialism, war, corruption and brutality—and the accompanying dislocations, diseases, poverty, underdevelopment, famine and internal conflicts—have practically destroyed the potential of these countries. Traditional societies have been brutally disrupted and ruthlessly repressed, creating populations in despair, prevented from natural development—and also creating an atmosphere of perceived impunity in which those who seek advantage through the use of force have been able to consider all possible options to achieve their ends, including the use of children as soldiers.

Hundreds of years of history can create a groundswell that finally erupts in ethnic conflict resulting from the subjugation of one tribe by another. But in other cases the source of the friction between the belligerents may be relatively recent. In the post-colonial era in Africa, disparities in power sharing and sheer poverty prevented democracy from settling in new sovereign states that were struggling to invent themselves within the artificial borders left behind by the colonial regimes. The fault lines in these new states were many, and violent outbursts were inevitable, leading in some extremes to ethnic cleansing and even genocide.

In the region's civil wars (as in civil war anywhere: remember the recent Balkan conflict), the general population became both the target and, in the jockeying for power, the essential resource to husband—by horror, threats, lies, brute force and fear. The low levels of literacy and the demographic pressures of overpopulation—including the huge numbers of unemployed and poor youths—provided fuel to smouldering fires of discontent over obvious economic and social disparities. This disenchantment and disenfranchisement of youths is palpable in all of the region's urban areas.

I witnessed this clearly in the Rwandan civil war and genocide. As the RPF was nearing victory, the extremists moved millions of citizens through narrow border openings into Tanzania and Goma in the DRC and through a newly established Humanitarian Protection Zone (created by the UN Security Council and enforced by a French and Franco-African peacekeeping coalition with a Chapter VII mandate that allowed the use of force). Hundreds of thousands of scared humans of all ages ended up in massive refugee and internally displaced persons' camps over which the extremists maintained brutal and near complete control. Still armed with machetes and some small weapons, the extremist hierarchy and minions ran roughshod over the distribution of aid, from food to medical supplies to wood and water. They overwhelmed the large number of NGOs that had deployed just over the border in Rwanda for security reasons, only to find themselves being manipulated and even cowed by the extremists into giving up their control of the distribution of humanitarian relief supplies, hoping that at least some of the refugees would benefit. Rwandans of both ethnicities were held hostage in these camps, prevented from returning to their homes by brutal application of such measures as cutting the Achilles tendons of those who attempted to escape.

We in the West bear the brunt of responsibility for this conflict in and around Rwanda (and similarly throughout Africa). The "ethnic" groups that still battle for supremacy there—primarily the Hutus and the Tutsis—were originally named for their occupation rather than their ethnic identity: the Tutsis were known for cattle ownership and herding; the Hutus were farmers. Prior to the colonialist invasion of the late nineteenth century, a Hutu could become a Tutsi through the acquisition of cattle, and a Tutsi could become a Hutu by cultivating the land.

At the time of first contact with Europeans, these groups shared the same language, religion, culture, music, rhetoric, poetry and customs.

Newly arrived European colonialists concluded that the Tutsis were a superior race to the Hutus, based solely on European stereotypes (in other words, totally arbitrarily). As a result, the Tutsis were given some access to schools, exempted from forced labour and allowed to hold minor positions in the civil service. They were also taught that they were superior and the natural rulers of the country (under the greater colonial power, of course) and that the majority Hutus were inferior and only of value as little more than animal labour.

For generations, first under the Germans and later under the Belgians, Tutsis and Hutus were taught this European interpretation of their history. Saddling these people with a false, and racist, identity led to devastating consequences: a civil war and genocide in which, along with the massive loss of life, many children, on both sides, were killed, orphaned or turned into killers.

In the rest of Africa, and elsewhere on the planet, the end of the Cold War created a perfect storm in which many nascent democracies fell victim to dictators who had been propped up by the West or East during the post-colonial period. When the West came out on top and the Berlin Wall fell in 1989, Western governments simply abandoned countries formerly in their sphere of influence to sort out the tenuous status of their systems of democracy, governance, rule of law and human rights on their own. The Soviet sphere similarly withered for lack of attention and for lack of money in the financial crisis that soon hit Russia and the former Eastern bloc.

To top off this act of abandonment, the West also imposed demanding and unachievable milestones on such countries: they had to get on with democratization if they wanted aid support from governments and from international financial bodies like the International Monetary Fund (IMF) and the World Bank. Our irresponsibility in the colonial, post-colonial and post–Cold War periods is staggering. Our governments created elites but turned a blind eye to leaders who failed to serve their people before themselves. We set them up for failure—we at worst nurtured and at best ignored corruption and graft, the illegal exploitation of resources by multinational corporations and the local elites, and the increasing misery of millions—and when we turned away, happy that the Cold War was over and claiming victory and the birth of a kinder, gentler era, a new world order even, they threw that rhetoric back in our faces.

In such states, the core of government soon collapsed; the police, judiciary and other bodies serving to maintain law and order have either ceased to exist or are no longer able to operate. For example, in the DRC (Zaire at that time), militias disintegrated into armed gangs of looters, and military commanders set up in business on their own account using army units as the muscle behind efforts to enrich themselves, while state-owned economic resources were exploited for the private benefit of those in power. Eyewitness reports from Liberia and Sierra Leone speak of the whole society—adults and children alike—falling into the grip of a collective insanity after government institutions broke down. The typical feature of such a "failed state" is the brutality and intensity of the violence its citizens face. These internal conflicts exhibit a highly unpredictable and explosive dynamic all their own and a radicalization of violence.

Such imploding nation states around the world—but primarily where the big powers had interests—created a wave of humanitarian catastrophes in the past twenty years, and in consequence factions in these failing states reverted to the use of arms to gain some advantages not available from incompetent governments. Global warming now threatens to bring the African continent, in particular, catastrophic famine and unrest.

And, at the heart of this tragedy are millions of children, too many of whom have suffered from one unique crime against humanity: namely being used as child soldiers.

We cannot undo what has happened to them, but we can commit ourselves now to aiming for a future in which children are never employed as soldiers in war. In this and the following two chapters, drawing on the initial research I led at the Carr Center, on the work of NGOs and journalists, and on the Child Soldiers Initiative (CSI) research project that I founded, I want to show you how child soldiers are made, how they are being used, and how they are being disarmed, demobilized and reintegrated— where that is possible—in an effort to deconstruct these practices and brainstorm solutions for their eradication.

—

What was it that created the child soldier as a weapon system, specifically? Obviously, the reasons were many and complex, and fundamentally tragic, but in the interest of necessary analysis for creating
solutions, I will attempt to itemize and exemplify them with only the
occasional diatribe or dissolution into a puddle of tears.

The reasons range from the social and historical (such as
poverty and instability, as I described above), to the practical and
tactical (such as the increasing availability of children in developing countries, their intrinsic malleability, and the accessibility of
small arms or light weapons easy for them to use), to the downright sinister (proven "successes" in the field, legal impunity, and
outright disregard for the humanity of individual children).

First I'd like to consider the life of an average child growing up
in any of the countries of the Great Lakes Region of Africa and
what makes him or her particularly vulnerable to recruitment as
a child soldier.

While children are naturally resilient and predisposed to hap-
piness—in my experience, all the more so in developing nations,
where children at play but with no toys to speak of rely deeply on
their ingenuity and curiosity—the instability of the region means
that the vast majority of children grow up in extreme and abject
poverty, undernourished, with poor survival rates, next to no health
care and sanitation, and limited access to any education, let alone
free schooling.

Imagine yourself as a child in this region. Chances are you live
in a rural community or on a small plot of land, and survival
depends on your family successfully planting and tending a crop
through to harvest. While the soil is very rich, and in a good year
your family can get two crops out of it, overpopulation has made
subsistence farming tenuous at best—larger families have access
to less and less land. Even if your harvest is successful, it will
provide only barely adequate sustenance for survival.

Basically, if the weather co-operates you eat, but if it does not, and too much or too little rain falls, then your harvest fails and you starve to death unless food aid arrives. You are constantly undernourished and are most likely to be stunted in growth and underweight, as well as suffering from any number of vitamin deficiencies and other ailments in consequence. Climate change due to global warming, deforestation and the soil erosion that results all point to a future of drought, famine and death, but those are the problems of tomorrow and you and your family are only thinking of survival today.

A successful harvest in itself is no guarantee that you'll eat. The crop could be stolen by bandits or soldiers, or destroyed by fighting, or abandoned because you and your family have had to flee from the inter-communal violence or catastrophic civil wars that are plaguing your homeland.

As a child in this region, you most likely have several brothers and sisters, but at least one in five has died at birth, and another one before five years of age, and a third before adulthood due to pandemics like HIV/AIDS and sicknesses like tuberculosis and malaria. Your mother has a one-in-thirteen chance of dying in childbirth, and your whole family knows well the impact of sickness and disease, and all too often death.

Proper sanitation and health care are almost non-existent, and even if medicine is available your family most likely cannot afford it. Your parents and sexually active siblings have approximately a one-in-fifteen chance of contracting HIV/AIDS, which is usually a slow, painful death sentence. In this area, I witnessed a whole generation of one family wiped out in a single year by AIDS; the grandmothers could not cope with the orphans and there was no government support system to help them either. In the past, when parents died there was always an extended family member to take a child in, which shows the overwhelming cultural strength and sense of responsibility of the family here. The concept of orphans is new to the region.

Water, a basic human need, is a daily challenge. A clean, potable supply is rarely within a reasonable distance of your home. The fetching of water is an oppressive chore, and if you are a girl, that chore falls squarely upon your shoulders. Many girls walk several kilometres every day to fetch filthy and contaminated water, encountering numerous threats to their well-being. Sometimes they begin the chore so young they become physically deformed by carrying the heavy loads. They are often prevented from attending school regularly because they simply do not have the time.

As a child in this region, you are most likely barely literate and have little or no access to the education or technical training that could improve your lot in life. You speak a family language of Kirundi, Kinyarwanda, Swahili or one of dozens of others among different groups in the region, but you are not able to read and write that language unless you've been lucky enough to be able to go to school. As the traditional oral transmission of history and customs is being eroded by pandemics like HIV/AIDS, where elders are overburdened and often sick themselves, literacy has become increasingly important even as it has become harder to obtain. Unless you can go to school, you will also not learn to speak, read or write one of the European languages, like English or French, which can also become a route to a better life.

Most children don't attend school because their families cannot spare them from daily survival chores or they cannot afford the fees they need to pay since the state pays teachers a pittance at most and doesn't supply school materials. Due to the conflicts in the region, children may not be able to attend even if they can afford the time or money to go because the local school has been shut down (the teacher may have died or been killed, the building may have been destroyed). Too often there is simply no school within walking distance (especially in areas populated by internally displaced and refugee families).

If you live in an area where a school does exist, and your family can afford to let you attend, you likely still have to walk a long

time to get there and back every day, risking attack from animals—
and from other humans. Packed into a one-room schoolhouse
with over forty students of all different levels, with a blackboard
painted on one wall and very limited access to paper and pencils,
you are fighting an uphill battle to get a modicum of education.
Homework is often impossible. So close to the equator, the sun
rises rapidly at six in the morning and sets abruptly at about six at
night. By the time your meagre supper is eaten and chores are
done, it is pitch black inside and out; candles are expensive and
there is next to no access to electric light. In the morning, you
need to be up before dawn to fetch water, or prepare the fire and
help with breakfast, so there's not much time to study then, either.

Still, an important advantage to the presence of a school in a
village or close at hand is that it is a significant sign of stability and
security for the children as well as for the parents. And no matter
how rudimentary, a school provides discipline, colourful uniforms,
friendships and a place to play and escape from the mundane but
essential daily chores—aspects of school that can be just as important to a child in a developing country as feeding his or her hunger
for learning. Where schools do not exist, children are often denied
their right to play, to dream and to grow.

But it is too often the elite children in urban areas, ones who
have proven their "exceptional" abilities, who actually get an education, subsidized by religious groups or NGOs. Imagine the overt
friction this style of subsidization creates within societies, the envy
felt by parents and children with no such advantage but the wit to
know that education is the only effective route to better circumstances. Add to this disparity religious, ethnic or tribal differences,
passed on both overtly and subtly in the curriculum, and you have
conditions that can synergize into the worst possible scenario, as
was the case in Rwanda.

As a poor, rural child who has not been able to attend school,
from your very early teens you would have a lot of empty hours
between your search for food, the odd manual job, and other less

reputable ways of surviving and helping your family to survive. Or you may not even be near your family anymore, having been pushed out by no food and too many siblings as soon as you had any chance of making it on your own, and ending up homeless and drifting in the urban slums.

In those slums, and even in the rural areas where farming has been increasingly marginalized and disrupted by climate change and war, there is no worthwhile or satisfying work for millions of essentially disenfranchised youths. Talk about a ready and willing recruitment base for any group that has an idea or an ideology, that can provide some sustenance, some means of bonding, and a bit of the power that comes from belonging to an organized outfit. Imagine arming these youths on top of that, and the dangerous ego trips that can result.

And so the constant companions of war, abject poverty, sickness and migration over the turbulent decades since independence in the late 1950s, make the children of this region particularly vulnerable to a myriad of tragedies, not the least of which is being recruited—willingly or not—into the fraternity of armed groups or even into the government forces as a child soldier. In fact, most of the conflicts, not just in the Great Lakes Region of Africa but around the world, that have employed, or are employing, child soldiers occur in countries where there is an unstructured political, economic and social environment. Ineffective and incompetent governments can't keep track of their voting-age citizens, let alone their children, and orphans are often not missed.

The historical and social circumstances I've just discussed set the stage for the abduction and recruitment of children, but there are also a number of practical motivations for governments, armies, rebel groups and even bandit gangs to choose to recruit children.

First and foremost among these practical reasons is numbers: the number of conflicts that require ever-increasing numbers of soldiers combined with the ever-increasing number of children.

Although the numbers of international conflicts are reported to be going down, according to a recent article in *Foreign Policy* magazine by Jeffrey Gettleman, called "Africa's Forever Wars,"

> There is a very simple reason why some of Africa's bloodiest, most brutal wars never seem to end: They are not really wars. Not in the traditional sense, at least. The combatants don't have much of an ideology; they don't have clear goals. They couldn't care less about taking over capitals or major cities—in fact, they prefer the deep bush, where it is far easier to commit crimes. Today's rebels seem especially uninterested in winning converts, content instead to steal other people's children, stick Kalashnikovs or axes in their hands, and make them do the killing. Look closely at some of the continent's most intractable conflicts, from the rebel-laden creeks of the Niger Delta to the inferno in the Democratic Republic of the Congo, and this is what you will find.

Ishmael Beah, a former child soldier in Sierra Leone and the author of the memoir *A Long Way Gone*, reinforced that point in an interview he gave to the *New York Times* after his book came out: "There might have been a little rhetoric at the beginning. But very quickly the ideology gets lost. And then it just becomes a bloodbath, a way for the commanders to plunder, a war of madness."

Outright bandits are taking full advantage of failing states—with their weak or non-existent import-export laws and lack of control over natural resources—to run criminal enterprises that trade those precious resources on the international market. The focus of this book is the use of children in armed conflict, but a parallel and reinforcing issue to keep in mind is the recruitment of children as slave labourers, moving such things as diamonds, drugs, precious woods and coltan—a mineral essential for cellphones—illegally to foreign markets. Ineffective border controls and weak enforcement agencies open the door wide for massive illegal employment of child labour in resource extraction, under conditions that almost defy description: children forced to dig holes metres deep and crawl along shafts barely big enough for them to move through, risking their lives in cave-ins to get at gold or other minerals. When shafts collapse on them, they are buried alive—abandoned in the "graves" they dug themselves—and the bandits simply start a new mine a few metres away and send in the next wave of child labourers. Many children, usually under armed guard and against their will, are forced to slide into the mud and seeping water where surface diamond mining is conducted, and often drown.

Children are extensively used by "non-state actors," as the jargon has it. According to the special representative of the secretary general of the UN for the DRC, "New cases of recruitment of children have been attributed to Coalition des patriotes résistants congolais (PARECO) (29 per cent), all Mai-Mai factions (32 per cent), CNDP [Congrès national pour la défense du peuple] (24 per cent) and Forces démocratiques de libération du Rwanda (FDLR) (13 per cent). A total of 1,098 children, including 48 girls, were documented to have separated from or escaped from armed groups." Imagine how many haven't escaped.

These forces fight for reasons that at times only they seem to be able to understand, and end up posing significant roadblocks to any peacekeepers or other actors attempting to prevent the failure of a state or to stabilize and reconstruct it after the fact. Such groups are ruthless, fully prepared to kill their own as well as the enemy in order to control their own areas of influence, outside any system of legal or democratic governance.

As well as the bandit gangs and wild-card non-state actors, there are the more classic freedom fighters or rebel groups, which use armed force in order to be "heard" on their issues and to protest injustices by the sovereign state to which they belong.

So the uses of child soldiers are multiplying even as the number of youths explodes compared to the rest of the population. Anyone who has visited the Great Lakes Region, or indeed many other conflict zones around the world, will be immediately struck by the sheer number of children. In most of these countries, children under eighteen years of age account for more than 50 per cent of the population. Rapidly falling fertility rates in most developing countries paradoxically have led to a "youth bulge"—the largest in history. The number of young people between the ages of twelve and twenty-four around the world stands at 1.3 billion and is expected to rise to about 1.5 billion in 2035 and then gradually decline. Fertility rates are declining but there is still a large child-bearing population, which means more babies born overall, until that point when the proportion of the population of child-bearing age begins to decline. Only then will the number of youths begin to drop.

In the meantime, the world around them makes no sense and offers little security, and so a large generation of youths, meant to be workers, teachers, parents, leaders, are ripe for the picking by those adults who seek to recruit foot soldiers and who can offer a bit of hope, inclusiveness, money, drugs, uniforms, chants, rallies, power over peers, and even a cause, no matter how warped (ethnic-based racism, for instance).

This simple demographic fact leads us to one of the saddest reasons why children are preferred to adults as soldiers: they are viewed as expendable, replaceable. Not in all cases, but too often, these child recruits are pushed to the front to take the brunt of an attack and the bulk of its casualties, because they can be replaced by the seemingly endless pool of available children. Children as young as seven are not viewed by the adult commanders who abduct or recruit them as precious human beings but as easily used, abused and disposable tools—cheap weapon systems that can be discarded when broken, and replaced. Tapping these child "resources" is like having a weapons arsenal in continuous production—a source of crass power available in limitless quantity, with no credible counter-weapon to neutralize it. Child soldiers are a commander's dream come true: the perfect low-technology, cheap and expendable weapon system, which can perpetuate itself ad infinitum.

Beyond their plenitude, children are also desirable because they are psychologically more vulnerable and can be easily manipulated, especially when they have been separated from their families. They will transfer loyalty to another adult, especially one who holds the power of reward and punishment. They can be psychologically manipulated through a deliberate programme of starvation, thirst, fatigue, voodoo, indoctrination, beatings, the use of drugs or alcohol, and even sexual abuse to render them compliant to the new norms of child soldiering.

Children, especially the very young, are also easy and cheap to maintain. They eat and drink less, they are not paid, they do not have to be particularly well clothed, sheltered, armed or logistically sustained. They can also provide advantages within an actual logistics system. They can be employed to do the kind of chores they have been doing since they were able to walk. They can carry supplies, they can fetch water, they can scrounge and prepare food, they can do laundry.

Certain groups, such as the Mai Mai (a general term for local militias in and around the Congo), seek out children to join their armed forces because they believe that children have mystical powers of protection, making them ideal guards for commanders and front-line fighters. The "purity" of these youths also renders them ideal to prepare and administer magic potions and tattoos to protect the adult soldiers without sullying the magical properties of these rituals. For the children, participation in such rituals is believed to make them invulnerable; under the influence of hallucinatory herbs and potions, they become fearless attackers.

Similar rituals and magic charms are used in areas of northern Uganda by traditional healers, who have been co-opted by rebel groups to make child soldiers "bulletproof." For many in the region, boys and girls provide good "juju" (spirit magic) simply because they are children. Girls, especially, are believed to be able to share these protective traits through sex—a belief that has dire implications for female abductees or recruits.

The most direct method of manipulating these children—more basic than drugs, occult rituals, charms and repetitive exposure to violence, both as victim and perpetrator—is simply fear. Drug- or voodoo-induced states of utter fearlessness are temporary: these children survive in a constant state of fear and vulnerability, with often irreparable damage to their minds and souls.

And, in their own right, they can become effective as weapons of terror and as weapons of hesitation, not to mention at honing skills in areas of logistics and reconnaissance. Adults do not usually view children, especially the very young, as a threat. This underestimation can be manipulated by ruthless leaders who will persuade their child troops to sacrifice their lives or use their age to strike blows of terror against their opponents.

In addition, the psychological reluctance of adults, including Western soldiers or police officers, to kill children in self-defence leads to situations where they at times hesitate to counterattack, which can provide a tactical advantage to the ruthless commander.

Children are also ideally suited to tasks of information collection or intelligence. Whereas adults hanging around a military establishment or forward line will generate suspicion, children in this region are ever-present, always inquisitive and watching adults. They can spy in an enemy camp, they can listen in a market, they can give warning—they can see without being seen or noticed and provide valuable information to their force.

In countries where the conflict has been ongoing for some time, this tactic can fail, as locals have become wary of groups of young boys, and sometimes girls, who appear in their villages or marketplaces. Even a lone child who is seeking nothing in particular but who is not from the area runs the risk of being treated as a threat, though he may be innocently lost, abandoned, hungry or otherwise in need of adult care and sympathy. The ultimate gross violation is that when child soldiers are demobilized and in the process of reintegration, adults fear them because of the risk that they will revert to the use of force to gain what they want.

The perversion of the common order of life is staggering—this in the region where the concept that it takes a village to raise a child originated. The fear of assault from armed soldiers, too often children, has upset the natural role of adults and elders as de facto guardians of all children.

All these reasons I've just mentioned have contributed to the creation of the child soldier. But the greatest tactical reason for the increased use of children in combat over the past few decades is the development and availability of small, lightweight weapons that do not require adult strength or skills to use and maintain. A child— boy or girl, even as young as nine or ten—who is used to hard physical labour can be easily trained to operate them.

The proliferation of light small arms, from pistols to assault rifles to light machine guns to rocket-propelled grenades, is one of the major vulnerabilities that can spark an easy descent into conflict in our world today. During the Cold War, both sides stocked huge arsenals of these weapons for rapid mobilization of the masses, and sold or provided them to so-called allies in the developing world. When the Cold War ended and the Eastern bloc (with its large arms industry and existing stockpiles) collapsed, many of these weapons found their way onto the international arms market, where merchants of death made them readily available at cheap cost.

Arms control specialists estimate there are over 650 million light, simple to use, deadly small arms cheaply available anywhere, anytime to those who wish to start, conduct and sustain an armed conflict. Responsible developed nations continue to manufacture about one million every year (the five permanent members of the UN Security Council—China, Russia, France, the United Kingdom and the United States—being the biggest weapons producers) and almost no one is destroying the older versions when weapons are upgraded. Responsible civil servants in signatory countries, not wanting to waste valuable, although dated, public assets such as these, go through a complex international arms control and limitations process in order to assess potential buyers and then, according to the established but still less than wholly effective rules, sell them for the best possible price.

We have struck some international conventions to reduce the proliferation of small arms, but too many of these weapons already exist, and the implementation of non-proliferation measures is uneven. To add to the toothless nature of it all, there are no sanctions against offenders except the occasional embargo that is difficult to supervise and enforce.

If we can't eliminate small arms, we could attempt to reduce their usefulness by cutting off the sources of ammunition, which is relatively expensive and not necessarily as readily available in the significant amounts required to conduct sustained combat operations. But once again, there are multiple producers and the scale of production is literally off the charts. Still, as I mentioned, belligerents need large amounts of cash to buy the projectiles of war, which brings us back to children again and the use of them— by both governments and other groups—as labourers mining and hauling gold, diamonds and coltan, or logging precious woods, to generate the cash. They become the instruments by which the funding is acquired to buy the ammunition so that other children can become instruments of war. A perfect circle of continued and sustainable war and death has been created.

So how can we effectively reduce the availability of the small arms and munitions that enables the use of child soldiers, among other evils? Strict enforcement of existing rules at the manufacturing and distribution points, strengthening embargoes, and enacting policies that require the outright destruction of decommissioned weaponry coupled with amnesty for anyone who turns in such weapons: these are all methods being applied in various conflict zones. But so far they have not proven their worth when it comes to stopping the flow. We need a much more deliberate political commitment to not only apply the rules as they exist today, but also to seek out and bring to justice illegal arms dealers, ending the impunity under which they operate. We also need to encourage our political leaders to tell their public servants to destroy surplus weaponry, not to sell it—except to legitimate states with legitimate security needs, and *in extremis* only.

Despite embargoes, there were so many guns readily available in Rwanda that I attempted to initiate a campaign before the genocide to buy all the weapons in the country. The result was similar to that of other such attempts in places like Sierra Leone, where the weapons that demobilizing soldiers turned in were junk— they usually hid the good ones in the bush "just in case."

Finally—unfortunately—rather than revealing the unthinkable nature of this crime against humanity, there have been many "successful" examples over the past twenty years of notorious groups that have used child soldiers effectively. To name just a few: the Lord's Resistance Army (LRA) in northern Uganda (and now southern Sudan and the DRC); the Interahamwe (in Rwanda and the DRC); and both the Revolutionary United Front (RUF) and the government militias in Sierra Leone.

As I wrote in the research paper I prepared on child soldiers for the Carr Center, it's extremely hard for rational actors to understand what is going on and why:

> Despite the fact that the children captured are of their own tribe, the LRA use[s] them mercilessly. To illustrate, the child sent to attack his own parents acts as both instrument of revenge and shield for the people standing behind him; the child driven to her death beneath a load of loot she can no longer carry is reduced to the status of disposable object; the girl

forced into "marriage" with an LRA warrior has value only as an instrument of labour and sexual satisfaction. It is hard to explain this conduct without resort to highly pejorative terms. To kill, to enslave, to torture with some overall goal in mind is at least explainable in rational terms, no matter how much one might deplore such activities. But to perpetrate atrocities without any externally understandable ultimate goal is to indulge in incomprehensible violence.

Horribly, child soldiers continue to be used in conflicts throughout the world because there are leaders—political and military, governmental or non-governmental, soldiers or thugs and thieves—who have achieved "success" through using them, and who are ruthless, apathetic and amoral enough to continue to recruit, employ, abuse and destroy children. These leaders are criminals who must be held responsible and accountable for their abuse of children and their violation of international law. Impunity must be erased and the legal consequences imposed so severely that the mere thought of recruiting children to fight will be a non-option. To see the International Criminal Court (ICC) finally bringing to trial some of these adult leaders who recruited child soldiers is a step in the right direction, but success in this formal process is not yet truly within our grasp.

Here's an example of how muddy the terrain can be, reported by the Coalition to Stop the Use of Child Soldiers in a briefing paper on Mai Mai child soldier recruitment released in February 2010:

Gédéon Kyungu Mutanga, the commander of a Mai Mai Group based in Katanga province, having fallen foul of the President, was prosecuted along with 20 others on a range of charges including crimes against humanity and with war crimes relating to the recruitment of 300 children in Katanga province between 2003 and 2006. Although Gédéon and his co-defendants were convicted in March 2009 of having committed crimes against humanity and other serious crimes, the charges relating to child soldier recruitment and use were dropped after the judge ruled that war crimes charges were not admissible in the absence of a declaration of war.

It is absolutely essential that we prosecute the adult leaders, but what should we do with the child soldiers? Almost all member nation states of the UN have agreed to formal processes to protect child soldiers from prosecution and to deem their use a crime against humanity through conventions and administrative procedure (see the appendix for a complete listing of these significant legal and administrative conventions and international processes). So has the ICC, which classified not only the employment of children under fifteen years of age in hostilities as a war crime and a crime against humanity, but also their recruitment, along with intentional attacks on hospitals or schools, rape and other grave acts of sexual violence against children.

And yet in the global report issued by the Coalition to Stop the Use of Child Soldiers in 2008, incidences of the detainment, prosecution and punishment of former child soldiers are numerous, including in Burundi, Rwanda and the DRC. From that report:

Burundi

After taking office in August 2005, government forces targeted real or suspected FNL [Forces nationales de libération] supporters, arresting, torturing, and even summarily executing those suspected of belonging to or supporting the FNL. Although the age of criminal responsibility was 13, children as young as nine were detained on suspicion of collaborating with the FNL . . . Captured child soldiers were reportedly severely beaten in detention, some with metal bars and hammers. Some were denied medical attention until human rights groups intervened on their behalf.

Democratic Republic of the Congo

Children captured from armed groups were detained by FARDC [the Armed Forces of the DRC] members in order to gather information on armed groups or to extort money from family members. Some had been beaten while in detention. Former child soldiers faced intimidation and harassment by FARDC members, including non-respect for their official demobilization certificates . . . Children were arrested, detained and tried in military courts for military offences and other crimes allegedly committed while they were in armed forces or groups. The trials contravened Article 114 of the Military Justice Code, which stipulated that persons below the age of 18 did not fall under military jurisdiction . . . At least 12 children were known to have been sentenced to death since 2003. The Child Soldiers Coalition was informed in mid-2007 that executions were no longer carried out in the DRC, but at least five children were believed to remain in detention under sentence of death in July 2007 in prisons in the eastern DRC.

Rwanda

Some Rwandan child soldiers repatriated to Rwanda were reportedly arrested and beaten by the authorities . . . Of the 120,000 people detained for involvement in the 1994 genocide, some 4,500 were reportedly below the age of 18 at the time of the genocide. Rwanda's president, Paul Kagame, ordered the release of all "genocide minors" in January 2003, but under implementing regulations only those who had spent the maximum possible sentence in pre-trial detention were eligible to be freed.

Child soldiers do, however, have some influential support in high places. David Crane, the American lawyer who served as chief prosecutor for Sierra Leone's UN-backed war crimes tribunal (and the person who issued the indictment against Charles

Taylor, at the time the president of Liberia), testified with me before the government of Canada's Subcommittee on International Human Rights of the Standing Committee on Foreign Affairs and International Development in 2008. In part, he said:

> [W]hen I was the chief prosecutor . . . I chose not to prosecute child soldiers, as it is my opinion that no child under the age of 15 can commit a war crime . . . I literally walked the entire countryside, listening to the people of Sierra Leone in my town hall meetings tell me what took place in that particular region. I was in Makeni, the former headquarters of the infamous Revolutionary United Front, and I was speaking to a group of about 400 people . . . I was answering questions about the special court and other issues, and a little hand came up from the back. I walked to the back of the room and this young man about 12 years old stood up. He had been injured and had become deaf from the conflict. He signed, but he also spoke, and in the atonal voice of someone who is deaf, looked me right in the eye and said he had killed people, he was sorry, he didn't mean it. He was 12, the conflict had been over about two years, so you can do the math. He was probably eight or nine years old when he was killing human beings. I went over to him, tears coming down my cheeks, and hugged him. He wept in my arms. That's a child soldier. There were 35,000 of them in Sierra Leone alone. So one has to consider, despite what he may have done, who is really at fault here. I would say that a child soldier and the victims of child soldiers all are victims, because they are usually placed in these situations in armed conflict, be it in Afghanistan, East Africa, Uganda, or West Africa, in situations they cannot control.

The international law in this area is pretty clear, even though it doesn't say that children are immune from their war-like acts. It just says that children are to be especially protected—as per the

Geneva Convention. That suggests that we shouldn't put them in situations that cause them to do these things, even if they do them voluntarily, because a child does not have the capability of making such choices.

Before I go further—having covered why children are being targeted in this fashion, next I want to explore how they are recruited—I need to reinforce the point that David Crane was making in his testimony. Whether commanders abduct children or recruit them voluntarily, using children as combat troops is always a crime on the part of the leaders. The child in either case should be viewed and treated as a victim of this crime and not be held responsible for decisions made under extreme duress.

It may be hard to imagine that children would voluntarily enlist as child soldiers, but remember the conditions under which so many children exist, in the Great Lakes Region of Africa alone. Such a challenging existence in and of itself can lead some children to volunteer to become soldiers. A war or conflict breaks out and a child sees a national army, militia or rebel force whose members seem to have plenty to eat, who wear attractive clothing, who get respect from wielding a gun, and who take not only what they need but what they want. Understandably, such a life, for a child who has only known poverty and hunger and disenfranchisement, can be alluring, especially considering the child does not know or understand the reality he or she will soon encounter as a child soldier. The disastrous economic and social conditions in regions such as this can and do significantly contribute to voluntary recruitment.

Another form of "voluntary" recruitment can occur as a result of displacement, which civil war in this region naturally occasions. A family may have to flee their home for somewhere they feel safe, usually a refugee or internally displaced persons' camp. At such camps, security is usually non-existent and rebel groups, bandits or even government forces can take control through the force of arms. They can impose rules, put taxes on families and conduct strategic violence, such as rape. The predominant ethnic group in the camp may have legitimate grievances with the government or the rebel force, may feel an extreme loyalty to their country or ethnic group and may willingly wish to join the fight for what they perceive to be their rights. Or a family or parent can lead their child willingly into service as a soldier, buying protection for the rest of the family and the village by providing a "volunteer."

A heartbreaking and far too common means of both voluntary and involuntary recruitment arises when children are orphaned or separated from their families during a time of conflict. Solitary children may decide that their only means of survival is to attach themselves to the nearest group of adults who appear able to protect and provide for them. Peer pressure or support inside the group can reinforce this sense of false security. Armed groups can replace the desperately needed family as well as prey on the child's sense of fear or revenge. The consequences for the child can be lifelong. As T.S. Betancourt and K.T. Khan noted in a paper on the mental health of children affected by armed combat, published in the *International Review of Psychiatry* in 2008:

> Armed groups offer access to food, shelter and other basic needs during times of conflict when access is difficult and when child combatants are taken far outside of their native homes and villages. Once a child is a member of an armed group, the child develops a "sense of belonging to something, when nothing else is functioning." The younger a child is at the time of their capture, the less likely they will have memories in the long term that reflect society before the war. This impacts their desire to end conflict and to return to their villages once the fighting is over. Consequently there is a need to ensure the youngest children are protected.

But by far the most common form of recruitment is involuntary. Children are targeted by government, police, army, rebels or plundering bandits who physically and psychologically sever them from their homes and families. Kidnapping or abduction is sometimes temporary—for example, when the child is used as a porter to carry supplies or wounded personnel, until the child drops and is left to die from exhaustion and starvation. But often the abduction is relatively long-term—a matter of years, not weeks or months—with the child taken to some sort of base for training and socialization.

An armed group may simply enter a school, village or farm and forcibly take the children. In these cases, parents and siblings are often murdered and the children's homes destroyed. In many conflict zones, children may be forced or tricked through the use of a blindfold to hold and fire weapons at their neighbours, friends and family members. Such an act, infamously employed by the LRA, is likely to irrevocably sever the children from their family and community, so even if they were to escape they would not be able to return home.

Girls represent about 40 per cent of all child soldiers and are often considered a more valuable resource than boys. Boys are generally limited to fighting and some support roles, but in these male-dominated societies where the women do most of the manual work of sustaining the "home," girls have many more useful skills than boys do. Far from being weaker or more passive, girls have proven to be as easily and effectively used in the same psychological, logistical, reconnaissance and combat tasks as boys—for instance, a significant proportion of the volatile and brutal LRA in Uganda is made up of girls. A perceived advantage of girls over boys is that they can be used as sexual rewards for the soldiers (though boys do not entirely escape that fate). They can be taken as bush wives (monogamous or polygamous sexual companions of a commander or leader) or used as sex slaves by the troops. Rape of girl child soldiers is a matter of course in most of these conflicts, and the resultant psychological damage, physical injury, sexually transmitted diseases, pregnancy, and childbirth complications are additional abuses the girls suffer.

And what about the children who are the result of these rapes and sexual abuse? There are reported cases of long-lasting conflicts in which the children of child soldiers have been trained and are now engaged in the fight. I cannot fathom the degree of human abuse and gross destruction implicit in the life of a girl soldier who is used to produce the next generation of child soldiers.

A warning: if contemplating the conditions that lead to the recruitment of children as soldiers is rough, exploring how they are trained and actually used in combat, as I do in the next chapter, is even rougher. And all the more reason why we need to marshal all our efforts to stop this.

6

HOW A CHILD SOLDIER IS TRAINED AND USED

EVERY MILITARY FORCE IN THE WORLD employs a formal training system to impart its knowledge, skills, experience and ethos to its recruits. From the basic training or boot camp through to the teaching of advanced leadership and technical competencies, the purpose of such training is to immerse recruits—and veterans—in the norms, identity, culture, values and beliefs of the military institution that safeguards the disciplined use of force within a nation state.

But the training that most child recruits are subjected to is often inhumane and gruelling, designed to separate the strong from the weak in the crassest of ways, in the shortest of time, using the minimum of resources. As the authors of Human Rights Watch's 2003 report, "You'll Learn Not to Cry: Child Combatants in Colombia," write: "From the beginning of their training, both guerrilla and paramilitary child recruits are taught to treat the other side's fighters or sympathizers without mercy. Adults order children to kill, mutilate, and torture, conditioning them to the cruelest abuses. Not only do children face the same treatment should they fall into the hands of the enemy, many fear it from fellow fighters. Children who fail in their military duties or try to desert can face summary execution by comrades sometimes no older than themselves."

Whether the children are abducted or volunteer to serve in a government army, a rebel group or any other belligerent armed cadre, they will undergo some form of training and socialization or indoctrination to ensure they become "good soldiers" or die trying.

Upon recruitment, the child will be assessed: those considered too young or too weak may become camp followers, employed in menial tasks like gathering wood, tending fires, cooking, drawing water, moving loot and supplies, taking care of the sick and wounded, performing latrine duty and so on. In return for performing these tasks, they will be provided with some water, food, hand-me-down clothes and a certain level of security. But these necessities are treated as rewards and may be withheld for lack of effort or failure to complete an assigned task. There are no rights for a child soldier, only privileges.

The *essence* of the training is to push the child to complete obedience and unblinking compliance to orders from a superior and also to forge the child's identification with the armed group. As the child ages, gains experience and grows stronger, they may receive more formal training in combat-related tasks.

Children who are too weak to carry loads or conduct garrison duties may, if they are lucky, be abandoned and have a chance to return to their home villages if they are physically able to get there—or if those villages still exist. (As Ishmael Beah recounts in *A Long Way Gone*, the factions fighting in his homeland of Sierra Leone habitually destroyed the villages from which they abducted children, leaving them no home to return to.) In other cases, such "weak" children may be abused or executed as an example to the others. The LRA perfected the technique of coercing children to carry heavy loads on a forced march back to its base.

Those unable to keep up were executed by the other children as a means of further separating them from their past connections, and hardening and familiarizing them with killing. The consequences for children who cannot keep up or refuse to do anything they are ordered to do are swift and terminal.

As I have mentioned in earlier chapters, rape is inevitable for the girls and sometimes for the boys. A resilient child soon learns that it is better to endear herself to one soldier with the gun and the power to protect her, than to be a communal sex object. The more power the adult soldier has, the better off the girl will be. As Chris Coulter writes in *Bush Wives and Girl Soldiers*, an account of the impact of ten years of civil war on the girls and women of Sierra Leone:

> Commanders' wives had the power to punish or reward and were often in a position to get everything they asked for: clothes, shoes, jewellery, music and videos, either by looting it them-selves or having it done for them . . . Those girls and women who did not become wives were forced into labor, which could mean domestic work, cooking, cleaning, and taking care of small children . . . [G]irls or women who had no "husbands" suffered physical hardship, lack of food, and frequent rapes. A "wife," on the other hand, would be protected from sexual abuse by other men and would also often have girls working for her, making her own situation less straining.

Boys are also forced to be creative in order to protect themselves. Emmanuel Jal, the former child soldier from the Sudan who is now a musician and the author of *War Child*, recently described in an interview how Sudanese boys would stuff their pants at night with paper bags and newspaper so that if a commander tried to assault them, the paper would crinkle and not only wake them up but wake up the others around them. As a result a com-mander could no longer rape the boy in the night with impunity and no witnesses.

Forced sex serves the needs of the adult leaders of these child soldiers, but its most insidious purpose is to undermine and alienate the child, making her (or him) a creature of the armed group. This form of torture also stigmatizes girls, especially within their cultural milieu, and makes it exceedingly hard for them to ever go home again.

In most standing armies, a formal basic-training course will be conducted at a school on an established military installation or garrison. With non-state belligerents, the training is less formal and often conducted on the move. In either case, where child soldiers are a significant component of the force, the methods used on children by government armies or rebel groups are largely the same. Training is violent, with the children experiencing blows or beatings for the slightest mistake or transgression. Threats, physical abuse, harassment and bullying by older and battle-hardened child soldiers against the younger children are encouraged. The new child rapidly learns that obedience and enthusiasm bring rewards and that disobedience and incompetence bring punishment. Serious errors, such as falling asleep on sentry duty, attempted desertion and insolence, are commonly punished by execution, often performed by their closest friends or even siblings.

After losing his mother and being discarded by his father, a commander in the Sudan People's Liberation Army (SPLA), Emmanuel Jal ended up a child recruit in the SPLA after a stretch in a refugee camp in which he nearly starved to death. In his memoir, he writes, "The SPLA made sure that discipline was strict. If you fought with another boy, you were beaten on the buttocks by members of your group; if you stole something, you were beaten again. I was often punished for forgetting to do jobs such as collecting firewood and water, sweeping and cooking, because I was interested in trying to find fun."

Children are frequently organized into small teams in which group punishment is administered for any individual shortcoming.

The mistake of one results in the punishment of all, up to and including the death penalty. Every child will rapidly become familiar with the chain of command (the hierarchy of authority and lines of communications) in their unit and will begin to seek a mentor or a role model, someone they can mimic to obtain praise, rewards and status within the group. In his rigorous study, *Children at War*, P.W. Singer writes, "Across regions, child soldiers typically take on nicknames. Some of the names are simply juvenile, such as 'Lieutenant Dirty Bathe' (because he never took a bath), while others are chilling, such as 'Blood Never Dry' . . . There is also often a physical aspect of reidentification in the indoctrination process. Many groups, such as the LTTE [Liberation Tigers of Tamil Eelam], shave their children's heads . . . This not only inculcates a break in identity, but also makes escapees easier to identify."

Canny leaders also subject child recruits to some form of brainwashing as to why they are fighting, in order to build fanaticism. Ethnic, tribal, political or religious rationales will be endlessly drilled into them, especially in times of hunger, fatigue or thirst, or with the reinforcement of drugs, be they marijuana, hashish or a mix of gunpowder with cocaine. Joseph Kony, the infamous leader of the LRA, combines ethnic hatred and religion in a toxic stew of hate, magic and twisted Christianity to empower his child fighters; he preaches that he is a direct conduit of the word of God, as well as a spirit medium, sent to found a Christian state based on the Ten Commandments and Acholi tribal traditions. How rape, murder and mutilation can serve such a "Christian" purpose is anyone's guess, but Kony's group is a splinter of Alice Auma's Holy Spirit Movement, which rose up to resist the Muslim advances of Yoweri Museveni's National Resistance Army, which in turn had overthrown the Acholi president of Uganda, Tito Okello. Children don't need to understand all the political ins and outs: they just learn to believe in the magic powers of their leader, or else. Creating "instinctive" reactions to stimuli controlled by the commanders is the essence of the unwavering and robotic discipline that will ultimately overcome fear in combat and horror at the slaughter of other human beings in the most barbaric of ways.

When it comes to actual skills that might save their lives when they are sent into battle, most child recruits are taught basic weapons handling, such as stripping and assembling an assault rifle; loading, aiming and firing it; and caring for and maintaining their weapon and equipment. Endless repetition makes such basic skills automatic, especially those related to killing on command. Children may also be taught some basic drills, such as movement formations, ambush tactics, navigation and bushcraft. But the training is usually rudimentary, relying heavily on "on-the-job" experience. There is no theory or pedagogy here.

In *Children at War*, a South American fifteen-year-old child soldier identified as "R." says, "My training was four and a half months. I learned how to use a compass, how to attack a police post, how to carry out an ambush, and the handling of weapons. By the end I was using an AK-47, a Galil, an R-15, mortars, pineapple grenades, M-26 grenades, and *taucos* (multiple grenade launcher)."

In the scheme of things, R. received extensive training for a child soldier. Usually the training process is short, because commanders regard these children as expendable and easily replaced. Only enough time and effort is spent on each recruit to achieve the minimum standard responses and blind reactions because there are always more where they came from. Those who learn quickly will survive their first encounters and gain experience in combat, and have a chance of becoming future child leaders; those who do not or who make mistakes will most likely be injured and abandoned or simply die in the battle zone. The commanders consider that the less time and resources wasted on training them the better.

Of note, however, is the amount of time such leaders spend on desensitization, as a method of indoctrination and a way to scare children into obedience. A twelve-year-old in Colombia recounts in *Children at War*: "If you join the paramilitaries . . . your first duty is to kill. They tell you, 'Here you are going to kill.' From the very beginning, they teach you how to kill. I mean when you arrive at the camp, the first thing they do is kill a guy, and if you are a recruit they call you over to prick at him, to chop off his hands and arms."

Also, children are made to kill and maim their own as a means to desensitize them. The twelve-year-old Colombian also told Singer, "Seven weeks after I arrived there was combat. I was very scared . . . They killed one of us. We had to drink their blood to conquer our fear. Only the scared ones had to do it. I was the most scared of all, because I was the newest and the youngest."

Ishmael Beah describes another, more familiar method of desensitization in *A Long Way Gone*: "We watched movies at night. War movies, *Rambo: First Blood*, *Rambo II*, *Commando*, and so on, with the aid of a generator or sometimes a car battery. We all wanted to be like Rambo; we couldn't wait to implement his techniques."

From reading memoirs and extensive interviews with former child soldiers, it seems certain these training and socialization methods are fairly common to all the forces that employ children. While some factions, such as the LRA, may be more extreme, every training "programme" tries to quickly create a combatant with the minimum necessary skills to fight or operate in a combat environment; an obedient soldier, often drugged and living in outright fear of his or her elders and veteran peers, who will fanatically, without question or conscience or hesitation or even afterthought, execute any assigned order, including murder or mutilation; a soldier loyal to the leader, the cause and the group; and most important of all, a soldier blindly and unconsciously prepared to fight and die for that group. Do or die, kill or be killed, make your victims suffer and plead for their lives or lose yours, humiliate and mutilate others or bear witness to your own degrading demise, instill horror and fear in others or become the victim of trauma and the machete's sharp blade.

What is the reaction of the children to this experience? Some will be brainwashed, suffer permanent physical damage to circuits in their heads and become fanatical soldiers—no, zombies—as the system intended them to become, however foreign to their natures that seems. Emmanuel Jal recalls in his memoir a night when an enemy had been killed, and people broke out in song: "Excitement rushed into my veins and the fear inside me trickled away as I sang. I was a soldier now. I could sleep with one eye open and stop myself from crying out even when I was beaten until piss and shit ran out of me. I knew there were eleven ways to attack a town; how to open, fuse, and throw a grenade; how to load and fire an AK-47; how to raise a machete and hack at an enemy or use stones as a weapon when my bullets ran out. There was nothing to be afraid of."

Not surprisingly, the nascent sense of values of children caught in these civil wars often becomes dramatically warped, devoid of any respect for human life and conventions of any sort. Right is wrong and wrong is right. Killing is good and mercy is bad. Life has no value and obedience and loyalty are paramount. The mental abuse, traumas and violence necessarily result in a child who is badly damaged, and possibly permanently psychologically injured.

The intentional attack on the child's sense of good and bad has complex consequences beyond simple destruction of the psyche. At a two-day round table that was sponsored by my Child Soldiers Initiative at Dalhousie University in August 2009, nine former child soldiers testified that they had volunteered because they had believed in the cause, that they liked their leaders and missed them when they were demobilized. After they left the field, they sometimes longed to go back: as with combat veterans everywhere, civilian life can be a pale imitation of war. Another complicating and particularly sad factor that affects and disorients child soldiers is that they are often recruited so young that they have little memory of life before they entered, either voluntarily or by force, the ranks of child soldiers.

The available literature rarely mentions the children who wish they could return to the field and to a time when they had comrades and power, no matter how misused and horrifying, but instead often concentrates on the damage done to the children and on the catalogue of rights abuses suffered by these children. While this is useful and necessary, more needs to be said about how children are actually employed in front-line combat operations. In other words, we need to understand how they operate as a weapon system and the doctrine that "governs" them so that we can successfully neutralize their effect, render them ineffective, possibly even make them a liability to the user. I think this is the most effective way to eradicate this weapon from the inventory of tools of war.

My research and experience have led me to conclude that child soldiers are used and abused in four distinct areas of most force constructs: as front-line fighters, psychological weapons, logistics support and reconnaissance or information collectors. I'll examine each category in turn.

Some non-state fighting forces in Uganda, Rwanda, the Congo and Burundi have been heavily dependent on children to provide the bulk of their infantry (such as the LRA and the RPF in their civil war). The Khartoum regime in the Sudan, for instance, did not set out to recruit children, but began targeting them after a recruiting drive designed to attract adult males into the armed forces failed.

The most common method of organizing child fighting elements is to put groups of children under the command of an absolute minimum number of adults. The basic organizational unit comprises ten to thirty children led by as many adults and older youths as are required to ensure sufficient control, intimidation and emotional authority. However, young boys and girls have been known to lead small groups of other children with efficacy, courage and relative competence. Quickly commanders learn to assess which children will be the most ruthless, which of them will make good leaders. Often they choose the most violent of a group.

The ruthlessness of these children can be breathtaking, impossible to take in. Mariatu Kamara, now a student living in Toronto as well as an ambassador for Radhika Coomaraswamy, the UNICEF special representative for children and armed conflict, grew up in Sierra Leone, and in her book, *The Bite of the Mango* (written with Susan McClelland), she describes how she became a double amputee:

> Three boys hauled me up by the arms. I was kicking now, screaming, and trying to hit. But though they were little boys, I was tired and weak. They overpowered me. They led me behind the outhouse and stopped in front of a big rock.
>
> Gunfire filled the night. The rebels were shooting up at the village, I assumed, and probably everyone left in it. "Allah, please let one of the bullets stray and hit me in the heart so I may die," I prayed. I gave up the fight, and I surrendered my fate to the boys.
>
> Beside the boulder, a shirtless man lay dead. Smaller rocks lay all around him. With a shock, I realized it was the pregnant woman's husband. He traded goods from town to town, like the man who had given me palm oil. The woman who had been killed was his second wife, and the baby would have been his first child. Now the man's face was nothing but a bloody pulp. I could even see parts of his brain. The rebels had stoned him to death.
>
> "Please, please, please don't do this to me," I begged one of the boys. "I am the same age as you. You speak Temne. So you might be from around here. We would have been cousins, had we lived in the same village. Maybe we can be friends."
>
> "We're not friends," the boy scowled, pulling out his machete. "And we're certainly not cousins."

"I like you," I implored, trying to get on his good side. "Why do you want to hurt someone who likes you?"

"Because I don't want you to vote," he said. One of the boys grabbed my right arm, and another stretched my hand over the flat part of the boulder.

"If you are going to chop off my hands, please just kill me," I begged them.

"We're not going to kill you," one boy replied. "We want you to go to the president and show him what we did to you. You won't be able to vote for him now. Ask the president to give you new hands."

Two boys steadied me as my body began to sway. As the machete came down, things went silent. I closed my eyes tightly, but they popped open and I saw everything. It took the boy two attempts to cut off my right hand. The first swipe didn't get through the bones, which I saw sticking out in all different shapes and sizes.

The hugely poignant last line of her chapter reads, "As my mind went dark, I remember asking myself: What is a president."

Most of the forces that use children as soldiers adapt their weapons and tactics to their use, which is why I argue that they have become a weapon system. My research at the Carr Center was what led me to understand child fighters in this new light. As I wrote, "Child soldiers are an effective weapon of terror and it has so far not been possible to develop an alternative that falls within the correct orientation of our moral compass." Rebel and other non-state organization leaders have quickly learned the impact that children with guns can have on adults, and they have mastered a tactical advantage by manipulating these little humans into leading the charge when they are facing armies of adults. P.W. Singer wrote that the "cover of children's assumed innocence is also often utilized to a force's advantage. In Iraq, rebel groups reportedly used children both as scouts and spies, particularly when targeting U.S. convoys"—presumably because U.S. soldiers would never expect children to be their enemies. Not only do children present moral dilemmas for legitimate forces, but they also throw the "game of war" into a tailspin. Gone are the days when our soldiers fought wars against enemies according to the laws of armed conflict, with clear battle lines and readily identifiable opponents.

In most cases, children actually begin their combat experience without weapons in hand but are introduced to them when they prove their reliability and when weapons are available. The ever-present AK-47 is the weapon of choice with older children, who progress to light machine guns like the RPK, rocket-propelled grenade launchers like the RPG family or even light mortars of the sixty-millimetre variety. Good performance is rewarded with a higher status weapon and increased responsibility and authority within the group. Most former child soldiers I have met have spoken quite fondly about their weapons and the power and security they brought them.

In actual combat, experience has demonstrated that children can typically be driven to emotional and even physical extremes more easily than adults.

After overcoming their initial reluctance and experiencing a favourable baptism by fire, many children become fearless and will actively seek the fight. Drugs are usually plentiful, aiding in the disinhibition and fearlessness displayed by these children and inducing dependency—another means of control used by the adults. In the conflicts of the Great Lakes Region, where operations have tended to be more fluid and less dependent on solid defensive positions that must be overcome by physical assault, child soldiers tend to be best employed in raids, ambushes, patrolling, and quick attacks on an unsuspecting enemy, in addition to looting and committing abuses of "enemy" civilians.

Some of the forces, like the LRA, employ child soldiers with no regard to their survival. Daily news releases, reports and testimonies speak to the fact that LRA commanders place no value on the lives of their soldiers. Children and adults are expendable and new recruits can be found just across the next border. Depriving their troops of food, water and medicine likely drives some of the violent looting when soldiers enter villages—pillaging being the only means of survival.

Other forces, such as the RPF, placed a high value on the lives of their soldiers and in return were rewarded with higher levels of loyalty and competence, as I observed when I conducted my reconnaissance before being posted to Kigali.

Nevertheless, the norm has been to push child soldiers to the front of offensive operations to draw fire, clear mines and booby traps with their bodies, and lead assaults. Such positioning usually results in children suffering the bulk of the casualties, leaving the adults to acquire the pillaged resources and reward the child survivors. For child soldiers, this may mean being forced into the attack by their commanders who stand behind them ready to shoot those who fail to show sufficient enthusiasm. Throwing children into battle and letting them fend for themselves seems to be the routine way for these children to get their bearings. This strategy is a modern perversion of the wise counsel of Sun Tzu, who advised in *The Art of War* that "troops in desperate straits know no fear. Where there is no escape, they stand firm; when they have entered deep, they persist; when they see no hope, they fight." When you're being shot at, you quickly learn how to avoid becoming an easy target and learn to combine the use of your weapon with evasive and advantageous manoeuvring. Kill or be killed.

Child soldiers appear to be as capable on the attack as adult fighters, and have regularly exhibited less fear and more aggression than adults when properly motivated. As P.W. Singer writes, "Children make very effective combatants. They don't ask a lot of questions. They follow instructions, and they often don't understand and aren't able to evaluate the risks of going to war. Victims and witnesses often said they feared the children more than the

adults because the child combatants had not developed an understanding of the value of life. They would do anything. They knew
no fear. Especially when they were pumped up on drugs. They
saw it as fun to go into battle." Or they had been reduced to a level
of desperation where the only survival option they could perceive
was to attack ferociously in hopes of victory.

Child soldiers can also be employed as psychological weapons.
Weak forces lacking the technical capacity to break the will of the
enemy by employing overwhelming force to shatter an opponent
must rely instead on human ingenuity—using the materials at
hand and usually in a fashion that has come to be known as terrorism. Child soldiers are a particularly effective resource in this
regard. The main, but not only, reason they can be employed as
suicide bombers or walking improvised explosive devices (IEDs)
is that, in most cases, they are forcibly drugged with stimulants
that make them impervious to fear or pain.

Chris Coulter, writing on the conflict in Sierra Leone, cited
"drugs as the main reason explaining the absurd level of violence.
'[T]hat is how they are brave to do all these things, without the drugs
they cannot do it. Because I cannot stand and see my mother and
kill her! But because of the drugs you can't recognize who is standing in front of you,' said Musu, one of my informants." According to
one former Mai Mai, cited in a briefing paper put out by the
Coalition to Stop the Use of Child Soldiers in February 2010, "After
taking a spoonful of [drugged] porridge, I cannot see the difference
between men and animals." Another former boy soldier described
how "after taking the medicine, as soon as you hear a gunshot, you
become crazy and seek it out, like a dog chases a hare."

Grace Akallo, a former LRA soldier and a founder of the Network
of Young People Affected by War (NYPAW), spoke to us during the
CSI's August 2009 round table in Halifax about how girl commanders would be especially brutal to their peers because they
knew it was the way to get to command a unit. Once they were

given command they would be sent off, at times with less than effective adult supervision and on rare occasions without any supervision at all, to do secondary harassment or scavenging tasks. Some of the girls would then attempt (and on rare occasions succeed) in leading their group to freedom.

In traditional African societies, age always was and still is greatly respected, and children simply do not disobey or cause trouble without risking instant discipline from elders. This feature of typical society has been even more instilled in the child soldier through training, socialization and combat experiences. At the NYPAW round table, participants told us how their leaders provided a sense of family and community to child combatants: "Children who come from a culture where they are accustomed to being raised in a communal environment and taught to respect all figures of authority are especially able to feel comfortable in this environment."

The corollary of this perversion of social norms is the shock value presented by child soldiers, simply because they upset the child's deference to his or her elders. An unruly child with an AK-47 is a terrifying sight if for no other reason than it represents an awful combination of unpredictable willfulness and naked power along with a complete reversal of the traditional role of children.

Knowing that there is a large pool of their own children who might be turned into soldiers—and that they can do little to prevent it—poses an added dimension to the terror such forces wield in these civil wars. The civilians of this central African region live among and love the same children who may one day come back and kill them.

Another dimension of the use and effectiveness of child soldiers is when they are used against rival or foreign fighting forces. Children pile an extra moral weight onto those they attack. Soldiers fighting against children must constantly question the legitimacy of their actions at the same time that they struggle to overcome their natural tendency to hesitate to pull the trigger.

The laws of armed combat explicitly state that the fundamental right of every individual combatant is the right to self-defence. Over the past twenty years, a full spectrum of foreign protection forces, with regrettably large variations in capabilities and effectiveness and involving well over 100,000 peacekeepers, has been deployed with nearly two dozen UN missions in conflicts where child soldiers are used in tactical altercations and yet their rules of engagement (ROE) do not specify any special procedure to employ when using force against child soldiers, either when the peacekeeper's life is directly at risk or when the task could be compromised. Any moment of hesitation on the part of the protection forces, be they foreign or national, can provide a tactical advantage to those who use the child soldier weapon system. The LRA's Joseph Kony pursued an added agenda when he frequently placed child soldiers at the front in battle in hopes that the media outrage over their deaths would hamper government military action against him. The Acholi people, who are preyed upon by the LRA and whose children are abducted by Kony's forces, became hugely critical of the Ugandan government efforts to fight Kony for just that reason: it was their children who were being killed, no matter that they themselves were killers. As P.W. Singer observes, fighting child soldiers "presents a public affairs nightmare that adversaries may seek to exploit. A primary worry for militaries facing child soldiers is that a traditional measure of success in defeating their opponent may end up undermining their domestic support, as well as sway international opinion."

There is a serious vacuum in the tactical responses by militaries and related security forces to the use of child soldiers in conflict zones. It is the aim of the CSI, as I'll discuss in chapter nine, to define this critical operational deficiency, develop a new conceptual base for neutralizing this very effective weapon system in the field and prevent its reinforcement by new recruits. From that rigorous conceptual base, we will develop the doctrines or principles required to create the tactics, equipment, drills and training, and organization we need to stop the outright slaughter of these children.

And there is a more insidious, and terrifying, impact on soldiers who have been attacked frequently by children from an unprofessional, borderline criminal force. Through fear for their own safety, the loss of comrades in battle, humiliating engagements that turn against them, and witnessing the scale of brutality drugged and indoctrinated children can visit on the innocent, they may begin to regard all children as potential opponents and commit abuses against any group of children they suspect.

Children are also employed in acts of terror, including suicide attacks against the opposing military or against civilians. Children are so plentiful in developing, overpopulated societies that one with a grenade can easily slip unnoticed through a checkpoint or loiter in an area and then use himself as a human bomb, destroying his target and in the process himself, out of some warped and drug-induced loyalty to the cause. They are also used as an instrument of terror against civilians through a combination of drug-assisted atrocities or whimsically savage attacks. The Mai Mai rebels and the Interahamwe militia in the Congo best demonstrate the continued application of this style of terror and have too often successfully destabilized the whole eastern region of that huge country and taken the civil war beyond national borders, with devastating consequences for millions of innocent civilians.

In addition to having combat and terror roles, child soldiers are the backbone of the logistics support train. Both government and non-state belligerents in the Great Lakes Region, for instance, lack transportation and even if they have transport, only a few roads can be used as main supply routes. The bulk of the road network, which traverses difficult terrain, is often impassible due to erosion and lack of maintenance. The best way to move heavy loads from place to place is along narrow tracks through forests and ravines and around mountains, employing large numbers of slender children as pack animals. Where the terrain allows, and the loads are very heavy—bulky munitions boxes, for example—commanders increase the load-bearing capacity of children by putting them on bicycles.

Where combat occurs in conditions of food scarcity, children are sent to forage for wild foods, barter for supplies in local markets, and steal food at the point of a gun from humanitarian agencies or local farmers. For example, both the government and the rebel forces in the Burundi civil war collected many child recruits during the drought of 2000 to 2001. Children were driven by insecurity, being orphaned or going hungry to attach themselves to these fighting forces, and though they were seldom used in actual combat, they acted as porters, errand-runners, launderers, cooks and sometimes even as nurses of the wounded.

Child soldiers can also be employed as spies or scouts in reconnaissance and information-gathering tasks. The particular advantage of children is that they can generally move without drawing much attention. This is particularly so in populous countries where children are found in large numbers and spend much of their day unsupervised. In normal conditions, most adults view children as objects of affection rather than fear or suspicion. To those who employ children as soldiers, this provides an advantage as the children can get close to security installations and other vital points, such as waterworks or electrical facilities, without attracting attention. They can become effective covert agents, spying or scouting for their superiors.

Similarly, children are also employed as couriers or messengers to deliver information from one location to another in the hope that they will not be stopped or even scrutinized by security forces or vigilantes at the ubiquitous road blocks. In Rwanda, in more recent times, attacks by the Hutu extremist group, the Army for the Liberation of Rwanda (ALIR)—whose aim was to bring down the government of Paul Kagame and restore Hutu power—were often preceded by scouting missions conducted by children in the hope that Rwandan forces would let them pass, so that they could gather intelligence for their commander.

To sum up, children have military capabilities, net operational advantages and tactical effectiveness that make their employment attractive to unscrupulous commanders. They can effectively fight with the light weapons most commonly in use in conflict zones and they have proven to be fanatically brave front-line soldiers. They are highly effective weapons of terror in failing states and have become the weapon of choice. They can perform a host of menial but essential logistics and support tasks that free combatants (soldiers and other children) for operational duties. They can also be effective when employed in collecting intelligence as spies, scouts, early warning systems, couriers or guards. The girls and some young boys are sexually abused and are traded like commodities to satisfy the perversions of men and older boys.

Given that all these children are considered expendable and easily replaced from a seemingly limitless pool of potential recruits, criminal commanders in the imploding nations of sub-Saharan Africa, especially, have developed child soldiers into a sustainable, low-technology weapon system of choice. They have come up with cunning and ruthless tactics, child-led combat unit structures, low-technology equipment needs, and rudimentary training methods and standards that maximize the effectiveness of the young bodies and minds at their disposal. These criminal commanders have in essence developed a child soldier doctrine that may vary slightly according to local custom but whose principles are startlingly the same: it's by understanding those principles that we will develop the most effective ways of neutralizing this relatively new and inhumane weapon system.

But first I'd like to explore one more aspect of the reality of the child soldier. As though the tragedy of their employment as soldiers is not enough hardship for these children to endure, the one thing we know about wars is that all of them eventually end. And when they do, what becomes of the child soldiers?

Children who make it out alive will most certainly have a myriad of social, physical and emotional problems to deal with. Often they have witnessed or been the perpetrators of unimaginable atrocities; also, they can be diseased, drug-addicted and suffering the physical wounds of war, which can become permanent handicaps due to a lack of medical care and unhygienic recovery conditions. They find themselves on their own, with no family or friends to speak of, and on the search for a means of survival. Some will return to their villages or drift to the big cities where they've heard work can be found, but civilian life is not so easy to adjust to, especially since most of them are illiterate, accustomed to using force to gain what they want and need, and have lost all proof of their identities and of their existence. They have been taught by their commanders that the end of the war is the end of their purpose.

The lucky ones (although they don't always know it at the time) are able to leave their roles as soldiers early because their release has been negotiated by UNICEF or other NGOs, international agencies and possibly even national and foreign politicians or diplomats prior to a ceasefire or the end of the conflict. Those who are not so lucky will be ultimately subjected to a demobilization process that does not clearly identify them for what they are or have been and as a result may totally miss the mark as it tries to restore these children to a semblance of normality in a country often still hovering between nation building and relapses into conflict.

The next chapter will look at how child soldiers are currently disarmed, demobilized, rehabilitated and reintegrated, and the ways in which they then need to fight to regain their childhoods. These bush-wise but still immature souls in small bodies have to slowly begin to unlearn the ruthless and perverse skills that have been inculcated in them, wean themselves from the drugs and booze used to control them, and forget—or transcend, with sometimes surprising resilience—the fundamentally predatory experiences that led to their survival in the bush.

7.

HOW TO UNMAKE A CHILD SOLDIER

WHAT I KNOW FOR CERTAIN from studying child soldiers for the better part of a decade is this: picking up the pieces of broken children after a conflict is hugely difficult, the necessary and ongoing effort is hard to sustain, and success is unpredictable to gauge. In this chapter I will sketch some of the features of this troubling terrain, which the UN, peacekeeping and humanitarian communities have labelled DDR, for disarmament, demobilization and reintegration. That final R stretches to cover many other *r* words—reinsertion, rehabilitation, reconciliation, reconstruction, repatriation—all of them so difficult to achieve. I will say it again: it's better to stop the recruitment and use of children within belligerent forces before it happens than to deal with the complexities of reintegrating children into their home communities—if they even exist—after the conflict is over. Former child soldier and rapper Emmanuel Jal eloquently captured the nature of the damage and the struggle of healing in the lyrics to his song "Baakiwara": "I'm in another war / This time / It's my soul that I'm fighting for."

The fact also stands that no matter the good intentions and agreed-to protocols, dealing with war-affected children and child soldiers is rarely a top priority among the international and domestic players as they attempt to put together the pieces of a viable nation state after a conflict has ended. This shouldn't be a surprise. What political entity in developed and stable countries actually pays more than lip service to putting the needs of children first or to "remembering" how important it is to our future to protect a child's sense of wonder and imagination, his or her capacity to dream and grow? No, we grow up and are told to put aside childish things, and we largely buy in to that: our education systems, in North America at least, have grown increasingly utilitarian and cost-sensitive, cutting libraries, art programmes, music, any essential that doesn't easily fit inside stretched educational budgets. We abandon our own poorest children to struggle on their own to lift themselves out of their circumstances; child poverty rates in the United States and in parts of Canada, particularly among aboriginal communities, are shocking in countries of such national wealth and resources. In my own homeland, one in nine children lives below the poverty line.

In a war zone finally grasping for peace, the tendency in the past has been to ignore the children: the "adults" basically decided that there were more important "adult" issues to be responded to than the fate of the children and youths who had been caught up in the fighting or who had been innocently pushed hither and yon as the conflict raged. But this near-automatic relegation of war-affected children—including child soldiers, the actual perpetrators of much of the human destruction—to the status of "we'll deal with them later" is slowly changing, as we realize how greatly such an attitude inhibits a stable reconciliation and rebuilding process. Or at least the language is changing. Most recent peace agreements include specific language on child soldiers, as well as outlining ways to address their needs in the demobilization and reintegration process. The implementation of these measures, however, is still shaky, and though the right noises are made all the way up the chain of command, and the UN appoints child protection officers to serve in its missions, the fact is these advocates for children often have to fight to gain the attention of the mission's senior leadership in order to claim their share of resources and effort.

It's so easy to fall into the old pattern of thinking, "Hey, they are just kids. Once we get the politics, the relief and the support structure that will appease all the main actors—from the ex-belligerent leaders to the NGOs to the nascent reconstituted government and its integrated security forces—we can deal with the 'social' problems, those softer areas that include women and children and community health and education." Generally speaking, the people running the show on all sides—both the strategic bodies, such as the UN Department of Peacekeeping Operations and the Security Council, which produce the peacekeeping mandates, and the field missions that attempt to enforce them and are always hard-pressed by time and resources to produce tangible near-term results—regard child soldiers as an annoyance, a pain in the side, a social-adjustment problem meriting a minimum of effort. The UN can only push an agenda if it has buy-in from its member nations, and if child soldiers are not a priority for those nation states, funding and resources for DDR programmes can be hard to maintain. In case that seems inexplicable to you, remember that child soldiers may have better access to food and medicine inside their armed groups than they will have after they've been repatriated to their home communities, and both the children and the people who attempt to demobilize them know that. These same child soldiers have been, and probably still are, wreaking havoc and reinforcing the power grabs being made by the leaders on all sides as the conflict winds down, which also muddies the situation for the people who have to deal with them.

I'm going to add an extra R to DDR, to stand for all those other r words, and label it "DDRR" here. In theory, DDRR should be among the first steps in helping a country rebuild, allowing its citizens to return home to some form of normality and justice after the conflict has ended. The reality is that things are never that simple. As laid out in the introduction to the UN's formalized standards for DDRR (called the IDDRS Framework, which was developed in the mid-2000s to share best practices in the world's trouble zones), the objective is to "contribute to security and stability in post-conflict environments so that recovery and development can begin." A great aim, for sure, but we must make sure these standards are well crafted to answer all the demobilized people's needs. Right now, some of the most vulnerable—the millions of war-affected children, the hundreds of thousands of child soldiers—have limited access to the DDRR process. And, in some cases, the very process that is meant to help them ironically pushes them back into armed groups—government, insurgent or paramilitary—or bandit gangs and a life of crime.

Much has been written on these issues, and my aim here is not to rewrite what has already been written, but rather to attempt to shine light on the areas that are the most challenging. And yes, these challenges have also been written about to no end, but even so, we are still dropping the ball far too often when it comes to dealing with some of the most vulnerable populations in conflict and post-conflict settings. The UN has taken a significant leadership role, supported by its own agencies, such as UNICEF, and within some of its missions by the special representatives of the secretary general, and by dedicated work done by several field-focused NGOs, such as Save the Children, War Child, Search for Common Ground, World Vision and a number of others.

But nonetheless, we responsible and reasonable adults still seem far off the mark when dealing with rehabilitating war-affected children and child soldiers. I would contend that most of the r problems stem from weak performance from the same agencies I've just mentioned, who enter the field with great ambition and resolve, and talk a great battle, but seldom manage to muster the capacity to sustain the fight to achieve their own declared objectives. They also risk being mired in dogma, which can hamper new initiatives. UNICEF, for example, operates on the firm conviction that family reintegration is the answer to the problem of child soldiers, but so many other factors—skills training and employment to name just two—need to align for reintegration to be a success. If you focus on only one aspect, that's where the bulk of your donors' dollars go, which results in an imbalance of resources that undermines creating the complete package the child soldier needs to re-enter normal life. And we're even further off the mark when it comes to addressing the complex needs of girl soldiers in DDRR programmes today (which I will specifically address at the end of this chapter).

Traditionally, DDRR programmes were created for adult male combatants in civil wars in order to disarm and reintegrate them into their communities after the war was over. However, increasingly over the last twenty years or so, women and children have also been taking up arms in war and, either voluntarily or by coercion, becoming combatants within the belligerent forces. They, too, need assistance once war has ended, but the needs of adult women, of boys and of girls are distinct from those of adult men. One size cannot fit all, but because of expediency and lack of resources, children and adults have often been processed under the same security and support conditions, which in effect ensure that the young ones remain under the sway of the adults who brought them such suffering and abuse. The early steps at establishing separate protocols for children suffered from the assumptions Ishmael Beah saw played out the first time he was offered up by his own commander to an NGO for DDRR: believing that all these children were longing to be "just kids" again, the aid workers housed demobilized boy soldiers from both sides of the conflict in the same facility, and the outcome was more violence. Those boys had to be taught, very carefully and with infinite patience, how to be boys again, how to give up their power as fighting units.

The UN's IDDRS Framework defines two categories with respect to children and war:

> Youth. While there is no internationally recognized legal defini-
> tion of "youth," young people associated with armed forces and
> groups make up an important part of society and can both fuel
> conflict and support post-conflict reconciliation and recovery.
> Many young ex-combatants may have been recruited as chil-
> dren, but not demobilized until they were young adults. They
> have therefore been denied normal socialization by families
> and communities, they have missed educational and vocational
> opportunities, and lack basic living skills. *The design and deliv-
> ery of DDR programmes shall consider the particular needs and
> potential of older children and younger adults associated with
> armed forces and groups.* [Emphasis added.] DDR programmes
> designed for youth can also have a positive impact on young
> people in the community who may be at risk of recruitment by
> armed forces and groups or organized criminals.
>
> Children. The recruitment of children into armed forces and
> groups is a serious violation of human rights and is prohibited
> under international law. The UN shall promote the uncondi-
> tional release of children associated with fighting forces at all
> times, i.e., during open conflict, while peace negotiations are
> taking place and before the establishment of a national DDR
> process. The identification and management of children associ-
> ated with armed forces and groups may in practice be quite dif-
> ficult. While the UN Convention on the Rights of the Child
> establishes 18 as the age of legal majority, concepts and experi-
> ences of childhood vary significantly among cultures and com-
> munities. Furthermore, children are likely to have taken on adult
> roles and responsibilities during conflict, either while associated
> with armed forces and groups or in war-affected communities.

Girl children in particular may be considered adults if they have been "married" during conflict, borne children or taken on respon-sibilities as heads of household in receiving communities. [Emphasis added.] Children formerly associated with armed forces and groups are stakeholders and must be carefully consulted when DDR processes are set up. To successfully cater for children's needs, programme development and implementation should be designed to ensure the participation of all stakeholders, and reinte-gration strategies must be adapted to meet the different needs, roles and responsibilities of children in each post-conflict situation. To ease their return to civilian life, former child soldiers should be integrated into programmes that benefit all war-affected children.

The age criterion is one of the most challenging aspects in DDRR programming. How does one determine the age of a child who arrives at a disarming post with no identification, a child for whom chronological age probably was never really that impor-tant? Chronological age figures in all international standards. The UN Convention on the Rights of the Child establishes the legal age of majority, but how is the concept of majority measured in reality? These children have often endured experiences that many adults in the developed world would fail to cope with, and as a result it is rare that the signpost of chronological age adequately captures their level of maturity. Age is not a universal construct delineating youth and childhood from adulthood. Though agen-cies are trying to recognize this issue, we still face considerable interpretive problems when we start drawing the age line among groups with respect to who is or isn't entitled to participate in DDRR programmes.

There are too many examples where children have fallen through cracks and as a result have not been able to benefit from education, skills training or adoption opportunities, mostly because they have been denied any recognition as having been a child soldier due to lack of proof and witnesses who would speak on their behalf. During the course of a conflict, the child soldiers who do escape from their armed groups do not always have a designated safe place to go. If they attempt to surrender to whatever recognizable authority exists, they are not necessarily turned over to a benevolent NGO programme for demobilized children. Instead, as I pointed out in chapter five, they can face summary execution or lengthy imprisonment for war crimes. Many child soldiers who desert have to flee in order to avoid both or all sides in the conflict and cannot return home. As I described in chapter six, many leaders force children to commit atrocities on friends, neighbours and even their own families expressly so they can't go home again.

The 2008 Global Report by the Coalition to Stop the Use of Child Soldiers estimates that "fewer than half the returning child soldiers registered for demobilization with the UPDF [the Ugandan national army], fearing the army itself, or rejection by their communities if they were identified as LRA members. In one study, returning child soldiers in the Teso region reported extensive and persistent stigmatization and rejection by their communities and constant bullying by their peers at school." This was aggravated by envy and jealousy in the community over the benefits these ex–child soldiers received in the DDRR programmes, which were not extended to war-affected children. How must it feel to be an orphan child, who has never raised a gun, and see a child soldier—who may have been the one to kill his family—receive food, schooling and support denied to the orphan?

The 2008 Global Report also showed that most female child soldiers in the DRC did not enter any official DDR programmes, "fearing stigmatization by their communities if they were identified as child soldiers. Others remained with their military 'husbands' for fear of violence and recrimination if they left. Only 12 per cent of formally demobilized children were girls, despite estimates that girls might have comprised up to 40 per cent of the total number of child soldiers during the armed conflict." More proof that the challenges facing the girls dwarf the challenges facing the boys.

In order to show you this terrain more completely, I want to dissect current DDRR practices, looking for what they actually provide children and youth and where they fall short. It is not all bad news, but it will become evident that the commitment of resources and the sophistication of the process still leave a lot to be desired, and permit the continued destruction of these youths at the hands of their own people or, far too often, spur them to rejoin the very groups that stole their childhoods.

The first D we must deal with in DDRR is disarmament. Traditional DDR programmes demand that a person has to hand in a weapon to gain access to the process. However, as in the case of the conflict in Sierra Leone, after a ceasefire was established, child soldiers were not obliged to bring in their weapons. As a result, many of them hid their AK-47s in the bush or sold them to adults who cashed them in under the adult DDRR programmes.

And what of children who do not have a weapon to hand in? Those who were never armed? The Paris Principles agreed to in 2007 define a child soldier this way: "A child associated with an armed force or armed group refers to any person below 18 years of age who is, or who has been, recruited or used by an armed force or armed group in any capacity, including but not limited to children, boys and girls, used as fighters, cooks, porters, spies or for sexual purposes. It does not only refer to a child who is taking, or has taken, a direct part in hostilities." But how are they meant to disarm if they do not have weapons to turn in? Chris Coulter explains the reality of this issue in *Bush Wives and Girl Soldiers*: "More than half of all female ex-combatants I interviewed said that they had actually wanted to disarm, but only a handful did . . . Some of those who had wanted to disarm said that the reason they did not or could not was that they could not access a weapon."

We have learned a lot about implementing DDRR, but we still make mistakes we are not learning from very quickly. "Cash for guns," for example, was a popular incentive for getting children, youths and adults to disarm. However, my CIDA field deployment and fact-finding exercise with the rebel forces in Sierra Leone showed me that issuing cash payments to demobilizing children only made them more vulnerable to abuse. The money turned them into targets of adult attention and did not help with long-term reintegration plans at all. My research at the Carr Center reinforced that finding. In Liberia, for example, cash for guns constantly put the children's well-being in jeopardy. As I wrote in my Carr Center paper: "Remunerating child combatants in this case seem[ed] to have been a naive gesture given the background level of corruption and the clear lack of complementary protective measures to ensure that the affected children's rights to the payment were respected." Today we find more innovative takes on this concept, such as "bikes for guns" or "goats for guns"—for the Mai Mai in the DRC, for example—all in a well-intentioned effort to get people to disarm. My long-time colleague Phil Lancaster (my executive assistant for the last two months of the UNAMIR mission in Rwanda, and a significant contributor to my research at Harvard) has worked extensively in the field with child soldiers, and in Burundi saw a bike programme work to the detriment of the children it was supposed to help—their older siblings or parents tended to appropriate the bicycles. But such new options have proven to be relatively effective when they are part of a larger programme to revitalize the whole community, and when they can be sustained and funded, no small task when you consider the vast number of weapons that need to be decommissioned in these conflict zones. The success of these new ideas really depends on the scale of the funding they receive and the consistency and length of donor commitment to sustaining that funding.

The question still stands: how do we effectively separate the guns from the children? The proliferation of small arms has put so many weapons at the disposal of armed groups that trying to stem their flow into any country in turmoil seems impossible. As I mentioned earlier, the production of these light and relatively cheap weapons as well as munitions did not decrease when the Cold War ended. And the Herculean effort on arms-control initiatives in the 1990s, led by countries such as Canada, seems to have lessened, even disappeared, without any outcry from different interested quarters on the international stage, even in normally very responsible capitals.

I think the best way to separate the children from the guns is to bring back a deliberate campaign for the reduction of the proliferation of small arms in illegal trade that goes well beyond the UN Security Council's action programme in this area, which began in 2001, and the subsequent reports from the secretary general on small arms proliferation and its direct links to conflict and the arming of child soldiers. One of the key problems here is that there has not been a comprehensive study of the subject, which once again seems to highlight the fact that the interests of children are low on the world's priority list. I was part of the Canadian delegation to the UN General Assembly several years ago as it considered methods of tracing the illegal trading of such weapons. Canada made the argument that small arms were the primary tool used by children and youths in conflicts around the world, putting a face to the subject as well as recommending registering the transit and ownership of these guns, and the destruction of them on the spot if they were found in unauthorized or illegal hands. In 2008 the secretary general's report finally widened the discussion to include issues of production, marking and tracing. But it is as if the whole exercise has really stood still, as millions of small arms continue to be produced and distributed with near impunity.

If we can revive the campaign against small arms, especially if we stress the link to child soldiers, we can end the overproduction of these weapons and munitions and start eating away at their distribution. The UN Office for Disarmament Affairs would have to be reinforced and would need more depth in the field, perhaps by establishing much more deliberate and innovative approaches through the hundreds of NGOs that could be engaged with the security forces to work with the local actors to create weapons-free zones. For instance, an initiative to create "zones of peace" in the drug wars in Colombia has achieved some success. Communities have taken it on themselves to declare gun- and violence-free zones in the midst of conflict, either literally and geographically, or with ceasefires on holidays. National NGOs have rolled the idea out across the country under the banner of "100 Peace Municipalities." Such campaigns are certainly worthy of serious re-engagement and priority of resources and effort. When one considers the number of people killed, injured and threatened every year, when we speak of "small arms" we are actually speaking of a weapon of mass destruction.

The second *D* is for demobilization—once again a term that implies a formal process. You have presented yourself to a DDR centre, handed in your weapon (or not) and are now leaving the armed group you were fighting with to enter an interim care centre. But what of the deserters mentioned above, the children who have run away? Those who may not have been released by commanders? What happens to them? Do they still get a chance to take part in educational programmes or vocational training? How do you prove that you were a soldier? Is the burden of proof on the child? It is so important that the personnel who come into contact with these children and youths know how to assess them properly, a difficult task when dealing with kidnapped children or children otherwise forced to flee their homes without a scrap of identification or any belongings. Many also come from countries where they had no access to documentation in the first place; South Africa, for instance, is still coping with providing birth certificates to millions who were disadvantaged by apartheid.

Conflict in imploding nations, which degenerates into civil war, is complex, ambiguous and rife with the unexpected. There is no one-size-fits-all solution to a no-size-fits-anyone problem. Children continue to this day to be somewhat marginalized by

DDRR processes. Although UN organizations such as UNICEF and NGOs such as Save the Children are hard at work trying to get children released from armed groups and then rehabilitated, their efforts pale in comparison to the continued efforts of armed groups to increase their ranks by kidnapping and recruiting children.

Complicating an already complex situation is the fact that the accepted UN standards state that the "UN shall promote the unconditional release of children associated with fighting forces at all times, i.e., during open conflict, while peace negotiations are taking place and before the establishment of a national DDR process." While noble in ambition, the release of children during a conflict presents many challenges for those trying to implement rehabilitation programmes. If they act on this recommendation, children might be released back to their communities while a conflict is still raging and either be kidnapped again or face such hardship that they return to the bush in search of the life they already know and have gotten used to.

Now we come to the many Rs of this process. The UN IDDRS Framework breaks down the reintegration process into two parts, short- and long-term stages. The first, *reinsertion*, is the assistance given to combatants during the demobilization process, meant to help with the child's immediate basic needs such as food, clothing and shelter. The second part, *reintegration*, is meant to be longer term and involves the ex-combatant's rehabilitation and reintegration into civilian life. The framework states that child-specific reintegration "shall allow a child to access education, a livelihood, life skills and a meaningful role in society. The socio-economic and psychological aspects of reintegration for children are central to global DDR programming and budgeting. Successful reintegration requires long-term funding of child protection agencies and programmes to ensure continuous support for education and training for children, and essential follow-up / monitoring once they return to civilian life." Successful reintegration ought to drive the overall DDRR process as it is the guarantee that we have been able to bring these children back from the extremes of abuses that they have both committed and survived.

But there have been many failures in this area and the reasons are innumerable, though I believe they all come down to the fact that if there is no acceptance for the ex–child soldier, no forgiveness and, worst of all, no opportunity to build a new life because the political and economic stability of their homeland remains at risk, a smart and capable child or youth will once again seek the opportunities offered by a gun. Where reintegration fails, there is considerable likelihood that former child soldiers will be re-recruited, voluntarily rejoin an armed group, or drift into a life of crime because they have no other means of survival.

Sometimes valid and worthy reintegration programmes for former child combatants fall apart due to erratic funding, irregular resource allocation and general impatience on the part of donors for immediate and measurable results. It's relatively easy for donors at a remove, no matter how well intentioned, to forget that instant gratification is impossible in this field. After a savage and catastrophic civil war has destroyed basic social order, decades are required to produce a stable citizenry again.

I believe that the key to rebuilding a shattered social order is repairing and restoring the lives of children who have been exploited as soldiers. The destructive impact of their experiences with violence, abuse and exploitation, if not redressed, will continue to ripple out into the wider community. As the American academic and child-protection worker Michael Wessells affirms in his 2007 book, *Child Soldiers: From Violence to Protection* (based on hundreds of interviews with child combatants):

> Children who spend their formative years in combat take on values and identities that are shaped by the military groups to which they belonged. Even at the end of conflict, children who can't see a future for themselves in their communities and

country, may cross borders to fight in neighbouring conflicts. While adults are also available for hire, they can only fight for so long. *Children who have grown up having learned fighting as their only means of livelihood and survival are likely to continue fighting for more years than adults.* [Emphasis added.]

Child soldiering is a serious threat to regional stability even in the post-conflict nation-building phase. Investments in effective, long-term reintegration programmes are investments in the security and stability of the nation and even the region. Successful reintegration plans must cover all the phases of the conflict, from the beginning of a crisis right through to the conclusion of a peace agreement and well beyond. And they must commit, with depth and sophistication, to the deliberate rehabilitation of conflict-affected children away from evil toward good, from abuse toward restraint, from survival toward living with hope that they can have a better future.

Take the case of a child soldier who has been a leader, who by the age of fourteen has gained extensive experience in command of his peers and even older members of his (or her) group. How do we keep this fourteen-year-old (going on twenty-five) from becoming disenchanted with rehabilitation programmes that offer only short-term schooling and skills training, with the more restrictive "normal" life of his home village, or even worse with the strictures of life in a refugee or internally displaced persons' camp?

He will soon realize that basic, elementary-level education won't provide him with the knowledge he needs to maximize his leadership skills to his own and his community's benefit. Three to six months of schooling with children much younger than himself in a temporary schoolroom set up in a DDRR camp will not persuade him to find the perseverance he needs to get ahead faster than his peers and go on to achieve with his brain and talent rather than with violence. How do we turn these very special children into catalysts of reconciliation and nation building, into the next generation of national leaders working for the democratic good of their fellow citizens? If we don't harness their potential for good, their societies will continue to reap their capacity for evil. As John Kon Kelei, a former child soldier from the Sudan, says, "Being associated with an armed group made the children hard, your heart had to turn to stone to be able to survive. What I fear most is myself."

Reintegration is an interesting word in that it presupposes that what existed before the conflict was adequate. It presumes that children are re-entering a previous life, returning home to loving parents and decent economic circumstances. However, in many cases life before conflict was not wonderful, and everyday life presented struggles. So what exactly are children reintegrating into?

How does a shattered community take in children who have been demobilized? How can a community that has not had the time to grieve and come to terms with what has happened, be expected to take in some of the perpetrators of the conflict? Where are these children expected to go? Who is expected to care for them? What protection mechanisms will have been set up to ensure that children are not snatched up to fight again?

If the conflict is ongoing, the social problems that allowed the children to become soldiers in the first place will barely have been addressed. How can we ensure that a child's rights will be upheld when the very fabric of society is broken beyond belief? These are the difficult questions that must be posed when looking at creating successful and effective DDRR processes. These are the questions we must be asking to ensure that no child be re-subjected to soldiering as an option. Until we face the reality of the situation and ask the right questions, how can anyone come up with the right answers? As P.W. Singer writes in *Children at War*, "Ultimately, a successful reintegration is as much about whether the families and communities are prepared for acceptance as about whether the children have been properly rehabilitated." We must find ways to break the re-recruitment cycle—make children and youth not want to go back, not *have* to go back to life in the bush.

One of the alternatives we can present children with is education. Education is a critical need of the former child soldier, but also a critical element for the prevention of the use of child soldiers. Careful thought must be given to the type of programmes offered. During the CSI's Ghana simulation exercise in Accra in 2007, several former child soldier participants spoke of their desire to pursue the education they missed because of the time they spent as combatants. The international community and local authorities must carefully consider the type of education to be offered. How many times have I heard youths say that the vocational courses that were offered to them in post-conflict settings were inadequate? How many cobblers, bakers and seamstresses does one community need? Are we actually paying attention to the needs of the children and the community or rather training children in short-term programmes that we deem cost-effective? Whose needs are we really trying to fulfill? In his book, *A Long Way Gone*, Ishmael Beah mentions the large number of boys who were trained as mechanics in Sierra Leone after the war—how many mechanics does Sierra Leone need for a population that can barely afford cars?

If we truly want to make a dent in the number of children who are re-recruited into gangs or other armed groups in post-conflict settings then we must make sure that the training we are providing is actually filling a need that either already exists or serves to improve the world in which these children live. We must be serious about moulding children and youth into productive individuals who can give back to their communities. In Sierra Leone some programmes have begun to train former child combatants for professions that are desperately needed. Water sanitation experts, agricultural specialists—these are professions that will make their graduates indispensable to their communities. As a result, the youths' sense of self-worth is improved because they quickly realize they are needed and can be useful to others, and the community may more readily accept children who are actively giving back.

Expecting these youths to take part in traditional paths of education alongside ten-year-olds, after they have commanded groups of their peers and fended for themselves for months and years in the bush, is not productive. How many eighteen-year-olds do you know who want to sit on a school bench reading picture books with pre-pubescents? This situation only sets the stage for frustration and helps clear the path for re-recruitment. In countries where conflict has occurred, we need pedagogical tools and co-operative institutions that would offer academic programmes with depth and reach, comparable to those available to youths in North America and Europe but adapted to reflect the experiences and expectations of these troubled and challenged former child soldiers.

Increasingly, I believe we must foster the leadership skills and knowledge of these often very experienced young bosses. They are the future of their countries and if we do not harness their potential then we have lost a chance to truly put an end to conflict. As former secretary general of the UN Kofi Annan has said, "Children are our future and if we use them in battle we are destroying the future. We must reclaim them, every one of them, one at a time."

Maybe we need to fund the creation of academies where such youths could be nurtured—integrated with other war-affected youths from IDP and refugee camps who demonstrate intellectual potential—over three to four years to refocus and get engaged in the rebuilding of their country, becoming examples for the rest of their generation. What a thought—to invest in academic institutions that would garner the vast potential of a society's young leaders and create the next generation of nation builders. What a challenge—to trust that these youths are not stigmatized for life as damaged goods and that they can become productive human beings. This is a worthy endeavour indeed if we could find the funds and the organizations that would be willing to take on the enormous task of reshaping these veterans from being a source of fear and abusive use of force into becoming the strength and backbone of a new national rebuilding.

Consider what could be done with veteran female child soldiers, who have had the strength to not only survive the usual sexual abuse but have led troops in combat, asserting leadership against all odds and cultural stereotypes. There is a potential here to create educational programmes that help these young women enhance their leadership abilities and figure out how to apply them to civilian life — to break the code that marginalizes women, perhaps even fostering a cadre of young leaders who could help revolutionize the developing world's approach to governance and peace.

But there is a downside here that cannot be underestimated and needs addressing. These nations, which have been so mired in conflict, also need to invest in themselves, working to create the productive capacity and steady tax base that will sustain them. If far-off donor money is relied on exclusively to retrain these youths into young leaders, we run the risk of distorting development again by footing the bill for something that ends up serving a new elite. This is a trap that could easily scuttle reconciliation initiatives, and even re-create the frictions that started the conflict in the first place. The local community and national government, as fragile as they may be, need to be completely involved in these educational initiatives.

As I mentioned earlier, I currently work with NYPAW. Grace Akallo, one of NYPAW's founders, said, "If someone had not sent me to school and shown me I am actually capable of doing something good, I wouldn't be standing here." John Kon Kelei, who also works with NYPAW, once said something that has stuck in my mind and rises as an answer when anyone accuses me of being unreasonably idealistic: "The reason why we believe that change is possible is not because we are idealists but because we believe we have made it, so other people can make it as well."

Every child should be allowed the chance to excel. Where you are born should not dictate your potential as a human being. The NYPAW members have managed to succeed despite their difficult beginnings. They have grown up to be productive leaders in their communities and are now helping others who find themselves in the situations they were once in. There are thousands just like them, still living in conflict, just waiting for us to finally get it right and provide the infrastructure they can build upon.

And it is not only the child *soldiers* we need to think about when it comes to DDRR. The Paris Principles noted the harm caused by focusing reintegration support exclusively on child combatants; other youths and children in need feel envious and abandoned. This tension between focused support for former child soldiers and wider support for all war-affected children, many of whom are discernibly worse off than those who fought, is of concern for those working on this issue. Moreover, attempts solely focused on the individual are doomed to fail since the child is not to blame for what's happened. It is not as simple as "fixing the children" and putting them into a community. The community also needs "fixing."

Reintegration is arguably the most important part of the entire process leading to peace, yet it is significantly underfunded. Long-term, flexible funding is often a problem for reintegration programmes, and donor support is sometimes not based on a sound grasp of reality on the ground. DDRR techniques are designed to address specific problems associated with absorbing combatants into civil society and are not, on their own, adequate tools for resolving outstanding conflicts that are fundamentally political and that demand more attention than any DDRR programme can provide.

As I wrote in "Children in Conflict," my own research at the Carr Center also showed that "later phases of DDRR processes are historically not well supported. It was suggested that this is because few donors are willing or able to sign up to support projects that may go on long after media attention has been drawn elsewhere. Though it may sound overly cynical to put it this way, money follows interest, and interest is largely driven by media attention, which is more easily captured by the drama of conflict than by peace."

Broadly stated, DDRR can seldom be isolated from the larger issues, often economic, that affect the security and the cohesion of embattled and impoverished states. If we continue to turn a blind eye to what is really needed because donors won't fund long-term projects or because a "sexier" conflict has turned up in another corner of the world, I am afraid that one day, our luck will run out.

And maybe one way to start thinking about DDRR differently, both as individuals and as donor nations, is to reinforce the UN missions to sustain them, and other UN agencies, through a more deliberate model of integrated NGO and government support. UNICEF coordinated the Sierra Leone DDRR programme with actors from all sorts of disciplines, including the security forces that were deployed in the country, with some success. Could we simply not formalize these sorts of arrangements, instead of always starting from scratch, recognizing that of course each case will have its own intricacies? It is true that disarmament and demobilization in a conflict zone struggling toward peace are easier done by outside entities, such as neutral peacekeeping missions. But years of work on the issue of reintegration have inexorably led to the realization that without consultation with community members, the process is doomed to fail. The design of the programmes must be the result of careful consideration of the nature of the society and the nature of the conflict. The design of the programmes must also engage all elements of the community, including the children and their families. Their support is critical to long-term success and sustainability.

Ultimately, one of the biggest barriers to successful reintegration programmes is the danger of broken promises. When the gap between words and actions keeps growing, people start to doubt your intentions. When promises of support have been made, it is absolutely critical that they be kept in order to avoid problems associated with mistrust. It is crucial that all parties involved in post-conflict DDRR programmes understand that their primary function is to help foster trust.

Too often, donors, NGOs and especially the media have difficulty committing to the recovery of a conflict zone over the long haul. They are drawn away by the next crisis, taking their funds, their programmes and their cameras with them—and the resulting blow to confidence and progress can be devastating. It is asking a lot from the ever-impatient and results-driven international community to commit for perhaps decades of rebuilding or of creating infrastructure that had never existed, but it is what is required.

Charles Achodo, head of the UN's DDR programme in Liberia, says that funding often dries up at the reintegration stage of the process. Donors "forget that these people need assistance to become productive members of the community—psychological counseling, trauma healing support, access to employment." When donors move away to address more pressing crises, as they are doing right now in Sierra Leone, they leave vacuums behind them that nothing can fill, because not much has been securely built. The idea is not to make communities dependent on aid, but self-sustaining—but it takes a long commitment from a lot of partners to help that happen.

In a case study on the reconstruction of Sierra Leone, posted on the University of Colorado's conflict resolution information site, www.beyondintractability.org, in March 2008, Christi F. Freeman writes,

> The failure of the donor community to provide sufficient infrastructure reconstruction and employment generation has made livelihoods in agriculture for ex-combatants and youth untenable . . . Opportunities in the agricultural sector have

been further stifled by international insistence on removing trade barriers, which has allowed cheaper Asian rice to swamp the local market, reducing the ability of small farmers to compete. A combination of the misguided reintegration programmes and the demands of international financial institutions have resulted in a lack of infrastructure and access to productive lands, a lack of appropriate training, and increased disappointment among youth.

Many children in conflict zones actually understand how to manipulate the system. Linda Dale, who works for Children/Youth as Peacebuilders, points to youth in northern Uganda figuring out how to get their school fees paid for twice and to children who never fought pretending to be child soldiers in order to access assistance. In Sierra Leone, schools actually receive goods or materials for integrating former child soldiers into the classroom, which is one of the good things happening in that country: if benefits flow to the community as well as to the individual child, it helps to de-stigmatize the children.

The largest truth here, which I've stressed a number of times so far, is that simple, technical solutions are rarely enough, and reintegration requires long-term commitment from donors and foreign agencies, yes, but also total dedication on the part of community and nation.

As terrible as the experiences of all child soldiers are, there is additional discrimination within that wider category. Roughly 40 per cent of child soldiers are girls, but their unique needs are often not taken into account by those attempting to address the issue of child combatants. One of the key failures of DDR and child-protection programmes has been the inability to adequately address the gender dimensions of child soldiering. Advocacy efforts have also failed to erase the idea that child soldiers are only male. Girls have gendered war experiences and specific reintegration needs.

Young girls who have been raped and borne children in inhospitable and unsanitary conditions have often suffered irreparable physical damage to their immature bodies, but they also suffer the cultural vulnerability of rejection by their society because of what has happened to them, even though it was not of their making. How do we break that code of silence, guilt and shame that they carry—often in their arms through their unwanted infants—and permit them a modicum of social acceptability and a future as caring and loving mothers?

DDRR programmes for girls require effort, resources and cultural adjustments that are rarely required to ensure the boys' return to the fold. The cultural fabric of many societies in Africa, in particular, is male dominated. When conflict erases or disrupts the cultural mores, as it has done so heartbreakingly in the Great Lakes Region, young men are actually rewarded by their commanders for their transgressions against women. One innovative suggestion might be to target young men and families with programmes aimed at erasing the stigma currently attached to girl combatants and to women and girls who have been sexually violated.

Since girl soldiers are not as visible as boy soldiers, and are less understood, they are often marginalized from the DDRR process. Despite being perceived as passive actors in conflict, girl soldiers can be highly active combatants during war. Conflict situations often allow girls to be taken out of their traditional roles and put in positions of power, independence and responsibility. The qualities they develop when forced to assume such roles do not simply go away when they are demobilized.

At the reintegration stage of the DDRR process many girls might be reluctant to go back to traditional female roles that they had willingly left behind. Often, due to their experiences girls can develop survival mechanisms that make them more aggressive and combative. They sometimes engage in behaviour that might not be seen as culturally or socially appropriate for a woman, such as cursing, drug abuse or promiscuity, and that further isolates them from everyday life in their home communities. They must have a say in what is best for them and their dependants. As Susan McKay wrote in "Reconstructing Fragile Lives: Girls' Social Reintegration in Northern Uganda and Sierra Leone," an article published in the journal *Gender and Development* in November 2004, "While girl combatants may have been equals as comrades in armed groups, many occupational paths are denied to them as girls during peace times." And sexually abused girls, who have become mothers of unwanted babies, find no accepted routes to rebuilding a life within the normal social structure. If they are not supported by long-term and innovative reintegration methods— for instance, teaching them non-traditional skills, such as carpentry, plumbing and small-scale financial management, that allow them to overturn old perceptions of what a woman's role should be—they and any children they may have been left to raise are often ostracized.

The stigma raped girls face is enormous. Due to the fear of being identified and prosecuted or stigmatized, many girls simply self-demobilize. Girls often re-enter their home communities or the camps under the radar, trying not to draw attention to their association with armed groups, but they often find it difficult to bond again with members of the community and end up living on the outskirts of society. Pregnant girls and those with children are often unable to attend school or skills training. Not only does the mere presence of an infant or toddler draw attention and questions they do not wish to confront, but school often costs money they do not have.

Increasingly, rape and sexual violence are used as a weapon in today's wars. Not only is sexual violence inflicted on villagers but very often within the ranks of armed groups themselves. Young girls in such conflict zones become victims of two dehumanizing tragedies: being forced into the life of a child soldier and horrific sexual violence such as rape. Although boys can also be the targets of sexual violence, they will not face the same stigma. The reintegration process for a boy will be very different. He can earn his keep and prove himself through work and his newly acquired skills. A girl, however, has lost her purpose at the heart of the community. She no longer has the same marriage value and her children are considered non-persons. An ex–girl soldier knows that if and when she returns to her village she will be seen as a disgrace to her family and her community, even if she wasn't to blame for what happened to her. In one blow, an ex–girl soldier has lost her innocence and the spontaneity of love. Her right to intimacy has been stolen from her.

Physically, her health is also at risk. She has often been battered and has contracted sexually transmitted illnesses such as hepatitis and HIV/AIDS. Because of the conditions under which she was forced to give birth, she may be afflicted with fistula, more common than anyone wants to imagine. The damage to her body can be so grave that a young girl may never be able to bear children again. She may suffer, along with her male counterparts, from malaria, tuberculosis and malnutrition.

Emotionally, she must deal with the memory of what has happened to her and her peers, the destruction of her self-esteem, and psychological trauma. She is shunned by others, laughed at and cast out by children who may not have been involved in the conflict. She is often disowned by her family. These aspects are not usually dealt with in the DDRR process.

And what of her children, if she has them, who were born in the bush, fathered by rebel leaders or as a result of multiple rapes? Young girls struggle to love these unwanted children. Some latch on to them as the only beings who will love them unconditionally, and others hate them for being a constant reminder of how they came to be. In the wider community, "rebel babies" carry a huge stigma, and will never be accepted, whereas within the armed groups themselves they are granted an elevated status. A young mother who loves her child may feel her child's future is brighter if she stays where she is, rather than trying to go home.

All of these physical and emotional traumas are compounded by the fact that in the usual DDRR programmes, girls are relegated to vocational training in traditionally female skills such as cooking and sewing, which render them essentially powerless once they return home, regardless of the positions they may have held in the bush. Girls actually help to sustain armed groups, almost literally—Joseph Kony is reported to have fathered at least 200 children. The NYPAW round table in Halifax last year reinforced the message that without girl soldiers most armed groups would fall apart.

Yet DDRR was created as a male concept. Men were and continue to be the perpetrators of war, and girls and young women are forced or coerced into joining them. Simply adding a gender component to DDRR will not address a girl's needs properly since the entire framework was built for adult males. A parallel framework needs to be created to address girls' specific needs.

Boys, too, pose health challenges that DDRR programmes are forced to deal with. Alcohol and drug addiction cross the gender divide. Heroin, marijuana and cocaine mixed with gunpowder dull these children's pain and hop them up for combat. Singer reports in *Children at War* that, at the end of the conflict in Sierra Leone, more than 80 per cent of the RUF fighters had used either heroin or cocaine.

Due to group sexual activities, sexually transmitted diseases, especially HIV/AIDS, are common among child soldiers too. While there are no formal statistics on HIV/AIDS rates in child soldiers, the UN has recognized the prevalence of the disease in former combatants in that it provides, according to the IDDRS Framework website, "policy makers, operational planners and DDR officers with guidance on how to plan and implement HIV/AIDS programmes as part of a DDR framework." Also, there is this passage on the website of the UN special representative on children and armed conflict:

There is a correlation between the spread of the human immunodeficiency virus/acquired immunodeficiency syndrome (HIV/AIDS) and sexual violence and the exploitation of girls and women in corridors of wars. The Joint United Nations Programme on HIV/AIDS (UNAIDS) estimates that rates of HIV among combatants are three to four times higher than those among local populations. When rape is used as a weapon of war, the consequences for girls and women are often deadly. Armed conflict also exacerbates other conditions in which HIV/AIDS thrives, such as extreme poverty, displacement and separation. Programmes for HIV/AIDS awareness, care and support in both peace operations and humanitarian programmes should be continued and strengthened.

This passage is in equal parts awful and self-evident.

Where do the ideas of accountability and justice sit in this realm of DDRR? I've mentioned that former child soldiers can be summarily executed for their crimes or sent to jail—never given a chance to reclaim their stolen childhoods.

Often, as part of reintegration, the ex–child soldiers—or at least the boys—go through forgiveness ceremonies where the community accepts them back. But what seems to be lacking is the opportunity for the children to forgive the community for having let them down and allowed the situation to progress to a point where fighting was inevitable. Forgiveness is not always one-sided, and there are issues of justice and redress on both sides of a conflict in which children have become combatants. Such serious societal issues of justice need to be addressed before a child can be successfully reintegrated.

Some countries create their own military tribunals, which can be biased against former child soldiers. But if a country does not have a proper government, judicial process, police system or security sector, how can we really expect its court systems to conduct fair trials? Rwanda and the Congo are two examples where military tribunals have scapegoated children in the process of assigning blame in the post-conflict reconstruction timeframe. Volunteer participation in the Interahamwe before the genocide automatically made Rwandan youth guilty of genocide, and huge numbers of them were arrested and sent to jail. However, with time, clearer heads prevailed and the Rwandan government instituted a policy that no one who had been under fourteen at the time would be held responsible for their actions. The government also reinvented a traditional justice ritual called *Gacaca* in which the accused and his victims were called to testify without lawyers in front of elders, which led to public apologies from the perpetrators, and forgiveness and reintegration into the community for many youths. Those accused of rape, however, remained incarcerated and were processed through the national judicial system (which banned capital punishment several years ago).

Sierra Leone turned to a special court, which was given jurisdiction over offenders eighteen years and younger, so that the people wouldn't seek vigilante justice for ex–child soldiers, but as I mentioned earlier, its special prosecutor, David Crane, refused to charge juvenile offenders, arguing that an injustice had been committed against them.

On occasion the community does take justice into its own hands, and when kids return to their villages they are physically abused, which might offer the villagers retribution for the pain inflicted by the child when he or she was fighting, but provides neither real justice nor a way for that child to come back to the fold.

And this is the final tipping point in the struggle to provide both justice and accountability for the wider community and healing for the children: how will these children come forward to register for DDRR if they know they face retribution at the hands of their family and neighbours or criminal prosecution or both? Would children with the capacity and the weapons to keep on fighting believe that it is better for them to lay down the gun?

Getting the word out about DDRR programmes is already a difficult task. If we condone the prosecution of children, we may have an even more difficult time persuading ex–child soldiers to come in from the cold. And at this point I can't help but comment on the stance the government of Canada has taken on a young man and Canadian citizen, who by every definition must be considered a child soldier. Canada—one of the drafters and first signatories of the Optional Protocol to the Convention on the Rights of the Child, an instrument to protect such children from prosecution and a guarantee that they should be put through a formal process of DDRR—has kept Omar Khadr in the illegal jail at Guantanamo for more than seven years without lifting a finger to repatriate him. And as this book goes to press Khadr is standing trial before a military tribunal at Guantanamo. The Canadian government insists it has confidence in the U.S. justice system and clings to the fact that though Canada has ratified the convention, we have not yet implemented it by legislation. (I will be introducing legislation in the Senate just after this book goes to press to rectify this loophole.) The Khadr case is a black mark on my own country's international reputation and standing in the fight for child rights and human rights as a whole.

Too few ex–child soldiers actually break out of the evil milieu in which they've existed for months and years, and even fewer actually thrive as they diligently, bravely and with a bit of luck, try to take advantage of any opportunity to succeed as a normal member of society. Many destroy themselves through crime, drug abuse or sickness, or because they have been abandoned. Others survive from day to day with no future and as such join the hopeless. A very few, again through luck combined with bravery and grit—and the generous efforts of foreign friends—escape from the region completely and build a new life from scratch in a new place, displaying extraordinary resilience.

But what of the child soldiers who paid the ultimate price? What can we say about those whose bones are spun across the landscape of these nation states at war or in civil conflict? We know so little of them. We don't even have decent statistics on where and when they fell to bullets, machetes, land mines and grenades in multitudes of ambushes, attacks, patrols and undercover insertions, or in the mining of gold and diamonds for the sustainment of their adult leaders' cause.

Who cries for them? Who accounts for their loss to humanity? In the scheme of important things to resolve when stopping conflict, who has stopped to weep over their unmarked places of death, the blood-soaked ground where they were abandoned by their "warrior" ethic, failed by their fighting machine, lost their drug-induced fearsome-killer mantra, and died—lonely, heartbroken children sacrificed to the evil ends of adults? Who actually sings their songs of sadness and promises, "We shall never forget"?

Probably no one.

8.

THE MOMENT: KILLING A CHILD SOLDIER

THERE ARE MOMENTS when time actually stops dead in its tracks. The moment becomes an eternity. The moment lives in your being from that point on, even when clock time starts up again.

The blue-helmeted peacekeeper who shot and killed the child soldier at the end of chapter four would have been dumped into such an endless moment. The account that follows is my best attempt at feeling, seeing and hearing what such a moment would bring that soldier, who is fictionalized here but is also as real as my intuition and military experience can make him. The violence committed against the world of a child when he or she is forced to pick up a gun is extreme, but at least most of us know in our bones that such a transgression is wrong. But our peacekeepers, facing child soldiers in the field, are told that they just need to do their jobs, trust their training, keep their focus on the mission and apply the rules of engagement. That doesn't seem to me to be all we need to tell them.

Facing a child combatant in battle strains to the limits the parameters we set for our soldiers. Often idealistic, our peacekeepers and peacemakers believe that they will use their training, their power, their expertise and their weapons to protect life, not take it. During training we teach our maturing recruits how to trespass against the instinct to protect life in order to do just that: protect life, home, country and the vulnerable in foreign lands. It's a powerful contradiction, drilled into the nerves and reactions of a soldier.

Using the instruments of death to defend one's life, or the lives of others, against other human beings who are your equal in species and evolution but who have been set up to be your enemy—your own potential destruction—defies the prohibition against killing that we have taken centuries to articulate in law, in philosophy, in religion and in written and accepted humanitarian conventions and procedures. To destroy another human in order to vanquish him or simply to survive to fight another day is an act that has no place in one's natural growth as a human being. I would argue—against the sociobiologists who reason that war is innate—that the killing impulse has been inculcated, instilled, drummed into our decision loop of actions, surrounded by justifications that enshrine soldiering as a higher calling. On the field of battle, we are trained to accomplish our duty not only at the risk of our own lives but also at the risk of destroying the lives of comrades-in-arms and foes alike. In our military institutions we are taught killing skills that become reflex from training, bolstered by moral defences of the highest order, so that we can kill if we have to and spiritually survive that act.

Every soldier who actually sees action, becoming a veteran of the fear, gore and unforgiving consequences of combat, still has to find ways to deal with the actuality of killing. To truly comprehend the reality of what you are doing—using your expertise to end another person's life—can create the most heinous of consequences on your mind, soul, moral fibre and humanity. You question endlessly if you really saw the other human being, the enemy, as a human being. Through your gunsight, you see arms and legs and a head and torso and all the normal body parts. Those body parts are most likely acting in a concerted and coordinated fashion to defeat you with extreme prejudice.

You may not even be able to tell whether your target is big or small, depending on how far away you are, the quality of the light, the clarity of the air, and the obstacles between you and a clear and unobstructed view. In a skirmish or set-piece battle, we don't often get the chance to contemplate the humanity of the targets picked out through our gunsights. With the cacophony of explosions, with earth and debris flying into the air and falling like rain on and around you, with the snap or crack of bullets whizzing by and the hissing sounds of super-hot metal fragments being propelled in your direction from rifles, machine guns, grenades, shells and bombs, adrenalin and the survival instinct kick in full force. Are you even thinking? You shouldn't be, or you may not survive. No, your senses are at the pinnacle of their sensitivity. You can discern the acrid smells of gunpowder, the pungent stench of burnt flesh, the wet-metal taste of blood, accentuated by sounds that eerily make their way to your ears through the impact of the explosions—voices screaming in fear or shouting orders, whimpering for help or crying out in grief. Shock waves from the exploding munitions stun you as you fall or are flattened to the ground, dizzy with your ears ringing. As you stagger to your feet, you are almost deafened, almost blinded, unable to speak—and deadly aware of your vulnerability.

It is then that you, the professional soldier, discover that you are moving again, adjusting to your situation according to the drills, the discipline and tactics hard-wired into your brain to override your basic instinct of self-preservation and self-effacement from this horror show all around you. You balance on the knife-edge of survival and you act according to your training. But does that training close down your mind, your heart, your soul, your morality?

Do such circumstances eliminate or at the least reduce soldiers' sense of humanity in order that they can employ destructive force? In the heat of the moment, can they still hear the orders, can they still understand the rules of engagement, can they objectively process ethical, moral and legal dilemmas? Is there still a track in their brains that permits some overriding constraints or limitations to what a human can do in combat? Can they still see the enemy as human or has the enemy become a target made of metal, wood, fabric and flesh, all of equal value and posing an equal threat? Is the enemy still human and are you still human too?

These questions arise from combat between equals. Here's another. Can you kill a child if that child is dressed and armed as a warrior? If so, how many times can you do that deliberately before revulsion and disgust and self-doubt fry your brain?

20.

There was no warning. The pounding of the rain on the metal corrugated roofing of the school and nearby church was deafening and had blotted out the normal noises of dawn breaking in the surrounding dense bush and of the villagers waking to start their day. Puddles of water formed instantaneously and we were awash in small rivers of reddish mud where the paths between the huts used to be.

We had arrived late the previous afternoon, after a long day on bumpy and dusty roads, weaving our way past endless lines of people milling and moving in every direction, crowding into every open space, as they searched for safer areas to settle until the aid agencies could get to them.

Rebel forces made up of a mixture of adults, older youths and armed children had already raided this hamlet with its small church and school complex before, seeking to create fear through horrific acts of violence and to steal whatever they could find—goats, maize, children—to sustain themselves. They had many uses for children—as porters, cooks, bush wives—but the most important was teaching them how to use their weapons in order to fight their war. I take that back: this was not war, as I would define it, but a descent into hell in a nation that was imploding. Opposing political forces, government troops and rogue rebel groups were all preying on the population, stealing, kidnapping, raping, mutilating and killing their own people.

These villagers had already paid a price: they'd lost several children, and the schoolmaster had been dismembered in the central clearing the last time the rebels hit. But the people had lived here for decades, as had their ancestors before them, and they did not want to run away from their school, their church, their land . . . and so the UN peacekeeping force commander had sent out a small patrol—twelve of us—to offer some protection until we could encourage them to move to relative safety in the nearest IDP camp.

The sergeant had spent most of the evening in discussions with the elders, who still hadn't resolved to go but said they would meet about it again in the morning. The rest of us had deployed in and around the village in what we thought were the most advantageous defensive and firing positions against a force that would attempt to attack from the bush. That thick bush line, lush and green, neatly isolated this hamlet from the closest village, about a kilometre away along the spine of the low mountain range, and provided great cover for the rebels.

Our rules of engagement were clear enough: we were to use deadly force if necessary to protect the population from any group that endangered them by the use of deadly force. We were to make our presence known by parking our white Jeeps with their light blue flags so that they could not be overlooked by any reconnaissance elements stalking the area. So far the rebels had steered clear of engaging with any UN forces, although bravado and lack of discipline on their part—among the younger ones in particular—had led to some hair-trigger confrontations where we had miraculously avoided opening fire on each other.

Once we had the elders' co-operation, we were to escort the civilian population to the closest camp, where aid and security could be guaranteed until the political situation stabilized. The work ahead was pretty straightforward, for me at least, if not for them.

This was not my first mission, and the rest of the patrol was at least as experienced as I was. Conflicts seemed to be exploding around the world, and all too often in impoverished countries like this one in central Africa. We had learned our trade diligently over the years, through trial and error too, learning ways to minimize the use of force and maximize the power of deterrence. All of us had seen our fair share of suffering and abuse and lack of success in other theatres of operations. But that night, for some reason, I was hopeful. Maybe because the air was fresh, the night sounds peaceful, and when I craned my neck to look up, the sky was clear and so full of stars it looked like someone had splashed white paint in great sweeping swaths across the sky. It never got stale, the way the stars shone in places like this, where there was little pollution and hardly any ambient light. It put the sky at home to shame.

After my first two-hour stretch of sentry duty—nothing moving but the usual, wild night creatures—I cleaned and oiled my weapon, then hit my folding cot to grab four hours of sleep. I huddled under my old mosquito net, which had its deficiencies: it let in just enough mosquitoes to buzz you alert every time you became comfortable enough to fall asleep. But at least I had a mosquito net, and anti-malaria medication, unlike the people who lived here. They suffered extensively from various insect bites and stings, malaria being the worst killer for the kids, along with lack of sanitation and clean water. Abject poverty was the curse of these innocent people, and their living conditions were becoming even more abject now that protracted civil war was tearing the place apart. Peace agreements had been negotiated but were unevenly applied and respected by the supposed ex-belligerents. Factions bred more factions, all vying for a piece of the power and loot, no doubt.

Both the rebels and the government forces were telling the people that they were the ones who offered the best path to peace and renewed prosperity, even as they regularly stole food and goods from them and killed them wantonly. Nobody meant what they said, and I would not bet on the ultimate outcome one way or another. I also wouldn't let myself think about the scale of the brutality in this place, especially what was being done to the women and children. If I did, I risked being overwhelmed with anger. To survive my tour, I concentrated on each task as it came up, keeping my focus squarely on the mission.

Yet everywhere around me I saw signs of people struggling to live an ordinary life, to plant their fields, keep their children safe, send them to school and secure them a future. I think they could have used more help from people like us, definitely more boots on the ground, but that was for the higher-ups to decide, I suppose.

I was so tired that eventually even the mosquitoes couldn't stop me from falling asleep. As I drifted off I thought of my own kids. Sara and Jeff had both had birthdays while I'd been gone. Twelve and fourteen now. So full of their music, their sports—not so much their school work—beating up the computer, their cellphones and every other possible shiny new gadget that came on the market with which they could talk to or text their friends. Their friends, the most important people in their lives these days.

My kids' lives were so full of entertainment and activity that I wondered at times if anything stuck in their memory or did it just float away on a wave of more new things? I know they got tired of lectures from me about how lucky they were, but I knew I was lucky too. They were good kids, both of them, and because of what I did they knew more about the world than most of their friends. I tried not to think about the price they were paying because of my long absences. Their mom did her best to hold the fort and keep emotions on an even keel even when I was able to get a call through to them. A good military family, stoically accepting the sacrifices.

It felt like I'd only been asleep two minutes when a downpour started so suddenly I was drenched before I climbed into my rainsuit. I ran for the Jeep anyway. Why be miserable and even wetter? The night was nearly over, and I dozed sitting up until the sergeant beat on the hood of the Jeep and made the sign to stand-to at first light. It was close to 0600, and another day was upon us.

———

21

I had just staggered sleepily through the red mud to join the sergeant and the rest of the patrol in front of the school when over the downpour we heard the first sounds of gunfire and rocket-propelled grenade explosions on the far side of the village.

They were not just a few shots in the air to scare people who were barely awake and in the most vulnerable of states. This was a sustained attack and the rate of fire was increasing in intensity as we heard the first screams. Those bastards came after this village even when they knew we were here. Clearly, they were defying us: looking for a fight over a small group of huts in order to prove they could push us back to positions defending the large camps. If they could push us around, these people would feel even more defenceless and would just completely give up.

We were on the move at double-quick time to our defensive positions through the small corn patches between the huts, past the loosely strung bunches of sticks that fenced enclosures for the goats and chickens, slipping in three to four inches of mud and rainwater that had turned the ground into a skating rink. We all took nasty falls, and scrambled to our feet again coated in mud and other substances that do not make your day, but I finally got to my position on the right flank of the forward edge of the huts and there it was: chaos, flashes and explosions, dirt and mud and water and maybe body parts or bits of debris flying ten to fifteen metres in the air and landing all around, the heavy smells of gunpowder and smoke choking the air.

The rebels, in wet, green camouflage, were here en masse. Like coyotes after their prey, they were conducting a direct assault from the length of the bush line about a hundred metres from the first line of huts. They seemed to be enveloping the huts, focusing on the centre of the village as they ran, screaming and firing their weapons.

From my flank position, I was able to engage some of the rebels in depth, but the first attack wave was already too close to the huts to open fire without risking direct or ricochet rounds cutting through the mud and stick walls and wounding the civilians still inside. I immediately moved from my forward position and lined myself up between the first and second line of huts and brick houses. This would give me a clear shot as the rebels continued their assault toward the centre of the village.

Turning the corner of a rectangular hut, I came within ten metres of a rebel who had come around the other corner with his AK-47 blazing from the waist. While his comrades were running straight to the heart of the village, this one was obviously responsible for securing the flank by laying down a wall of fire to protect the others and to ensure no one was left alive inside the huts closest to me.

I opened fire instantaneously and deliberately, hard-wired for this type of combat situation, the adrenalin rush making my heart pound loud and fast. The rounds were relatively accurate and the rebel was hit with such force that it countered his forward movement and flung his body backwards like a football player being clotheslined.

One down, I thought, as his machine gun flew in one direction and his body tumbled in the other. As we continued to advance, firing on the other rebels from our flank position, I glanced down by instinct to ensure that the man I shot posed no further risk.

That glance downward was surreal. I got my first good look at the warrior, lying there on his back with his arms stretched out and his legs half folded under him in the mud, and I froze, against all common sense and orders. The rebel with the blazing machine gun who had raced around the corner of the building firing away at anyone and everything, including me, now lay face up and dying in the mud, twisted, bleeding and barely able to breathe. But that was not the horror that instantly burned so many circuits in my brain that it ended up turning me into a casualty too.

The torn uniform was there in the mud, and the machine gun, but the warrior had vanished. Lying in his place was a youth, a young teenager, at most thirteen or fourteen years old. A child. A girl.

I had shot a girl, dressed as a rebel and acting as a warrior and projecting all the attributes of a rebel combatant bent on killing. I tried to doubt the evidence before my eyes: maybe it was a boy—the hair was cropped so short and the smooth facial lines could be male or female—but as I bent close, totally ignoring the firefight still going on around us, I noticed that her raggedy jacket had been torn open by at least two rounds, and that just above her left breast was blood and torn flesh and splintered bone. There was another bloodied area in her abdomen but I couldn't make out the extent of that wound.

I was paralyzed by what I was seeing and what I had done. I stared and stared and stared. I was witnessing the opposite of a miracle. I was witnessing the grossest of human indecencies. I was, for probably only a few seconds but for what felt as long as my whole life to that point, observing the transformation of a warrior back into a child and that child was now dying—of wounds that I had inflicted on her child body.

22.

I could not move on, I just stared at the girl. She caught my pant leg and I finally met her dark brown eyes, and it was as if I could hear her shock and cries of pain and fear. But there was more to her expression—she seemed to be pleading with me to restore her childhood, her innocence, her mythical world of dreams and wonder, the time when she was serene and protected and loved and cared for in the circle of affection that was her family. To restore her to the girl she really was.

The gentle grip of her fingers drove giant needles of excruciating pain deep into me. Around us, the battle was still going on, but it barely broke into the exchange I was having with this little girl dying in the mud and dirty water, inside a torn and soaking-wet camouflage jacket that had identified her as a warrior for all to see and fear. It had actually camouflaged an abandoned little girl who would soon die for no reason understood by her—nor by me anymore.

My brain stuttered excuses, raced through the logic. If you are being fired upon, you fire back or die. It was self-defence. Of course it was. No one could argue that this presented an ethical or moral or legal dilemma. But if I had done nothing wrong, why was I so sick to my stomach? I had just shot a young girl who was dressed like a rebel soldier and armed to the teeth and had been shooting at innocent villagers and had shot directly at me but had missed. I shot back and I did not miss. That's what happened.

Her eyes kept yelling message after message at her killer, the only person at her side as she died. In her eyes, I could still see signs of her resilient youth trying to repel the horrors she had been living for God only knows how long. But coupled with that flash of resistance was the realization that there was nothing left for her to do: her life was over. She knew she was dying, if a child can know that in a fully conscious way. Pain, loss, resignation, memory, love: an overwhelming torrent of emotion and history spoke to me from her eyes, which would not close, that could not close, that could not yet give up on life. Yes, her suffering and humiliation and trauma were also coming to an end, but so was everything else, positive or negative. And I had been the one to end it all for her.

Kill or be killed. That just didn't sound right to me now. It felt completely foreign to everything I had lived by, even before I became a soldier. Yet I had done that: kill or be killed. And the result was the death of this young girl who was still holding on to my pant leg, her eyes wide open but now suddenly totally silent. There were no more messages. She had died without making a sound.

Held in place by her fingers, I finally looked up and around at my position. The battle was over and although we had won the day and saved many of the villagers, there were losses among the civilians and even more terrible losses among the rebels. They had been stopped dead in their tracks after they crossed the first line of huts and had withdrawn in panic and disorder, leaving their wounded and dead in the red mud, which was getting redder by the minute as the blood of all the victims spread in the little rivers of water still flowing toward the centre of the village. It was dead silent and that is how it is after a firefight, dead silent.

23

Everyone still standing seemed as caught in a stunned stoppage of time as I was—the post-combat silence was deafening and disorienting. I smelled gunpowder on the grass and in my clothes, and burning flesh coming from inside the hut beside me. I felt like I was suffocating, but in order to find myself some air, I had to release the girl's grip on my pant leg—I didn't have the heart to touch her. And so I pulled my leg away from her, shuddering as her body twisted even more grotesquely in the mud.

Then the silence was broken by a songbird, and I felt like I was being released from a binding spell. I began to walk, looking for the sergeant and the rest of the section. We had to deal with the wounded and move these people out: they couldn't stay on here now. I spotted the sergeant and my heart rate spiked in exhilaration. All the bullets and grenades that had been looking to tear us apart had missed: we were all standing and my own flesh was intact. For one moment I felt invincible, a rush of relief and release that was startling in its intimacy.

But then it was as if the girl had grabbed my pant leg again, and those few precious seconds of renewed contact with life were shattered. I felt a wave of complete unease, of total transgression. I was parched, my tongue glued to the roof of my mouth. The thirst was so intense I could hardly speak, but thirst was nothing compared to the sudden onslaught of mental pain and anguish and guilt and even a sort of fear, which literally bent me in two. I threw up the bile in my stomach and had difficulty regaining my breath, my warrior ethic, my veteran composure.

I told myself to get it together, and managed to straighten up and look around. The villagers were moving around shakily now, and over the moaning of the injured, civilian and rebel both, the sergeant was issuing orders and speaking on his vehicle's radio. Other members of the patrol were responding, fatigued but determined to do their duty, helping to stabilize the survivors, to comfort the panicked, to assist in providing medical aid right there in the mud beside the mostly destroyed huts. So much activity and yet I couldn't seem to join in, to get on with the next phase of the security and support job that I was mandated and ordered to do. When I finally began to move, I felt like an imposter. I felt like nothing would ever be the same.

24.

Shortly after that engagement, my tour was up and we were driven to the airport for the trip back home. The mission was not over—in fact, the fighting was spreading. At best, we had stymied it for a while, had helped some civilians not get killed and helped others get to the camps where they would exist—only exist—aided by numerous

NGOs and donations from far-off countries like mine. Countries that generously poured out their hearts for a time and then forgot the poor people again and carried on as if nothing much had really happened in the scheme of significant things in the world.

Yes, we'd safely conducted convoys of essential aid to those camps, so the people could eat and not die of cholera and typhus. It was something at least.

Not much of a welcome party at our home base after six months away on another planet, but I was just as glad that it was low-key. Much as it was great to see my wife, to hug my kids, I felt as if I wasn't really home.

People talk about culture shock and I had it in spades: it struck me as weird that the streets were safe, and even our little house seemed revoltingly opulent compared with where I'd just been. The pace of life seemed insane, and I couldn't find any way to cope with the demands coming from my family, my bosses, even the bank teller. I yelled a lot. Or hid.

I tried. I went to watch Sara play soccer, delivered Jeff to his guitar lessons, sat at the kitchen table chopping vegetables for the stew I always made when I was home, as my wife browned the meat on the stove and I tried not to react to the smell. Other times when I'd come home, I slipped back easily into our family life and felt nothing but unrestrained joy and relief to be back with them, especially when I hung out with the kids.

But this time I couldn't make that easy connection. There was a wall between me and them, and to be honest I didn't really want to climb over it, and doubted that I could. That surreal action in that far-off village had killed more than that girl child soldier. She was embedded where my heart used to be, had caked all my senses with the red and slippery mud of brute reality. I simply could not feel the way I had before.

I also thwarted all attempts by my loved ones to get close. I didn't want them polluted by what I'd seen and done, and didn't want to explain what I was constantly remembering. I didn't want my daughter and son to know I had caused the death of a girl the same age as them. This was not their picture of who their dad was, of what their dad did. The same went for my wife: would she ever be able to look at me with any love in her eyes if I told her? We all were caught in a vicious circle where I wouldn't tell them what was haunting me and at the same time rejected their every gesture of support as inept and superficial. In the court of judgment inside my head I convicted them of being grossly ignorant of the ugly extent of the wound I'd brought back home to them. The psychological wound. I did this even though I knew it was irrational and unfair.

All around me at work were lots of people who didn't even try to offer support, who seemed willing to believe that the wound was only flesh deep and that if I left it alone, it would heal in the fresh air and sun of home. I just needed to wait for the great equalizer called time to do its work, and I'd forget that young girl's eyes and I'd be as good as new, possibly even better because I now had unique experiences of life behind me.

Those arguments sounded so plausible I wanted to believe in them. But they were too facile, too cozy to provide any comfort. I knew that my brain had been physically injured and that the damage was preventing me from handling the stresses and pressures of life as people normally lived it. This operational stress injury was festering, causing a sort of emotional gangrene that ate away at all reasonableness and my sense of security. The events of that day in the village kept coming back like a steamroller to crush all other thoughts, feelings, desires and logic out of me, and I felt too vulnerable and guilty to put up any defence. It seemed to me that it was only fair that I should suffer, though I kept searching restlessly for some peace, some relief.

Late one night, when everyone I love was safely asleep, I picked off the shelf in the den a huge poetry book illustrated with pencil sketches, which for a time kept me intrigued. I didn't remember where I'd gotten the book as I wasn't really into poetry. In school I'd been told that poets were the voice of a culture, a society and a people, and I guess I paid lip service to that concept in front of my teachers. When my eyes drifted from the sketches to the words, a verse caught hold of me, caught hold of something like what I was experiencing. The poem was Coleridge's *The Rime of the Ancient Mariner*:

> I closed my lids, and kept them close,
> And the balls like pulses beat;
> For the sky and the sea, and the sea and the sky
> Lay like a load on my weary eye,
> And the dead were at my feet.
>
> . . .
>
> The look with which they looked on me
> Had never passed away.
>
> . . .
>
> But oh! more horrible than that
> Is the curse in a dead man's eye!

Home to me now meant the exercise of maintaining a veneer of normality so I wouldn't upset my wife and children, my parents. They wanted me as I used to be, and I was sure they didn't want to know that for me that "foreign" place was far more real than my life here. When you've been caught up in the extremes that humans endure, it's hard to give this padded world of serenity and comfort any credence.

Part of me—possibly my soul, for all I could tell—had stayed in that faraway place, reliving the assault on the village and the shooting of that young girl soldier, that moment when she metamorphosed from a warrior into a child, that instant where death appeared in her eyes and then disconnected them forever. That was now the most real of worlds for me.

There was no escape from that moment, and because there was no escape, I was uncertain about the future, whether I'd ever be whole again. Sometimes I tried to hide from the memory when it came, but other times I pursued it in anger, reliving every moment in order to see if it was really true. Other times I persuaded myself that if I could stay with it long enough, maybe I could finally correct what had happened, or at least do penance for it. In that village, in that moment, my life had changed inexorably, and most of the time I believed that I would never really make it back.

I know that child soldier, that girl rebel, that martyred youth was killed legally and ethically. But no amount of time can dampen the impact of that act on this soldier's psyche. I can't find any possible penance to reconcile me to this sin against humanity. What has caused us to be trapped into having to do such bad things?

9.

THE CHILD SOLDIERS INITIATIVE

N O CHILD SHOULD HAVE TO DIE the way my fictional girl soldier, Rose, died. No peacekeeper should have to become the agent of such a death. After six years' work on the Child Soldiers Initiative, I wish I could tell you that we are on the verge of eradicating the use of child soldiers in conflict. We know a lot more, it's true—I've shared much of that knowledge with you, along with some new analysis, in the previous chapters. But we are not there yet. The one big certainty I've come to as a result of launching the CSI is that we still face a significant challenge—both in the field and inside large and small organizations, agencies and NGOs, security forces (military and police), and political and diplomatic circles—in changing many minds and many old ways of doing things when it comes to the issue of child soldiers.

Before I take you into an account of the sometimes mind-bogglingly frustrating roadblocks we are attempting to find our way past, I want to share some ideas of how we can shift the whole exercise of dealing with child soldiers from the current mode—which is still mainly reactive, designed to pick up the pieces through DDRR—to a prevention mode, where all our efforts are designed to stop belligerent forces from using children in any capacity and to prevent child recruitment or abduction from occurring in the first place.

In the best-case scenario we are trying to achieve, no peacekeeper would be so surprised by ending up in a firefight with child soldiers that when shot at by a ragged kid with an AK-47, he'd react in self-defence with lethal force. Instead, my peacekeeper would have been trained, mandated, deployed and possibly armed differently, and would serve as part of an integrated operation where political, security (military and police), humanitarian aid and development workers all pulled together, along with the NGOs and local authorities, to prevent conflict rather than react to it. They would all understand that ending the use of child soldiers in the area is a primary way to prevent the conflict or stop it from escalating. They would aim to both protect children from abduction and to persuade parents that they don't have to trade their children to the leaders of armed groups for a little money and a promise that their village will be safe. They'd communicate this message of protection in many ways, including over the local radio, which is often the best means of getting news and ideas out in areas where roads and infrastructure are lacking. The Washington-based NGO Search for Common Ground, which is one of my partners in the CSI, developed just such a radio program, designed and executed for local youths in South Kivu in the eastern Democratic Republic of Congo by fifteen- to seventeen-year-olds. In a survey, 14 per cent of the children who demobilized from armed groups in that troubled place reported that they were inspired to do so by information that the program, called *Sisi Watoto* (Swahili for "We, the Children"), broadcast. (Unfortunately, the program is on hiatus as this book goes to press because of lack of funding.)

Peacekeepers would take every opportunity to talk to locals face to face, too, and the mission's civilian and military members would have studied the best ways to connect and talk with the people of the region, especially the kids. In this best-case world, NGOs would have no qualms about letting military and police forces in on any crucial intelligence they'd gathered when moving through the conflict zone, because they would have established a relationship of trust based on shared aims and understanding of each other's operational needs. As a result, they wouldn't feel that aiding the mission "tainted" them with politics and the use of force. In such an integrated mission, there would actually be less risk of the use of force, because the troops and their leaders would have other options in their repertoire, and would only use their weapons as the very last resort.

The military leaders of the mission would reach out to establish commander-to-commander links with the heads of the armed groups, rather than leave them to the political side and to at times ethically questionable negotiations with aid workers over access to humanitarian food and medical supplies. The military mission would make it clear to these leaders that using children to fight their battles was about to become a losing proposition. They would be clear about the sanctions they faced: prosecution for crimes against humanity; the threat of arrest if they tried to cross borders; the apprehension of their child soldiers, who would be taken away from them and placed in DDRR programs; the vow that from here on in, the mission would make it very difficult for those leaders to abduct or recruit replacements.

Ideas like these could go a long way to eradicating the use of child soldiers and some of them are gaining ground. But for much of the time that I have been wrestling to find solutions, I've been trying to bridge a gulf between the security forces—both military and police—and the NGO and humanitarian communities that, in my view, really needs to be eliminated, but sometimes feels totally unbridgeable. We are still at the stage of getting people to accept the hard fact that we have to do these missions differently, and not yet at the place where we can get total buy-in on new operational tactics. And so the lives of our peacekeepers and peacemakers, and those of the people they are trying to protect, are being put on the line every minute of every day in conflict zones around the globe.

But at least we do know where we need to go—which is more than I could say when it all started, at the end of my Carr Center fellowship in June 2005. In the CSI we have built something that, against pretty incredible odds, has brought all the necessary players into the room to talk to each other, has sponsored research in the field, has found an academic home at Dalhousie University in Halifax, and is about to conduct trials of the working field guide we're developing for military and police forces and NGOs alike. And we have recently decided that beyond this useful work, what we really need to do in order to eradicate the use of child soldiers is to expand the CSI from mission to movement.

I will challenge you in the next chapter to get involved in that movement. But first, I'd like to sketch what I've been working to build. I think that one of the benefits of optimism and idealism is that they lead you into things you would never have tried if you'd let yourself imagine how hard it was going to turn out to be. I knew, from my work at the Carr Center in 2004 and 2005, that my research team and I had stumbled on a way of thinking about child soldiers that cracked open the problem in illuminating ways. Until we began to apply that language to the issue, no one had ever really conceptualized child soldiers as "weapons systems." To most, they were victims of horrible abuse, not agents of conflict: but the truth is that they are both. This was a hard reckoning, I was to discover, and the first meetings I convened were interesting, to say the least.

The hushed, tense voices inside the glass-windowed, high-rise boardroom ceased when I came through the door. On one side of the heavy oak conference table was a group of men in military uniform with polished shoes and solemn faces and on the other side, a more motley crew of young women, scruffy young men and grey-bearded older chaps in bright, somewhat wrinkled, collarless shirts. Even the tabletop spoke of the chasm between the two sides: standard notepads and reference documents, sharp pencils and ice water on the uniformed side and on the NGO side a potpourri of papers and paper scraps, weathered notebooks, eye-catchingly colourful ballpoints and paper coffee cups.

I had interrupted a not-unanticipated exchange, typical of many to come. They always followed the same path:

"But these children are people, not weapons! You can't seriously expect us to discuss shooting children!" This from the NGO side.

The uniforms' response: "Well, *you've* never been in a situation where keeping some people alive meant having to use force to stop others from killing them!"

"Who do you think was on the ground before you got there, providing medical aid and support with the bullets already flying and casualties mounting—and nothing more than our white T-shirts and logos to protect us? We were! We're the ones able to respond in hours to a crisis, while you wait around for your mandate. Our colleagues are already there on the ground, and know the players and the terrain."

"Right, and what did your presence do to stop the escalation of the crisis? You had to pull out and abandon the people you were promising to help while we were stuck waiting for the politicians to fiddle with the mission mandate, meaning that the people ended up with no one on the ground to help them."

And there they found at least one area of agreement: the uniforms and the blue jeans both end up getting shot at because mandarins advise their political bosses to show concern but not too much of it, especially for people in places where there is nothing strategic at stake, as the UN canvasses its member nations for commitment and troops.

As I approached my place at the head of this table—or rather great divide—the military noticed me first and rose to greet me, while the NGOs continued to argue, acknowledging my presence with a nod.

Great start, I said to myself as I sat down and put a pile of my Carr Center research papers in front of me. How was I to get these typical representatives from two so opposite—and self-protective—cultures to even want to work together, let alone start doing so? Every one of these people was dedicated to alleviating the plight of innocent citizens in troubled nation states and to assisting them in achieving peace, good governance, justice, security, human rights, gender equality, democracy and education within a renewed atmosphere of hope and optimism. I knew I needed smarts and commitment from all sides if I was going to have a chance at achieving the mission. My research at the Carr Center had already identified the dearth of rigorous data and ongoing research into the uses of child soldiers in the field, and the particularly blinding gap when it came to the challenges girl soldiers faced. To cure a disease, you have to know its causes, what feeds it, and subsequently, what destroys it. No single group—the humanitarians and NGOs or the security forces—was capable of solving the problem alone; each required the others' knowledge and skills.

But to that point (and to a large extent this is still the case) humanitarian groups and child rights activists had never trusted militaries to be sensitive to children's needs. In their heart of hearts, even at those meetings in which I sat at the head of the table with military personnel who had been actively involved in DDRR in some of the most dangerous places in the world—risking their lives to help children—most of the NGOs didn't think the military at large really cared about the issue. They didn't know who they could collaborate with in the military and security forces in the countries where they were working, or even how to approach them. Since children fell in the realm of the social sciences, the argument went, human rights and child protection agencies had taken on the issue of child soldiers as their cause and responsibility, and rarely considered the military as a potential ally or as a part of the solution. Until now, most believed the only role for uniformed actors was one of protection—of refugee and IDP camps, compounds, civilians and NGO workers. Since they also believed that such protection could not be perceived to impinge on the aid group's neutrality, the relationship between NGO and aid groups and military protectors was a well-enforced one-way street. Neutrality, they believed, was their protection in conflict zones, the only thing that allowed them to work for the betterment of the innocent in and around the contending armed groups, and as a result many of them would do everything they could to keep the "outside" security forces (the ones who were actually working to end the conflict) away from children—never considering actually giving them a role in their rescue.

Of course, as a result of the NGOs' historical insistence on neutrality, many in the military and police assumed any interventions they launched around child soldiers would be viewed with suspicion by the humanitarian community. And they weren't that sure they wanted to collaborate with such "undisciplined" groups anyway. Military eyes tend to view the humanitarian world as "soft" and unorganized, unversed in the "hard" realities soldiers face, and even the military personnel I brought to our many CSI tables thought it unlikely that their disciplined, organized and protocol-oriented groups could really collaborate with "bleeding hearts" who didn't pay due attention when a general walked into the room. Out there in the larger world there were a lot of single-minded military and police who saw use of force as the only solution to dealing with armed children. You shot at someone who was trying to kill you and the people you were protecting as a matter of training and self-defence, but they also pointed out that beating them in a fight, in their view, was the only way to "persuade" the leaders that child soldiers couldn't handle the job. They considered broad rules of engagement (meaning ones that allowed the use of lethal force *in extremis* to achieve the mission's objective) the only means by which we could actually put a stop to recruitment of children and influence the leaders using them.

As both a retired general and a committed humanitarian—with credibility as an advocate of human rights and conflict prevention as a result of my experience in Rwanda and the work on genocide prevention I'd been doing since—I was in a unique position to talk to both sides, because I was an amalgam of both. I had been a soldier for most of my adult life and so was slightly suspect still in the eyes of most humanitarians, but I had witnessed a massive, brutal genocide of a scale and from a vantage point no other military commander had experienced in the post–Cold War era. I had seen the best and worst from humanitarian and NGO workers in Rwanda, and they had seen my efforts to bridge the gulf between us to save lives where we could. But I suspect that both sides remained unsure as to whether my scales tipped to favour one side more than the other: too military for the humanitarians, too bleeding heart for the military. Did these ideas we were kicking about mean inventing a new military and police entity that would be too soft to be effective? Or was I on a mission to subvert the vaunted neutrality of the NGOs and bring them into an alliance with uniforms that would, in the end, only hurt their organizations? Well, I am neither one nor the other, yet I am both. I am attempting to be an amalgam because I suspect that to help resolve the complex situations of failing states, we need amalgams, especially when it comes to the issue of child soldiers.

Still, on the one hand persuading military forces to consider psychosocial factors and, on the other, convincing a rights-based NGO that the use of lethal force against some children might be unavoidable, in some rare instances for the greater good and safety of many other innocent victims, was a challenge to say the least.

I am not going to recount here every step of the journey we've been on with CSI. Six years, now, of meetings, conferences, round tables, war games, draft working documents, reviews of those drafts, and redrafting. This is what it takes to try to change minds and hearts: endless, incremental, effortful attempts to bridge gaps and bring all parties into the full light of each others' knowledge, and then create innovative action out of those new understandings.

Referring to children as a *weapons platform* continued to make collaborators physically react, squirm in their chairs, mumble under their breath. How could someone refer to a child as a weapon? Such language had never been used before and thus became the subject of much objection and discussion.

People are extraordinarily sensitive to words, and some are not willing to take the time to examine the new word suggested before drawing conclusions. In many sessions, we were caught in a linguistic and cultural divide that prevented a true meeting of the minds.

The military and police stakeholders wanted clear definitions to words that permitted some flexibility but were not ambiguous in their intent. For the military, words allow you to figure out how things work and thus how to take them apart. They are accustomed to defining and analysing tasks so as to avoid confusion, because when it gets right down to it, they bear the responsibility for the disciplined use of lethal force and its deadly consequences. They need to know exactly when, how and how much is required, with as little doubt as possible, or (as we saw with my fictional peacekeeper) their soldiers pay the price either with their own lives or with physical or psychological injuries. But NGOs and civil society actors had an almost allergic reaction to the language of soldiers, finding it too strong, deliberate and unequivocal—lacking sensitivity to human and social factors.

In turn, the military broke out in hives over how words could take on a fluid identity for humanitarians, with circumstances dictating definitions. In session after session, they rendered themselves tone-deaf to the nuances of humanitarian language and grumbled over the way it seemed designed to avoid the specific.

I didn't think it would be productive if, in order to talk with each other, everyone had to put a lot more water in their linguistic wine, because I thought we'd lose the real information and insight each discipline could bring. Who really wants to drink watered-down wine? The taste is blah and you are left with the firm impression that you have been had by the barman, which only leads to more friction and even blows. Essentially, if you're constantly editing your language, you're not bringing your true self and all you know to the situation, just a version of your self that seems safe enough to offer. I didn't think we could get at real solutions until we understood each other, but in too many sessions our words seemed to keep us apart, not bring us together. Even over the very word I proposed to describe our coming together: *integration*, which I saw as a step beyond coordination, cooperation and collaboration, and which I hoped could give birth to a new conceptual base.

Much discussion was held around various tables over several years about the concept of integration—bringing the NGO community and the uniformed members together in one concerted mission. Humanitarians were quite fearful of that term since it implied to them that one discipline would be swallowed up by another, leaving the people with the guns and the people without them in unequal positions. Countless discussions about this issue boiled down to the fact that we had to coin a new descriptor for the same idea that didn't carry so much baggage: *cohesion*. We started focusing on "cohesive" plans of action using child soldiers as the catalyst that all stakeholders were working to help.

No one said this would be an easy task. Finding a way to get these disparate actors on the same side of the argument has kept me both frustrated and determined since 2005.

Helping me keep the faith, though, was the simple fact that from the very beginning I had a strong NGO partner. In 2005, Sandra Melone, the executive director of Search for Common Ground, based in Washington, D.C., heard of my work on the child soldier issue and brought a group of her colleagues to meet me and my research assistants, including Phil Lancaster, in a small classroom

at the Carr Center at Harvard. The idea of describing child soldiers as more than victims—as utilitarian tools of war—intrigued
them. Melone and Search for Common Ground are still key collaborators with the CSI to this day.

As a result we organized a one-day round table at the Brookings
Institution in Washington, D.C., in June 2005 to introduce my
research to the major agencies and NGOs in the capital who were
working on the topic of war-affected children. About forty people
were around that first table, including Mike Wessells, a leader in
research on child soldiers, and Peter W. Singer, who had been
looking at the impact of child soldiers on American soldiers and the
trauma that dealing with them caused. During this meeting I drilled
home the fact that until that moment, we'd only had marginal successes in confronting the child soldier phenomenon in over thirty
civil wars, primarily in DDRR efforts after the conflict ended. It was
time to listen to new perspectives, debate and try to create concepts
and methods that had never been considered before.

We decided on a phased approach, starting with a conference
in Canada to follow up on the Winnipeg conference on war-
affected children that I had spoken at in 2000. Our conference
would be called "Expanding the Dialogue: Preventing the Use of
Child Soldiers." It would concentrate on naming all the gaps in
our efforts to end the use of child soldiers and our deficiencies
when it came to stopping recruitment and DDRR, and generating
ideas for new approaches. Afterwards, we would collate the results
and proceed to the second phase of the research, which would test
our ideas in a war-game scenario as close as we could get to the
conflict zones on the African continent, where child soldiers were
used most extensively. We settled on the Kofi Annan International
Peacekeeping Training Centre in Accra, Ghana, as an ideal venue
that also had relatively easy access to child soldiers and even their
commanders. And finally, after we'd digested the results of the war
game, in phase three we would move the solutions into the field,
conducting a year-long trial in a conflict zone, such as the DRC,

and produce a set of initiatives that we would disseminate to missions already deployed.

Armed with my Harvard research and the alliance with Search for Common Ground and UNICEF Canada (its CEO, Nigel Fisher, had been with me during the Rwandan genocide), we secured support for the week-long conference in Winnipeg, slated for August 2006, from some of the major NGOs working on this issue, and also received a substantive study grant from CIDA to pay for much of the conference. I reached out to the military, and approximately ten reserve officers were sent by the Department of National Defence to participate. I asked them to come in uniform, figuring that the civilians needed to get used to talking to military in full garb, which didn't turn out to be such a good idea. Back then, I hadn't really taken on board how much of an impediment the outward signs of military life could be to communication with people who didn't wear uniforms.

Though the Canadian minister of foreign affairs at the time, Peter MacKay, agreed to give the keynote address at the conference, we had trouble getting some other crucial participants—ex–child soldiers from various African countries that were now into rebuilding their nations after years of conflict—into the country. The Canadian government was reluctant to give them visas, arguing that they were a risk to national security. I was indignant that the bureaucrats we were dealing with did not realize that these youths were *ex*–child soldiers and believed the real reason that they didn't want to let them in was the fear that they might bolt and then ask for refugee status. Even if they did bolt, I didn't see that as such a bad thing, since a life in Canada might be more secure and fulfilling for these young people than life at home. In the end, the dozen or so youth participants at the conference were former child soldiers who had already entered Canada as refugees, most of them living in the Winnipeg area.

MacKay opened the conference with a speech that emphasized how important child protection was for Canada, and how important it was that we fulfill the promise of the conference by working together to help solve the issue of child soldiers:

> A robust legal regime is in place, a series of Security Council resolutions has established a framework for implementation, and a broad array of international and non-governmental organizations are working ever more closely to provide protection for children caught up in armed conflicts. Yet the nature of the abuses faced by children in dozens of conflict zones remains unthinkable. Concerted action is required by actors at all levels to prevent and respond to violations of the rights of children. An investment early in conflicts will pay huge dividends in [preventing] future abuses.

During the ensuing week, more than a hundred participants went to work in discussion groups to hammer out innovative ways to advance our quest of neutralizing the use of children on battlefields around the world. Despite endless arguments leading to many communication breakdowns, we came out of it with some ideas: mission commanders should engage in military peer-to-peer dialogue with rebel leaders; procedures needed to counter this weapon system should be elaborated; sound military tactics and strategies to prevent recruitment must be developed; issues of small arms and light weapons must be addressed, as their proliferation was linked to the use of child soldiers; media strategies (at both local and international levels) had to be created to raise awareness and provide information on a range of rights issues. Most importantly, this conference pushed for a more deliberate research plan, demanding a shift in focus to the task of understanding recruitment strategies, ways of avoiding recruitment, military uses of children and gender dimensions, and it called for this research effort to be part of an integrated, interdisciplinary analysis of the conflict—basically an endorsement of the mission we had set for the CSI.

—

A war of words followed the Winnipeg conference and carried on well into the following year. If the military were being pigheaded about the use of force (maybe too many still dreamed of a return to the "good old days" of the Cold War, where we pushed high-tech equipment forward and the enemy actually dressed up for the showdown), our NGO colleagues were entrenched in the human-rights-based position that forbade even contemplating the use of lethal force and enshrined neutrality.

Joe Culligan, a retired Canadian colonel I'd asked to be the CSI's diligent scribe, produced draft after draft of the conference's fundamental findings and also the results of several multidisciplinary working groups held at the Pearson Peacekeeping Centre at Carleton University in Ottawa, with inputs from organizations such as UNICEF, Search for Common Ground and War Child, diplomats with UN experience, the military, humanitarians, police officials, academics and other experts. We never had a lack of involvement and review of our work: people genuinely thought we might be on to something essential in regards to the child soldier problem. But they were very uneasy with this more security-based approach. I argued vehemently that though DDRR was essential for those child soldiers already caught in conflict—and we could not turn off these wars until we got organized—we had to leap ahead and stop children being used in the first place.

With so much effort in coming up with a formula, a format, a method, an instrument, even just a paper listing a bunch of things to do and not to do, we kept whirling around on the merry-go-round of consultation. Then an old colleague and friend, Major Ken Nette (Ret 'd), came up with the idea that what we needed was a bunch of tools at different levels to fix the problems and that the tool box we put together needed different drawers, from one labelled "framing the mandate of a mission," so that child soldiers become a priority; to one called "assisting the senior leadership of the mission," in the case of a UN deployment; to another labelled "helping the troops in the field" with the practical tools they needed when they came face to face with the child soldiers and had to implement the operational tasks assigned by the mission headquarters. The tactical level of the tool kit would help them sort out who to talk to, who to seek information from, how to establish links with all the other actors in the area, and where to fit into the process of neutralization of the child soldiers and stopping their recruitment.

But when the first drafts of the tool box were circulated, all hell broke loose again. Some felt we shouldn't tackle the mandate or strategic level at all but should concentrate on the nuts and bolts of field work, while others were equally certain we had to stay away from the nuts and bolts and focus instead on moving political leaders and the UN into deliberate action against the mere concept of the use of child soldiers.

To say that frustration with turning in relentless circles was overcoming my enthusiasm would be a gross understatement. For a time, I felt I was treading water, and only hoped to be able to do it long enough to keep from drowning and ending the whole affair. We were supposed to be launching the war game soon in Accra, Ghana, to test the tools in the tool kit. As the debates went on, I was concerned that we would not in fact have anything of real substance to study.

Then there were the ongoing funding problems. I was certain that I had a surefire humanitarian project that was intimately linked to security problems in a number of developing states. But I was finding that donors did not, as a rule, wish to invest in a project that was extremely long-term, scattered around the globe, and still uncertain as to how it would achieve its aim. As a result we were always in a money crunch, and fundraising became my most necessary and least-favourite part of the job. A good portion of the royalties I earned from my first book, *Shake Hands with the Devil*, has gone to the CSI over the years (and also into my own foundation, which helps Rwandan orphans as well as children in Canada). I also poured in the fees I received from speaking engagements. Sandra Melone and Search for Common Ground built an extensive fundraising campaign in 2007, in which Ishmael Beah and I spoke at several events in North America and the United Kingdom, with rather limited success. We brought in thousands, for which we were grateful, but we needed hundreds of thousands if we were ever to get to the stage of a field trial. The lack of funding limited our scope of research and slowed us down: at times, we could not even afford paper and phones, let alone the salaries of a small core staff of two persons earning starvation wages as they put in an average of sixty hours of work a week.[1]

The subject of child soldiers was captivating and donors felt empathy whenever Beah and I presented our experiences and the situation in the field. But we were working on a project that was still trying to figure out what the answer would look like. I did not have a bona fide new "medicine" to plop onto the table to assure people that if they funded my work, I could "cure" the world of the use of child soldiers. So, dollars dribbled in, and we were trapped in a cycle of creating funding proposals to all sorts of foundations and potential donors, which was taking the precious time of the staff away from the research to advance our goals. That staff and volunteer commitment was never in doubt, but with so little in the way of resources they could not sustain their effort. Many came and went as the years flowed by. As the body count of child soldiers kept creeping up, especially in Africa, we were caught in a labyrinth of words, egos, endless arguments and cash crunches, and stuck at home with no sense of when we might actually reach phase three, the year-long field trial.

---

[1] It was very hard, under the circumstances, to retain staff, or to pay them what they deserved without bankrupting the rest of the organization. In 2007, Nicole Dial left us to take up a humanitarian post with an NGO in Afghanistan. Three months later she and two colleagues were killed by the Taliban. What a terrible and senseless waste of lives; what terrible payback for dedication to helping others.

Contrariness kept me going. Quite frankly, I was pissed off that even with my background, I could not get any military or police force at home or abroad to engage in a serious way with this problem. To most of them, the solution was obvious: child soldiers were simply members of the belligerent forces and were to be treated like any other threat. I knew that was too simplistic, and vowed that I was not going to let more and more uniformed personnel find themselves facing the ethical, moral and legal dilemmas of having to kill kids to achieve their aims of security in a mission area.

That we managed to get to phase two—role-playing solutions in the week-long simulation exercise at the Kofi Annan centre in Accra, Ghana, in July 2007—is a miracle I credit to some very innovative support from the exercise group at the Pearson Peacekeeping Centre in Ottawa.

I assembled a multidisciplinary group to take part in the war game (the non-military types were more comfortable with the term "simulation exercise"), which we called "Prodigal Child." Fifty participants came from all over North America and the African continent to engage in a simulation we devised, whose setting was Fontinalis (a fictional imploding country caught in social breakdown and civil war, whose features had been sketched out over some years at the PPC's operational centre in Cornwallis, Nova Scotia). Fontinalis's political disintegration and economic and social collapse made a fertile ground for child recruitment. Three teams of about fifteen participants each were challenged to come up with collaborative ways to prevent child recruitment or abduction.

We ran up against many obstacles: the military was used to the idea of role-playing—many training situations are role-playing writ large—and had no problem absorbing some of the "un-real" parameters of Fontinalis as the basis for the exercise. The NGO participants, I soon realized, were experience-oriented people, who were more used to confronting real situations in real places and jerry-rigging solutions to fit the circumstances. They and the ex–child soldiers both had trouble throwing themselves into the role-playing, and as a result, the sessions could be ragged affairs. Some team members would express their discomfort by not showing up to their sessions, or by voting in their chairs by actually falling asleep. And everyone wanted to argue, demonstrating clearly the ever-present rifts between the camps.

The use of force was a flashpoint. Nigel Fisher, who came to the table with unequalled field experience and international HQ knowledge, nailed it bluntly: "The biggest spoiler," he said, "is [the disconnect between] humanitarian principles and use of force. Until we can find some way of agreeing on this issue there is going to continue to be a problem." NGO members just could not bring themselves to accept that the use of force could be an option, and the security types could not accept that it wasn't an option, vividly aware of what it was like to be shot at by anyone wielding an AK-47, child or not.

In *Killing in War*, Jeff McMahan argues for a moral requirement of minimum force against child soldiers (which is already in all mission rules of engagement) but then makes a significant observation: "[J]ust combatants . . . may be morally required to fight with restraint, even at greater risk to themselves . . . [W]hen child soldiers are conspicuously young . . . just combatants should show them mercy, even at the cost of additional risk to themselves, in order to try to allow these already greatly wronged children a chance at life . . . I suspect that any commander would earn the respect of his troops if he were to order them to take additional risks to try to drive back, incapacitate, subdue, or capture child soldiers, while sparing their lives." We still have a long way to go to persuade military forces around the world of the justice of such a position.

I'm a passionate humanist, and while I long for and strive for universal peace, as ex-military I understand that my resolve to protect and preserve human rights must be tempered by the sad reality that lethal force is sometimes necessary. As much as I attempted to argue that, even so, we had to avoid using lethal force against children in all circumstances, in the end Phil Lancaster (who had by far more practical experience with child soldiers than most of us) did win me over to the fact that we may, *in extremis*, have to look at the most horrible option of actually using force against some of the children in order to stop the killings, mutilation and horror of the many. And that by doing so we would finally be foiling the adult leadership using and recruiting these children. (This point would come back time and again and is still a very contentious subject, many years later, in my continued work on the CSI.)

NGOs might eagerly embrace the option of using non-lethal weapons in combat against child soldiers—rubber bullets, tear gas and the like—but experienced soldiers did not take so kindly to it, not because they wanted to kill children, of course, but because they knew how hard it would be to equip missions with effective non-lethal weapons, enforce their use and then deal with the real possibility that using such weapons would put our soldiers in graver danger. The leaders who sent kids into battle weren't stupid: they paid attention to a mission's rules of engagement, and if they discovered that soldiers were mandated to use non-lethal weapons against children, they'd be sure to sprinkle enough children into the front ranks to protect their adult fighters from harm.

After a week of role-playing and informal discussions, we basically proved one of my major contentions: there was truly a fundamental lack of co-operation, of coordination, let alone col-laboration, in the field. It was a critical weakness plaguing even the newest UN peacekeeping missions, which on paper at least were "integrated." Individual NGO workers, security personnel and politicos in the field were able and willing to work together informally, and as a result, sometimes collaboration worked. But that all depended on the personalities of the people involved. When a crisis escalated, each group crawled back into its own silo and reverted to its disciplines' traditional communications.

I also came to realize that most of the actors deployed in the conflict zones and up to their necks in child soldier problems felt that they already had the insight they needed to resolve the issue. They didn't really see that an innovative, cross-disciplinary approach was needed for conflict resolution, or that they needed any new tools, though they were always willing to agree that the uniformed forces were a problem. They felt that if we could simply tweak the training and education of the military personnel and police to enlighten them about the needs of child soldiers, the uniformed players would know how to properly protect the DDRR efforts of the humanitarian workers, who could then comfortably concentrate on fixing the social problems faced by demobilizing child soldiers.

I knew that this was limited, ineffective, status quo thinking. But coming out of our session in Ghana, I doubted my own abilities to break down the barriers between soldiers and humanitarians. My doubts were fed by the fact that in March 2005, while I was getting the CSI up and running, I had been appointed to the Canadian Senate, and my workload as a senator meant that I just did not have the time to commit to the day-to-day strategic thinking that the project required. I felt that the CSI was stalling because I had not given enough time and thought to the proposals, options and research focus so that I could push the agenda effectively. The frustrations of a debate that never seemed to evolve was eroding my ability to grasp the holes in processes and find a way to bridge the gaps.

I'm fighting off the desire to share the rest of the ups and downs of the CSI to this date, but I don't think I really need to take you through all those bumps in order to explain where we are now.

Just as I was ready to throw in the towel over lack of funds, time and consensus, a report came out from a NATO task group on "Child Soldiers as the Opposing Force." The CSI team and I, who over all these years had been in and out and up and down every possible trail only to so often find ourselves nearly back to the starting point, were elated that the report recommended the development of military doctrine on the phenomenon of child soldiers, that it noted that a successful doctrine required a comprehensive approach that would bring all the players in a region into the solution, and that "isolated application of the recommendations [would] not be fruitful." The real vindication of the CSI came in the last pages of the study:

> Such co-operation has been demonstrated in 2007 where a group of specialists assembled at the Kofi Annan International Peace Operations Centre in Accra, Ghana, in exercise PRODIGAL CHILD. The group consisted of humanitarian workers, child protection specialists, police and professional soldiers, lawyers, UN political affairs officers, and NGO mediators [they forgot to mention the ex–child soldiers and a few of their commanders]. The exercise was organised by Canadian Senator, the Honourable LGen Romeo Dallaire (Ret'd).

The next part of the study could have been written by the staff of the CSI:

> In order to be effective in operations, military personnel need to understand and be engaged in all stages of the phenomenon of child soldiers. A fire fight is just one of the stages in encountering child soldiers. The prevention of recruitment or abduction, the reception and treatment of detainees or escapees, demobilization, disarmament and reintegration in society are evenly important aspects in the handling of child soldiers in which military and other agencies are to play an important role. This is referred to as the Comprehensive Approach.

The recommendations go on regarding training and support:

> Close and regular inter-agency communications, including NGOs, is required to raise mutual understanding of competences,

identify common goals and fields of co-operation, and avoid duplication of effort. In that respect the efforts of the different Centers for Peacekeeping Operations are to be combined.

After absorbing this shot in the arm from the NATO report, followed by more meetings and a diligent academic review, I realized that our lack of progress was due to the fact that we were trying to roll too many balls up the hill all at once, and had lost sight of our primary strength, that we existed in a niche that nobody else was really tackling: the security dimension of the problem. The CSI was in an ideal position to move the whole security agenda of child soldiers into the forefront—and was also poised to move the uniformed disciplines much closer to comprehending the complexity of the issue and to accepting that some ways of thinking and acting needed to drastically change.

We would keep as a primary aim the continued enhancement of a practical field guide for missions at the operational and tactical levels, which we would continuously upgrade. But we would also commit ourselves to creating the climate of change and funding that would help us to make the CSI really happen, by building a movement with the youth of the world itself. Who better to react to the plight of children forced to pick up the gun than their peers who had so many more options in life? At the strategic level, I would lead a campaign at the highest political, military and humanitarian levels to advance the cause of eradicating child soldiers sooner rather than later. We'd reinforce both those efforts with steady operational research that would remain field-oriented.

What ultimately clinched this refined course of action was the fortuitous arrival in the project-cum-nascent movement of Professor Shelly Whitman from Dalhousie University, an expert on war-affected children and international affairs, introduced to us by the CSI's director at the time, Brigadier General Greg Mitchell (Ret'd). Shelly was soon followed by her boss, the director of the Centre for Foreign Policy Studies at Dalhousie University, Dr. David Black.

His engagement with us, in turn, was supported right up the decision chain through the dean to the university president himself, and the result was that the Child Soldiers Initiative found a permanent home at Dalhousie. This became the North Star we needed to move the project into its new incarnation, and from our current stalemate to the dynamic force I hoped this movement would become.

A first step in this direction was the second venture on the African continent. In November 2009, we hosted an executive seminar in Gaborone, Botswana, on child soldiers and security forces. Participants included military officials from Botswana, Zambia, Zimbabwe, Mozambique, South Africa, The Gambia, Angola and the DRC. Botswana's minister of defence attended and spoke of the risk child soldiers posed to the fragile stability of this region of the world.

Covering topics such as international legislation on child's rights, gender dynamics in conflict, negotiating release of children in combat, as well as a personal account of life as a child soldier, this seminar proved to be instrumental in engaging the Southern African sub-region defence forces on this issue and set the stage for repeat productions in other regions of the continent with military and police alike. Most participants had stories to tell of encounters with child soldiers, but they had no training to speak of when it came to coping with that particular challenge. For some of the countries represented, child soldiers were not considered an issue, but the representatives at our session understood the vital importance for all to be engaged—whatever hurts your neighbour hurts you. Conflicts can occur quickly, borders are porous, and trouble can land on your doorstep: it is in everyone's best interest to assist in finding effective solutions. This was an extremely heartening session.

We've also been witnessing a new phenomenon caused by a big shift in attitude and operational concepts over the last year or so, closer to home. The military, and the Canadian Forces in particular, are beginning to support the ideas on conflict resolution that have been driving the CSI. They are coming to understand that the use of force is perhaps not the first and best option in many situations for the armed forces and their political masters. The source of this sea change are the lessons learned in current real-world operations in conflict zones such as Iraq and Afghanistan.

Lieutenant General Andrew Leslie, who commanded the NATO forces in Afghanistan and has recently stepped down after four years at the head of the Canadian Army, has recently stated exactly what I have been espousing, but in military terms. He says that introducing the philosophy of conflict resolution to training and practice is essential in the complex and multidisciplined environment in which militaries are now employed. Quoted in an article on training for counter-insurgency operations, published in the November–December 2009 issue of *Vanguard*, he recommended that at the earliest opportunity, "all agencies and civilian and security forces should come together to conduct joint training." He went on to say that there is an overall need for "a more comprehensive approach [to missions] that requires greater awareness of intelligence information and [the] social cultural milieu of the area of operations. Commanders must come to understand the overall environment, its systems and its overall culture."

A more recent article in *Vanguard* ("Complex Solution" by Chris Thatcher, in the May–June 2010 issue) quotes the U.S. Secretary of Defense, Robert Gates, who says:

> The greater collaboration in operations is prompting nations to re-evaluate how the concept [of collaboration] might be institutionalized . . . on the surface it sounds simple and obvious: integrate the work of various players in conflict zones, both at national and international levels, to achieve a coordinated, collaborative and more effective outcome . . . but the

efforts to integrate the roles of various players—military, diplo-mats and aid agencies, to name just some—are still largely sporadic due to the lack of long-term effort to institutionalize coordinating mechanisms.

He goes on to recognize that the contentious aspect of the "comprehensive approach" remains the relationship with NGOs, many of which require neutrality in order to function.

This is what the Child Soldiers Initiative is attempting to achieve: build that new doctrinal base and lexicon of action verbs to bridge the gaps between the different actors so that they feel comfortable with candidly exchanging information; help integrate their efforts to produce cohesive plans that are then applied and implemented in the field with the appropri-ate priority of resources to successfully curtail the use of chil-dren in conflict; reduce the availability of small arms and light weapons; and ultimately stop the recruitment of children as instruments of war.

Encouraged, even elated, by the vindication of the CSI's objectives by the uniformed side of the house, we are launching a global humanitarian movement to eradicate this scourge delib-erately inflicted on children by adults in order to cement these gains and to inspire our leaders to find the political will to follow through. By securing the buy-in of world leaders in a movement to eradicate the use of child soldiers, I believe we will eventually be able to do what the Lloyd Axworthys of the world did with land mines in the 1990s. There was a day when land mines were part of the inventory of available tools one could use in warfare. The international movement, which roused public and media support around the world, led to a ban that took this weapon completely out of the inventories or arsenals of most nations.

We aim for the day when the use of children provokes the same reaction. If we can do this for a chunk of metal, surely we can do it for living beings who are the most vulnerable in our society.

—

The Child Soldiers Initiative continues to pound the pavement in search of ways to creatively solve this issue. Throughout the years, it has remained clear that the CSI is a worthy and positive addition to the spectrum of means by which one day we will stop conflicts from happening due to the frictions of our differences. A project to stop the use of child soldiers will go some way in preventing conflicts in the first place. And that is the part that I want the CSI movement to be totally committed to.

I finally feel the project has matured enough that we can start going into the field to assist in building the necessary capacities for change. The practical details—the "hows"—are being worked out as I write these lines. Movement director Shelly Whitman and Tanya Zayed, a young staffer, are in the DRC right now, gathering essential data from all the actors currently engaged in a conflict that is continuing to cause so much human suffering and destruction. Yes, we are finally getting into the field, entering the phase three stage of field trials and capacity building that we dreamed up at our first conference in Winnipeg.

I'm bruised by the ride we've had, but not beaten, and I have to say that now I am more broadly experienced in the ways of the various disciplines in the field, with a more focused sense of how we tackle the ultimate objective of eradicating the use of children as instruments of war. I firmly believe that concerned individuals can come together and defy the norms and challenge expectations. If we open ourselves up to learning about others and share a common goal of child protection, it is possible to make a difference. I still believe I can make a difference and I am going to continue working to achieve that aim in the case of child soldiers around the world. I believe without a doubt that you can make a difference, too.

It will be a long struggle with evil and ignorance and often seemingly implacable intransigence and downright pigheadedness. But so what if we have to battle? So what if it takes forty or fifty years to end the use of the child soldier weapon system? It will have been worth it for the betterment of humanity and the protection of our youths.

10.

WHAT YOU CAN DO

As the world grows smaller, our common humanity shall reveal itself.
—BARACK OBAMA (INAUGURATION SPEECH, 2009)

S HE FOUGHT AS A SOLDIER but died as a child. And the professional soldier deployed to implement a mandate of protection ends up a casualty, having been forced to face an armed child as the enemy. The act devastates the adult peace-keeper as it destroys the child, eating away at a grown man who cannot forgive his own action, no matter how hard he tries to frame it as part of an overall mission that brought some stability to a nation in turmoil. He doesn't have internal tools to deal with killing a child combatant, because no such altercation should ever take place—it should be totally inconceivable. And yet adult soldiers are repeatedly meeting children in combat in conflict areas around the globe today and have been for the past twenty years.

Peacekeepers are still not formally or properly prepared to expect this encounter. Despite issuing protocols and passing legis-lation condemning those who recruit and deploy children, politi-cal leaders fail to take action against these criminals. Even the presence of the ICC does not seem to deter rogue commanders.

Agencies neglect to address the source of the issue, merely its aftermath. Why? This is a complex political, security and social issue, indeed, but the use of child soldiers is not a subtle or surreptitious practice of which experts can claim ignorance. It is a brutal crime against humanity being perpetrated in the most blatant and provocative fashion against the most vulnerable people. How many more thousands of children have to be recruited, how many raped, wounded, killed, before we become engaged?

Where is the urgency? Where is the outcry? Where is the will to act?

Maybe it lies in me—I've described what I'm attempting to spark with the CSI, with the help of the academics, NGOs, ex–child soldiers, the military, the police and the donors who have rallied to these ideas. And maybe it lies in you.

Through history, there have been individuals who have overcome seemingly insurmountable obstacles to achieve milestones of human rights. They have exhibited the necessary strength, eloquence and presence to influence others (and ultimately those in authority) to create revolutionary action. We may need just such a revolutionary in order to stop the impunity of adults who use children as soldiers, and to ultimately eradicate from the human mind this practice as a potential option. We definitely need a movement, not just a one-time surge, to sustain and build a marathon of hope.

I have witnessed the destruction of children who have been recruited as child soldiers—not only the bodies of the dead, but the living souls of these once-children who have been influenced to commit such horrific acts. In Rwanda, I saw child soldiers in action and met the adults who directed them, and I was unable to engage and to stop them, leaving me with a rage that remains unabated nearly two decades after the fact. Despite my efforts, I have not yet been able to significantly influence action against the use of child soldiers, let alone eradicate their use. But that has not deterred me from continuously seeking means and ways of attacking the problem—or from hoping one day to succeed. I keep searching for the code we need to break to put this crime against the vulnerable on the world's radar once and for all, to push our governments and leaders into action.

Now that *you* are aware of the horrific abuses inflicted on these children, where do you fit in to the solution? Will you rely on old excuses: that these children are too foreign, too far away to matter? Or will you recognize that these children are exactly like the child you once were, maybe not so long ago, like the children you love. These child soldiers once lived in the safety of their parents' care, played in their schoolyards, learned in their schoolrooms, explored the magical freedom of their minds. What is distance anymore? The conflict zones of the world are only a few hours away by plane, seconds away by Internet. Too many people are living in them.

I'd like to believe that you and I are on an ancient journey together—a journey that begins with a promise made to our fellow human beings. In *Freedom's Battle: The Origins of Humanitarian Intervention*, Gary J. Bass writes of how timeless this promise is: "The basic ideas go all the way back to Thucydides, who, horrified at bloody ancient civil wars, hoped for the endurance of 'the general laws of humanity which are there to give a hope of salvation to all who are in distress.'"

They are not laws that all humans choose to adhere to or even believe in. Every day, conservative "realists" make the pragmatic argument that we shouldn't get involved, that to aid the world's failing states is beyond our capability, that it is innate savagery that leads military commanders to go so far as to use children to kill innocent civilians, that such savagery has nothing to do with "us," is not our fault.

But I believe that you are like me: now that you know of the terrible reality in which these children exist, you can never un-know it. You are involved now, and once you are involved it is impossible for you to remain aloof, impassive, detached or uninterested. We both understand that no human is less human than any other. And you have also made a friend of the little soldier I tried my best to describe, and of all the boys and girls she represents. Our responsibility to them is our responsibility to all humanity.

I remain indefatigably positive. After all I've seen, I still have hope and I still take action. Do you? Will you? I sense that you will—particularly if you are of the generation that has come of age since the turning of the millennium. And though I encourage older readers to continue to "eavesdrop," what I have to say from here on in is directed at the young.

Your generation seems to have something beyond a passive sense of hope. You do not wish merely to avoid despair, but rather to understand your obligations. You have the tools, you believe the time is right, you see the future up close and you want to shape it. You are not going to merely hope for change, you will make it. As my father would have said, you are full of piss and vinegar.

Over the past twenty years, which have seen such massive abuses of human rights, especially of children, in Rwanda, the Congo, the Sudan and other conflict zones around the world, we have also been witness to seismic revolutions occurring all around us in the way we connect and perceive our world. And within this dizzying revolutionary era, we can sense a radical shift in our civilization's powers to eliminate evil and to hold those who conduct crimes against humanity accountable for their actions.

Revolutions in human rights, global awareness and communications technology have created an atmosphere ripe for action, giving you and me the opportunity to find a new path away from the well-travelled and corpse-laden byways of old regimes that used force and abused the innocent as a means to gain, maintain and sustain power.

But in order to appreciate this revolutionary position, we need to take a moment to consider that brutal past and the status quo that at times still seems an overpowering hindrance to positive change.

Only three hundred years ago, human beings in the Western world were ruled over by god, by king, by master. Most couldn't vote or own property. They rarely raised their voices to question authority, and if they did they were brutally put down. There were no rights, only service and obligation. No equality, only servitude or tyranny. No progress, only acquiescence to the existing system. The Enlightenment introduced ideas of reason, education, equality, freedom, progress and rights, which did not prevent the rise of the great colonial powers and the subjugation of millions of humans considered to be below the threshold of "reason," but which also gave the subjugated the ideological ammunition they needed to break their chains.

The slow evolution of these enlightening concepts led most significantly (for our purposes) to the idea of individual self-realization. Despite (or perhaps because of) the global polarization and subsequent unity around the world wars and the formation of the UN, this concept of individuality came to a head in the 1960s, when young people took to the streets in countries throughout the Western world, demanding their civil and individual rights. And then "one small step" led to an important clarification of this concept: just over forty years ago, a human being walked on the moon for the first time. The astronauts photographed our planet from space, and humans saw the evidence of their collectivity. Our geography, our culture, our equality, our personal humanity make us unique individuals, but also bind us together: we are humans. Each one of us.

The planet Earth is no more an utter mystery. What once was considered foreign is now known to be ultimately familiar, intimate, connected. Though many desperately and relentlessly cling to old divisive ideas in the face of a future that looks complex and uncertain, no one can legitimately portray themselves as members or practitioners of the one true faith, the superior race, the best culture. No one can say, with the image of the blue and green Earth floating in their heads, that others don't count as much as "we" do, that others don't hold the same status as we do, are not as significant as us, are ultimately just not as human as us.

You children born in the last decades of the twentieth century are part of a generation that need not be restricted by perceptions of "the Other" (a term coined by the white European philosopher Georg Wilhelm Friedrich Hegel over two hundred years ago to mean people who are different, i.e., non-white and non-European). It was only in the late twentieth century that we collectively began to end the subjugation of the Other. Significantly, the modern French philosopher Emmanuel Levinas (quoted by Ryszard Kapuściński in his 2008 book, *The Other*) has redefined the Other as "a unique person whom we should not just notice but also include in our experience and for whom we should take responsibility."

As the title promises, Kapuściński devotes his book to explaining our era's new relationship with the Other:

> For five centuries Europe dominated the world, not just politically and economically but also culturally. It imposed its faith and established the law, the scale of values, models of behaviour and languages. Our relations with Others . . . were invariably imperious, overbearing and paternalistic. The long five-hundred-year existence of such an uneven, unfair system has produced numerous ingrained habits amongst its participants. A new world is taking shape, more mobile and open than ever before as the Cold War was ending . . . This pro-democracy atmosphere has been enormously conducive to human mobility. The world is in motion on an unprecedented scale. People of the most varied races and cultures are meeting each other all over this more and more populated planet. While formerly the Other meant the non-European, now these relations are as extensive and varied as they can be on a never-ending scale of possibilities covering all races and cultures.

Your generation takes this democratic philosophy to heart. Many of you already think in terms of the globe, not a patchwork of nations; of humanity, not Us and Them. You innately understand that we are all the Other to someone else, and that in this way we are all the same. Great concepts like human rights and preserving the global environment are in the atmosphere you breathe; your generation seems able to grasp these concepts and knows that you can manage them and influence the future. You are not defeated by the parameters that limit your parents—ideas like the nation state, sovereignty, the hugeness of the planet. You understand that a large portion of humanity lives in inhuman conditions, and you are uncomfortable with that knowledge because your world is small. Humans in places once considered "far away" are real, they are at hand, and they are your peers. And you don't just *know* this metaphorically, you know it viscerally, thanks to your ability to go online and communicate directly with them if you choose.

I marvel that we actually live in an era when technology potentially allows us to communicate with every person on this planet. Granted there are regimes that spend a lot of brain power and resources on preventing their citizens from participating fully in Internet culture, but they are constantly faced with subversion of their control. The potential may seem commonplace to you, but it is astounding to me. While some of us are still trying to master typing, *you* are the masters of this information age. This places a burden on you, too, in that you must maximize what this rapid technological change can offer humanity. You must harness the power of the information revolution to communicate ideas and experiences worldwide. And you must take the time to listen to the ideas of others.

Consider this: it is completely within your potential to gather together some of your peers and fundraise for a small, cheap, solar-powered computer to send to a school in the Congo. This is just one small example. Imagine the potential for growth, for understanding, for solution building, if once a week your class or youth group were to meet electronically with a class or youth group in Africa.

If this level of global intercommunication were properly nurtured and developed, it would eventually be possible to create a movement that would influence every human being who exists or will exist in the future. Such a movement could facilitate a grand design for the application of human rights and justice around the world—a global appreciation that all humans are equal, that all humans are human, and that no one human is more human than any other.

With all these new philosophical and technological advances that are available to humanity as a whole and to individuals within humanity, there must be a way to bring about solutions to those conflicts and abuses of power that continue to plague us. With worldwide communication tools and innovative social networks popping up at a breathtaking pace, we could create a virtual headquarters of engaged individuals to focus attention and guide action on the issue of child soldiers, to reach out to build direct connections with youth in conflict zones. A virtual worldwide movement could constantly monitor and connect victims, could target the perpetrators and also the political leaders of the developed world, who have the power to make the risky decisions to intervene in conflict zones. The power of such grassroots connections was demonstrated in the election of President Barack Obama, whose campaign team built a coalition of voters linked by cellphone, BlackBerry and laptop, in which all that communication turned into real votes. We can argue about how path-breaking Obama's presidency has turned out to be, but how it came about is a wonderful example of the effectiveness of using the new channels of communication to motivate and inspire a new generation of voters.

As this book has revealed, I am working at coming up with some answers. What we now need to discuss is not *how* to eradicate the use of child soldiers, but that we will *commit* to doing so.

We need to decide whether we are finally on a mission, you and I, inspired by our empathy for human life, whoever and wherever it is.

Since the beginning of recorded thought, there have been accounts of greed, brutality and the destruction of innocence, to the point that too many in the human race—too many leaders, too many pundits—firmly believe that the natural state of humans is a combative competition for survival. The architects of the Rwandan genocide to this day, even while standing accused of crimes against humanity in the dock at the international tribunal in Arusha, Tanzania, believe that their plan to systematically destroy another ethnicity was justified by their own people's need for security, opportunity and serenity of mind and soul against a history of oppression. "Us against Them" turned into evil of unimaginable scale. They killed and mutilated hundreds of thousands, using their own youths, their own future generations, as their instrument, driven by fear and insecurity, and a perverted drive for peace for their own kind.

But another narrative has always existed alongside the fear-driven, utter selfishness of Us versus Them. It has been called by many names: social responsibility, altruism, the golden rule, *ubuntu*—an Africa-born concept that Archbishop Desmond Tutu has described as the essence of being human, the fact that you can't exist as a human being in isolation, that you, too, are humiliated and diminished when others around you are humiliated or diminished. All of these ideas inspire individuals to look beyond themselves to others; to take personal responsibility for the larger social good; to act on the ethical obligation we have to our neighbour; to assist in building the means to advance this quest to protect the peace and humanity of all human beings.

Over two thousand years ago, Aristotle asserted that human beings aren't at their best when they stand alone, and that excellence can't be achieved by hermits. I love how that sounds, though he was actually speaking of small states working together. In the last century, Mohandas Mahatma Gandhi advised each of us to "be the change you want to see in the world"—a line now posted on undergraduate walls in student residences everywhere. He knew the limitations of the individual—"whatever you do will be insignificant"—but believed that those limitations are not an excuse: "it is very important that you do it." The civil rights leader Dr. Martin Luther King, Jr., had a dream "that one day this nation will rise up and live out the true meaning of its creed: 'We hold these truths to be self-evident: that all men are created equal'"—a beautiful dream for his country, which in some ways has been realized forty years later by the election of Barack Obama.

Individuals who possessed no apparent power, wealth, influence, connections, or even the technological tools you have at your fingertips today, harnessed their passion and changed the world. Seismic change can happen over a lifetime, or in an instant.

In the 1960s, an important revolution was brewing in the United States. Black Americans were fighting for their rights, and many African-American athletes heading to the 1968 Olympic Games in Mexico City wanted to draw attention to the unfair poverty and injustice afflicting them back home. Community leaders and athletes, most of them African-American, came together in the Olympic Project for Human Rights to arrange a boycott of the games by all black American athletes. They were unsuccessful. Despite the fervour of the civil-rights movement on American streets, no protest of any kind succeeded on the Olympic world stage. Runners Tommie Smith and John Carlos decided to change this. After winning first and third place, respectively, in the two-hundred-metre race, they stood on the podium to accept their medals without shoes—to symbolize their poverty—then raised their black-gloved fists in pride and defiance. Their simple gesture rocked the world, and brought the terrible injustices of black America to global attention.

How could such a singularly simple gesture have been so powerful? It was not an act of terrorism, of destruction of other human beings or infrastructure, or of themselves in some form of self-immolation by fire or dynamite. It was a powerful symbol that shifted focus effortlessly from their physical prowess to their cause.

Raising their fists had the impact of a nuclear bomb on those with political, social and economic power. That ever-so-simple gesture, protesting the exploitation of millions of abused humans and the injustice that dogged their every day, helped to topple evil and abusive laws that kept so many humans in a state of less humanity than others. Imagine if we could define the right moment and harness such powerful energy to eradicate the use of child soldiers. What would our symbolic action be?

Of course, change is rarely instantaneous. In a longer but no less revolutionary way, another man helped to change the world through defiance and refusal to accept the status quo. Rolihlahla Mandela was born in 1918 in a small village in South Africa at a time when apartheid—an Afrikaans word meaning "separateness"—denied black South Africans basic human rights and forced them to live segregated from white South Africans. Mandela was the first member of his family to go to school, where he was given the English name Nelson. Despite the heavy oppression of apartheid, from a young age Mandela worked with others of like mind to overturn the racist status quo. He was suspended from his first college for participating in a protest boycott, which was only the beginning of his lifelong struggle for equality for the black citizens of South Africa.

Mandela helped form the African National Congress Youth League and tried to encourage the ANC itself to become more radical in the fight against apartheid. Even after his first arrest and trial, Mandela continued to follow the rules and try to create change peacefully. But at every step, he was a victim of apartheid— he was constantly being banned, arrested and imprisoned—and it further radicalized him. "When I was first banned," he said,

"I abided by the rules and regulations of my persecutors. [But] I had now developed contempt for these restrictions . . . To allow my activities to be circumscribed by my opponent was a form of defeat, and I resolved not to become my own jailer."

In the early 1960s the National Party banned the African National Congress, and Mandela made the difficult decision to change his tactics and promote the use of sabotage and violence against government and military targets. Mandela wrote in his autobiography *Long Walk to Freedom*, "I did not plan it in a spirit of recklessness, nor because I have any love of violence. I planned it as a result of a calm and sober assessment of the political situation that had arisen after many years of tyranny, exploitation, and oppression of my people by the Whites." Arrested and on trial again for subversion and treason, Mandela closed his defence with the following statement: "During my lifetime I have dedicated myself to the struggle of the African people. I have fought against white domination, and I have fought against black domination. I have cherished the ideal of a democratic and free society in which all persons live together in harmony and with equal opportunities. It is an ideal which I hope to live for and to achieve. But if needs be, it is an ideal for which I am prepared to die." Despite his passionate plea and massive support from the black population of South Africa, Mandela was sentenced to life imprisonment and spent the next twenty-seven years in jail.

But his resolve not to be defeated, even in jail, slowly led over the decades to an international movement to "Free Nelson Mandela" and end apartheid in South Africa. Even after his release from prison in 1990, Mandela continued to acknowledge the unfortunate need for violent action to combat the violence of apartheid. He was often misunderstood as a terrorist, but he maintained his resolve to bring justice to his country. In 1993 he won the Nobel Peace Prize. In 1994 South Africa's first multiracial elections were held, and Nelson Mandela, at the age of seventy-five, was elected as the country's first black president.

Like Mandela, many revolutionaries—think of Burma's Aung San Suu Kyi today, or even Dian Fossey, who was murdered for her campaign to protect the gorillas of the Great Lakes Region of Africa—pay a high price for holding to their convictions and attempting to share their beliefs with others. Why would anyone want to be out in front of the pack, trying to influence its direction and its capacity to perform beyond itself? What logical, responsible individual wants to submit to ridicule, to ruthless cross-examination, to physical attack, to incarceration, to risk that his family, friends and associates will suffer too? What is the trigger? What keeps him going?

In his award-winning 2009 book, *Murder Without Borders*, journalist Terry Gould explored what compelled ordinary local reporters in dangerous and corrupt places to keep doing their jobs in the face of death threats. The answers for each of the journalists he profiled, in Colombia, the Philippines, Bangladesh, Russia and Iraq, were individual to a certain extent—bravery, stubbornness, guilt, bravura and, in one instance only, saintliness. But they were all only people, people like you and me, who shared the stubborn belief that life in their hometowns needed to be fair, needed to be free of the impunity of criminals and overlords, needed to be organized so that the poor had as much right to safe and fulfilled lives for themselves and their children as the rich. It was not some rarefied quality that drove them to sacrifice themselves, but an insistence on justice for their neighbours.

Whenever I falter, I think of the people I met before the genocide began in Rwanda, so human, so full of hope, so deserving of life. I reread a passage written by Elie Wiesel, published in an anthology called *What Does It Mean to Be Human?*: "To the homeless, the poor, the beggar, the victim of AIDS and Alzheimer's, the old and the humble, the prisoners in their prison and the wanderers in their dreams, it is our sacred duty to stretch out our hand and say, 'In spite of what separates us, what we have in common is our humanity.'" I also remind myself of the old saying, attributed to "Anonymous": "We are told never to cross a bridge till we come to it, but this world is owned by people who have 'crossed bridges' in their imagination far ahead of the crowd."

Revolutionaries such as Gandhi and Mandela were called to use the tools that were available to them, to overcome the obstacles of racism, sexism, national politics and international apathy. They each helped change the world in their own ways, and you and I are their heirs.

Given that it is so easy to find out about the world we live in, is it even conceivable that, going forward, any one of us could actually abandon other humans to their brutal fates? Not just by living as if they do not exist, but by acting as if you are the only one who really counts, as if you can actually detach yourself from the rest of humanity and be purely an observer, a hermit cut off from the suffering of others—an audience of one, watching with varying degrees of interest the screen in front of you where humanity is playing itself out.

I know people regard such isolationism as a real option—I see detachment all around me. I can connect to the world at the click of a mouse, and I can disconnect exactly the same way. Why get involved, why be bothered by what other human beings are doing to their fellow humans? Why should I want to be an actor in the film of the human race?

If we in the developed world don't like what we see, a thumb or index finger quickly removes it from in front of our eyes. Having the world at your fingertips can take you down a dark path as easily as it can take you toward engagement with that world. I see lots of evidence of instant, anonymous communication over the Web being used to foment stupidity, ignorance and hate, or to mire people in intellectual futility, serving up endless helpings of celebrity gossip or instant reinforcement of ignorant attitudes, or worse. Illegal material, such as adult and child pornography, colonizes much of the Internet, the latter being a form of child abuse that perpetrators can now easily share all over the globe, creating a virtual community of pedophiles. Youths in the developed world sit in their bedrooms imbibing the hate represented by videos of beheadings, being recruited to a cause that has little to do with the realities of their own lives, but much to do with the perversion of youth's sensitivity to injustice, and longing for action.

Many of your peers fall into the dark side of the Web because we adults—as teachers, as parents, as community leaders—have not been able to show them an alternative, to prove to them that they are needed and wanted, and that there are opportunities all around them that will stretch them to their limits in the cause of humanity rather than hate. We adults need to show that it is possible to be as energized by empathy, compassion, courage, determination and altruism as by negativity, narrowness and self-ishness. Though it can be daunting, it is also invigorating to try to change the world for the betterment of humanity.

But I can see where anti-hope and anti-idealism grow. I mean, if our duly elected leaders can shirk their collective responsibility to intervene in any number of conflicts and humanitarian catas-trophes, even when the evidence of flagrant need is presented to them—selectively engaging only when they perceive a national interest—why should a lone individual think she or he could influence the situation?

In 1994, sovereign nation states around the world decided that the only reason to intervene in the Rwandan genocide would be to protect the human beings at risk. Since there was nothing to be gained other than saving a million black Africans from slaugh-ter, the powers-that-be decided that the risk to their own troops was too high a price to pay. The leading voice in the debate at the UN Security Council was the United States, which in 1993 had pulled its forces from the peacekeeping effort in Somalia after eighteen of its soldiers were killed during a raid to try to capture a warlord in Mogadishu. President Bill Clinton and his administra-tion decided that the American people would not permit casualties in a mission that was purely humanitarian, a rationale he enshrined in Presidential Proposition 25: going forward, the only missions the United States would risk shedding blood for were ones that also served American strategic or national interests. Rwanda had nothing to offer the American people. It lacked resources and strategic value. Someone from the U.S. military at the time of the genocide had the audacity to tell me that there was nothing in Rwanda except human beings, and there were too many of them.

As the genocide began, the United States informed the UN Security Council that it would also oppose any effort to preserve the presence of UNAMIR, the peacekeeping mission I was leading in Rwanda. We were physically protecting thirty thousand Rwandans from immediate slaughter, but the Americans wanted UNAMIR abandoned and all the remaining peacekeepers withdrawn because of the risk of non-Rwandan casualties, and the fact that no American national interest would be served by intervening in the war. A few people, such as the late Alison Des Forges of Human Rights Watch, tried to get that decision reversed; she was told that Rwandan citizens weren't a significant enough political constituency in the United States to justify changing course.

Deciding not to intervene is as much a course of action as choosing to leap into the fray. Governments tend to hide behind the skirts of their citizenry, insisting that "we" don't care, that "we" don't want to take such risks. But in my experience, it's chicken and egg. As editors I. William Zartman and J. Lewis Rasmussen wrote in *Peacemaking in International Conflict*:

> The lack of a clear sense of interest and legitimacy results in an absence of public commitment. All these doubts and arguments, repeated authoritatively by world leaders, feed the reaction behind which the leaders hide. Yet many polls have shown that the public is strongly committed to the management and resolution of international conflicts for reasons of both morality and interest, under these specific conditions:

when leaders show that they know what they are doing, have a plan, explain it confidently, and pursue it deliberately . . . A commitment to these goals allows leaders to turn conflict into an occasion of decisiveness and allows parties to get on with productive activity. It is a calling of courage and compassion, a hard defence of basic interest under dangerous conditions, a contribution to local reconciliation and global leadership.

Intervening when a massive abuse of human rights is the essence of the conflict is still a hard sell, especially when the lives of our soldiers are on the line and the end of the mission is not in sight. It seems that governments (and most individuals, too) are prone to act only when there is a threat to themselves. As a result we need to demonstrate that abuses of human rights elsewhere have ramifications in our own lives, too. They clearly do, no matter how we attempt to turn a blind eye. As Strobe Talbott, president of the Brookings Institution, wrote, "Inhumanity, when it is system-atized as it is in dictatorial and genocidal regimes, is not only an outrage against common human values, but it also carries very real security implications." Gareth Evans, past-president of the International Crisis Group, spelled it out even more plainly: "States that cannot or will not stop internal atrocity crimes are the kind of states that cannot or will not stop terrorism, weapons proliferation, drug and people trafficking, the spread of health pandemics, and other global risks." As we've seen more and more, all of the threats Evans listed do not respect borders.

Despite the evidence of change all around us, we have a ten-dency to view our political "verities" as unchangeable and time-less. For roughly three centuries, national sovereignty has been held to be above all other principles and laws of humanity. Hiding behind this powerful, fundamental and long-standing international respect of nation states' autonomy—which is also enshrined in the UN Charter—world leaders have freely abused their own populations within their borders while other nations bowed to their sovereignty. But as Gary J. Bass argues in *Freedom's Battle*, the very idea of national sovereignty grew out of European reaction to the devastating Thirty Years War, in which "perhaps 40 per cent of the population of central Europe perished in the name of competing versions of universal truth." In other words, the idea of the nation state was created in large measure as a response to an annihilating assault on the lives of individual citizens and was actually designed to better protect them.

By the late twentieth century, though, the concept of national sovereignty could not contain our outrage any longer. The genocide in Rwanda and other horrific crimes against humanity around the globe demonstrated that armed conflicts *within* a single country, not between nations—and with mainly civilian casualties—were the new standard for warfare. And it was clear we needed to invent a new doctrine that could engage the political will of nation states to prevent future massive abuses of human rights and destruction of human life on the scale of Cambodia, Rwanda, East Timor, Kosovo, Bosnia, the Congo and Darfur.

In response, Gareth Evans led an international group, funded mostly by Canada, that conducted a seminal study on the interrelationship between sovereignty, massive human rights abuses and the impact of those abuses beyond national borders. (I was asked to provide input to that group.) The year-long study, the results of which were published in 2001, produced a paradigm-shifting concept: nations have a "responsibility to protect" suffering humanity in any country on the planet.

The doctrine of Responsibility to Protect (R2P) states that no sovereign state or its authorities can deliberately abuse the human rights of its citizenry and claim that no other state has a right to interfere. It says that should such a scenario present itself, or in the case where a government cannot stop such massive abuses of innocent civilians, then the international community has a responsibility to protect those civilians under a mandate from the UN. In other words, the protection of individual citizens is paramount over the sovereignty of a nation state. The doctrine contends that if innocent people are being abused, we do not have a choice about whether or not to intervene; we have a fundamental responsibility to humanity to intervene *in extremis*, even with force.

The principle of R2P, endorsed at the UN World Summit in New York in 2005, continues to be controversial. Smaller developing countries at first feared—citing historical example—that world powers would abuse such a doctrine and simply invade at whim to depose regimes that were dictatorial, or even rogue. And, as I mentioned above, using the example of the Rwandan genocide, world powers are reticent to embrace the concept of R2P, which they perceive to be a near-open door to involving them in trouble spots in which they have no compelling interest—beyond the saving of human life. The old attitudes and reflexes and excuses linger, exacerbated these days as NATO in Afghanistan and the U.S.-led coalition in Iraq try to figure out ways to responsibly exit from conflict zones that the major powers had deemed to be within their national interests.

Concurrently with my work on eradicating the use of child soldiers, I was also nominated by the UN secretary general to his advisory board on the prevention of genocide, mass atrocity and abuse of human rights, which was designed to assist him in moving the UN, its agencies and member states into prevention. mode when it came to genocide. Having embraced such a doctrine doesn't mean that we have worked out how to apply it or how it should be integrated with other radical initiatives of the last decade, such as the ICC, which has been establishing jurisprudence for prosecuting crimes against humanity and even indicting heads of state. We are on a steep learning curve when it comes to applying these new international tools and figuring out the resources we need to use them effectively.

For instance, the 2008 indictment for genocide of the president of the Sudan, Omar al-Bashir, was designed to bring a halt to the slow-acting ongoing slaughter in Darfur. But when the ICC brought down the charges, al-Bashir immediately threw a large number of foreign NGOs and humanitarian support out of the Sudan, depriving millions of his own people of the means of survival. That act should have been enough to further indict him, but where does the escalation end?

Glen Pearson, a Canadian member of Parliament with deep humanitarian ties to the Sudan, wrote in A *Land of Designs: The Saga of Darfur and Human Intentions*: "Before any nation or group of nations can intervene, there must be a full and proper humanitarian assessment undertaken to determine the effects on the citizens of that nation." Every indictment, every sentencing, he continues, "carries stupendous recriminations; for one or a few brought to justice, thousands could be consigned to their deaths. No decision that could result in the privation of hundreds of thousands, even millions, can be truly just unless the people making the ultimate decision provide for the full protection of those who will surely endure terrible consequences of such a complex choice." If we are going to indict the leader of the Sudan, we have to be ready to step in so that the Sudanese people don't suffer repercussions. Who is ready, however, to go in and arrest a serving president and bring him to trial, along with the other fifty-two members of his government, his military and police, in order to break the back of an evil regime and stop a genocide that is already seven years old?

I have been doing operational research on this very question with colleagues at Montreal's Concordia University: the will to intervene based on the principle of R2P. I felt that I needed to bring rigorous thought and options to the UN Advisory Committee on Genocide Prevention on top of the in-the-field knowledge gleaned from my experience in Rwanda. I approached Dr. Frank Chalk of Concordia's Montreal Institute for Genocide and Human Rights Studies to strategically develop the will to intervene (W2I) in international humanitarian crises. What became clear to us, as we wrote in our 2010 report, is that we can't wait for our leaders to take action: "When leadership at the top is absent, civil society . . . must strongly pressure governments to broaden their concept of 'national interest.'"

This is our responsibility, as much as our leaders'. For the most part, we continue to watch the world passively and permit our leaders to respond with no response. By not raising our voices, we as citizens allow the political elite to get away with inaction even after they have signed on to the concept of R2P. I believe our governments cling to their own sovereign status and allow others to do the same so that one day they do not find themselves being accused of crimes against humanity by fellow members of the UN.

Because of this fear we continue to not only witness immorality in action in those countries that allow the use of child soldiers and other abuses of human rights within their own borders, we also continue to participate in immoral inaction, either standing on the sidelines or paying lip service by donating hundreds of millions of dollars in an attempt to wash our hands of these complex problems.

Clearly, we need to become individually engaged in influencing the decision makers of our own countries to actively participate in the R2P doctrine to which they have formally agreed. This is an instrument of enormous power in the hands of the populations of the world, of the citizen juries of the world, of the NGOs of the world, to go forward and pressure the political decision makers to take the action they committed to on our behalf in front of the international world body. It responds to a crying need. It is the essential requirement for protecting millions of human beings from being abused, mutilated, raped, killed, slaughtered, displaced from their own homes and turned into refugees in other countries for the rest of their lives with absolutely no hope of a future for their children.

Some people mistakenly blame international failures and inaction on the UN. But the UN is only as effective as its member states allow it to be, by approving robust mandates, providing multidisciplinary and progressive mission leaders (civilian and military), contributing sufficient funding up front and guaranteeing the logistics essential to sustain the mission in the field for the length of the mandate. Effective action depends on the political will of sovereign states, and on those countries acting according to the will of their populations. The failure is ultimately not the fault of the UN but of sovereign member states whose peoples choose not to act.

As we bore down to what each individual citizen can do, we have to figure out how to compel our politicians to act. The way to drive the political will to intervene here at home is to find inventive ways to describe the impact that the conflict abroad will have on our lives here, making the risk-taking more palatable and easier to explain. We must help our politicians—who ultimately are the ones who must make the difficult decisions of investing resources and the human lives of soldiers, diplomats, humanitarians and police—establish clear objectives, reasonable means to achieve them and clear exit routes if the situation turns completely sour. The more an intervention seems manageable and limited, the easier our leaders will find it to commit. They are the ones who bear the electoral heat for unpopular decisions, who need to take pragmatic, tactical and short-term action to survive in their positions. We need to help them do it.

There are two goals you must keep in mind as you venture forth on your mission to eradicate the use of child soldiers and to encourage our political leaders to accept the responsibility to protect. You must be a leader, and you must influence leaders. There are many ways to do both. But two important places for you to start are in the voting booth and with the media.

In my home, Canada, people between the ages of eighteen and thirty make up about 35 per cent of the population. But voting patterns show that barely 15 per cent of them exercise their right to vote. What a waste, to fail to use this peaceful political process to shape the great democracy we live in. If young people coalesced around key issues and voted, they would change the face of Canadian politics in one election. Why? Because *you* hold the balance of power in this country. Each young person represents a brand-new vote that has never been counted. It is tragic that Canada's young voters, the eighteen- to thirty-year-olds, have never stepped up to the democratic challenge of influencing the path they believe this country (and humanity) will take into the near future. Voting patterns in the United States, the United Kingdom and Europe don't vary much from Canada's.

Don't tell me you're not being heard—it's that you're not speaking. You may roll out to the streets of Toronto to protest G20 meetings or travel to Copenhagen to voice your opinion on the climate change conference, but overall your age group is letting political leaders off easily because you aren't forcing them to craft a vision of how we are going to move the country forward. So far as I can tell, you aren't consistently demanding your rightful place in the political process. The political elite thrive on the non-participation of the vast majority of citizens and end up being driven more by the media than by the individuals that comprise a country.

You have been *allowing* traditional media (television, radio, newspapers, magazines) to speak for you and to influence you rather than the other way around. Governments are strongly influenced by the media—and largely define what they perceive as important based on coverage in the press. You need to make the media report on youth-led priorities.

Through voting, through affecting media priorities, through activist commitment and constant engagement with political leaders, public opinion will jell into a solid front that can influence public policy and garner political leadership and action. Without your voices and leadership, the political will to intervene in the world's toughest and most intractable hot spots will simply not materialize.

As the great American philosopher Yogi Berra once said, "The future ain't what it used to be." He was right, but I'd add a significant qualifier: it is a lot closer than it was.

When I was graduating from military college, a very senior officer asked me what I wanted to achieve during my career. I immediately assumed that we were talking about a future twenty years down the road. It was a given that I would have a lengthy, demanding period of apprenticeship upon which I could establish my credentials, build my experiential base, hone my skills and acquire the knowledge I required to be an evolving asset to my organization and the community.

This slow and predictable progression is no longer a given for young people today, born into a wide-open and limitless world. When we speak of *your* future, we're speaking three, four, five years down the road, because we're not in an era of evolution or even in an era of change or reform. We're actually in an era of revolution. There's nothing static or stable about the status quo anymore. It's shifting all the time. The future will be in your face so soon that you will wonder how you got left behind.

In the decades to come, it will require more of your time and intellectual efforts to keep up and survive, let alone master and lead. Your challenge, then, is to *lead* in a time of perpetual and rapid change. You need a vision that will inspire others to maximize their potential, not just survive by sitting on the sidelines. There are no sidelines anymore. And you need to do this, even as you understand that eradicating a horrific abuse such as the use of children to fight dirty civil wars may take decades of steady effort.

To lead must be your aim, and you also have many more tools than did past revolutionaries to enable you to achieve it. You don't have twenty years to work out your priorities, dreams and passions in the comfort of your milieu. Everything is changing, and you must participate in that change so that it does not happen at your expense, or at the expense of the rest of humanity.

You are looking at a future that is not only very near but one that is within your power to affect. The Internet seems to have no limit on providing you with information, and you seem to feel there is no limit in moving toward all the knowledge and awareness of the world, the whole of humanity, and all that it has produced in thought, research and development, and accomplishments, good and bad.

Just think back for a moment to the last communications revolution, which your parents witnessed and which you may regard as a birthright: television, which brought the world's wars, famines and natural disasters into people's living rooms. Michael Ignatieff, in *The Warrior's Honour*, describes the impact of television on the concept and practice of humanitarianism:

> Television is . . . the instrument of a new kind of politics. Since 1945, affluence and idealism have made possible the emergence of a host of non-governmental private charities and pressure groups . . . that use television as a central part of their campaigns to mobilize conscience and money on behalf of endangered humans and their habitats around the world. It is a politics . . . that takes the human species itself rather than specific citizenship, racial, religious, or ethnic groups as its object. It is a "species politics" striving to save the human species itself. . . . It is a politics that has tried to construct a world opinion to keep watch over the rights of those who lack the means to protect themselves. Using the medium of television, many of these international organizations have managed to force governments to pay some degree of attention to the public-relations costs of their exercises in domestic repression.

But as Ignatieff also points out, "television's morality is the morality of the war correspondent, the veteran who has heard all the recurring justifications for human cruelty advanced by the Left and the Right, and who learns in the end to pay attention only to the victims." But it's not the correspondents' morality that rules what gets on the air. When the international community effectively abandoned UNAMIR, I turned to journalists and their cameras and tape recorders, helping them as best I could to film and record the unfolding genocide and get the tapes to their producers at home in London, Paris, New York and Toronto. I figured that if what was happening could be seen, my calls for support might trickle up to the political elite, who couldn't then ignore the slaughter. My soldiers risked their lives to get the tapes out, but much of the video, film and audio tape ended up on the cutting-room floor when other stories were deemed more immediate and interesting for the audience. It was censorship by ratings in the service of making money.

The Internet and social media are not run by that particular profit model, and information over the Net cannot be stomped on by media bosses who assume that people won't be interested. In this new era of social media and YouTube you decide what to disseminate and how to do it in order to achieve our ends.

The only impediment in this new era of global connectedness may be the risk of being overwhelmed. As technological mega-companies like Google advance the digitization of all materials that have been written and printed, from fiction to the most complex scientific matters, access to information is limitless. You also have access to online, real-time observation of any specific spot on Earth—you can even check out what the locals are drinking at the cantina. There are downsides to this, but there are also tremendous upsides: we are entering an era in which evil has no place to hide and there is no limit to how we can present the good.

The ancient rule of borders and boundaries, which have separated and split humanity into boxes, is broken—despite the last-ditch attempts of barbaric regimes to cling to them. Can you grasp that there are practically no limits—except those we wish to impose upon ourselves, individually and collectively—that can prevent us from influencing the whole of humanity, from initiating and sustaining reforms from anywhere we live and work? With these tools we can attempt to extricate ourselves from those constraints that have driven us as a species so readily to evil and conflict and greed, and to express and make real our desire for improvement and serenity for ourselves and others around the world.

Recognize the enormous potential this gives you, the influence you could muster. You'll be able to change things faster, shifting more paradigms than your parents could ever imagine. In fact, the intensity and magnitude of the revolution is already beyond a mere "shift." To express this limitless potential, we require a new lexicon: new action verbs and terms to guide us. You cannot allow anything, not even the limits of language, to hold you back.

So go forth and invent, create and become a new generation of multidisciplinary individuals dedicated to ensuring that all members of the human race thrive on our vulnerable planet in peace and serenity. Attack with courage and energy those hangovers of the past that put the whole exercise of universal humanism at risk. Inventions like the child soldier: an insidious threat to humanity that you can aim to eradicate.

You could create a global accountability process that would so overwhelm those in power that they would agree to the eradication of the use of child soldiers. This is an objective as tangible as was the elimination of slavery, or the pursuit of human rights, and it is within our grasp. Not only *can* you make a difference, you are ethically responsible to do so. Your generation must be a generation of activists. I have offered you some suggestions for how to proceed. But what is most important is that you develop your own ideas. You know the problem, you have the tools, and you have the will. You are more than halfway there.

In this period of blistering change, persevere in your aims. Beware of fleeting popular interest. As quickly as you can bring an issue to the world's attention, it can just as quickly be distracted. As I struggled against the Rwandan genocide in 1994, the world's eyes flitted past Africa to American celebrity car chases. Be prepared.

People sometimes get stuck in a rut doing nothing because their ambitions are too large: they won't act until they discover their life's purpose. I'd argue that it is only through action that we have a hope of discovering our purpose. Instead of asking yourself, "What do I want to do with my life?" ask, "If I had one or two years to devote to something, what would that something be?" What would you do? The great ones—Gandhi, King, Mandela—devoted their whole adult lives to creating "impossible" change. Your world is so much faster and smaller and the impossible seems so much more plausible, and you do not have to wait to be an adult to take a leadership role. (In fact, it is the adults who created child soldiers in the first place.) The action you commit to does not have to be large. It does not have to cost much money, or take much time or effort. It can be free and fast. You don't even have to get out of your chair.

As I discussed earlier, we have shamefully abdicated to the media our democratic responsibility to guide our politicians. They're telling us what's pertinent; they're choosing the issues. What can you do to change this? Well, the media reports on what's hot, what they think people are interested in. Let's show them that we are interested in the children of Africa.

Let's say, for example, each day this month you emailed your local media outlet and asked them to tell you what was going on concerning the use of child soldiers in Uganda. At the end of that month, they would have received thirty emails. If everyone in the country did this, at the end of the month, they would be inundated with 996,380,880 emails. If everyone in France, Japan and Australia did this as well, in one month 7,291,402,320 emails would have been sent—and the Western media would surely have begun reporting on Ugandan child soldiers.

Does this sound naive? It's true—I have been accused of naïveté. But I hope that you, too, are a little naive, a little sensitive, a little hopeful. These qualities make us human, make us able to hope, to care, to act—not for profit or politics, but for humanity.

I am not asking you to take action alone. I am asking you to join me, going forward, in the CSI movement, and all the other initiatives that are finding ways to enact and embody and enforce the human rights conventions and laws in the field, bringing to justice the perpetrators who use and abuse children as soldiers. It will not be easy and we will not be successful overnight; even though we are in an accelerating era, it will take time and concerted effort to shift our political leaders away from the status quo. But our efforts will be just and right and ethically responsible. To protest, to confront, to disturb, to argue: these are all gestures of a mature, democratic society. What an impact you will have on your elders, too, if you find ways to raise your voice. Don't be torn by dilemmas of guilt and commitment. Get engaged in fighting to stop the conflicts adults create, in which children are forced to do the reprehensible dirty work; help me to eradicate the use of child soldiers.

When I led the international peacekeeping mission in Rwanda, I was given strict orders from the highest commanders of the UN *not to act*, merely to observe. It was a legal order, but I refused to obey it because it was immoral. I didn't hesitate to disobey, because I knew it would be a death sentence for the thirty thousand men, women and children—from both sides—we were protecting from the génocidaires. In the first days of the genocide, some troops pulled out without orders and the two thousand people they were protecting were slaughtered within hours. I simply refused to add the 30,000 humans under my protection to the 800,000 people who were ultimately mutilated, raped, traumatized by indescribable evil acts against family and friends, and ultimately slaughtered.

I stress one more time that many of those génocidaires were children, forced to act against all moral references and instinctive feelings. Thousands of youth, indoctrinated, drugged, and overcome by mass hysteria created and sustained by adults who were aided and abetted by the rest of the world's nation states, who refused to provide any assistance to stop this human catastrophe. Adults who pursued relentlessly their objective of destroying all humans they perceived as "different" from them, as a threat to them. They decided that they needed to exterminate them and that their most effective means of mass destruction were children, who they encouraged to be imaginative, energetic, deliberate and effective in inflicting physical and psychological pain.

I will not rest from my goal of eradicating the use of child soldiers. I ask you to join me on this mission. The humanity of these children is as real and valid as your own, and I know you will not fail them. However you proceed, never let it leave your mind: all humans are human; not one of us is more human than any other. The challenge is before you, screaming for you to take it on. Become an activist: inform others, influence public policy and public opinion, join an NGO's efforts, and get engaged in advancing humanity beyond the evil that it does.

The time is now and the moment is yours to grasp. Go and get your boots dirty in the field. Go and smell, taste, feel, see, hear and cry with your peers, so many of whom are starving for love, aching for release from the grip of conflict, hoping that one day they will find again their inner world of childhood—that they will be aided in their desire to grow into mature, responsible adults, parents of future generations of children with a chance at being safe and happy. And then return to your own safe and happy home and take up the cause of the advancement of human rights for all with a passion, transfigured by witnessing with your own eyes the impact on your peers of being used by rogue adults as instruments of conflict.

Bring your new-found depth of argument to the political elite of our nations and remind them day in and day out of their enormous responsibility to protect, to assist, to intervene.

Peux ce que veux, allons-y.

APPENDIX

INTERNATIONAL ACTION ON CHILD PROTECTION AND CHILD SOLDIERS

In recent years, international attention on the issue of children in armed conflict and child soldiers in particular has increased dramatically, thanks in large part to the groundbreaking report Graça Machel presented to the UN in 1996. Legal standards since then have improved markedly, and international attention on children affected by war continues to grow, as is evidenced by the following chart. It is my sincere hope that this groundswell continues, and more importantly that these international laws and protocols are enforced so that perpetrators no longer feel impunity and the use of child soldiers is eradicated entirely.

26 June 1945   **United Nations Charter**

10 Dec. 1948   **Universal Declaration of Human Rights**

12 Aug. 1949   **The Geneva Conventions**
(especially, Convention IV relative to the Protection of Civilian Persons in Time of War)
Relevant Passage: *Requires special considerations for children under fifteen in times of war (e.g. protection if orphaned, adequate food and recreational space if detained). No mention of children active in combat.*

20 Nov. 1959   **United Nations Declaration on the Rights of the Child**
Relevant Passages: *"The child shall enjoy special protection."*

"The best interests of the child shall be the paramount consideration."

"The child shall be protected against all forms of neglect, cruelty and exploitation."

"The child shall not be admitted to employment before an appropriate minimum age; he shall in no case be caused or permitted to engage in any occupation or employment which would prejudice his health or education, or interfere with his physical, mental or moral development."

8 June 1977 **Protocol Additional to the Geneva Conventions of 12 Aug. 1949: relating to the Protection of Victims of International Armed Conflicts**
Relevant Passage: *"The Parties to the conflict shall take all feasible measures in order that children who have not attained the age of fifteen years do not take a direct part in hostilities and, in particular, they shall refrain from recruiting them into their armed forces."*

20 Nov. 1989 **United Nations Convention on the Rights of the Child (CRC)**
Relevant Passage: *"State parties shall take all feasible measures to ensure that persons who have not attained the age of 15 years do not take a direct part in hostilities."*

11 July 1990 **African Charter on the Rights and Welfare of the Child adopted by the Organization for African Unity (now the African Union)** Note: Charter does not come into force until 29 Nov. 1999.
Relevant Passages: *"For the purposes of this Charter, a child means every human being below the age of 18 years."*

"States Parties to the present Charter shall take all necessary measures to ensure that no child shall take a direct part in hostilities and refrain in particular, from recruiting any child."

29 Sept. 1990 **United Nations World Summit for Children**
Document produced: "Plan of Action for Implementing the World Declaration on the Survival, Protection and Development of Children in the 1990s"

Relevant Passage: *"Children need special protection in situations of armed conflict."*

2 Dec. 1993   **The General Assembly of the United Nations recommends the secretary general appoint an independent expert to study the impact of armed conflict on children.**

26 Aug. 1996   **"The Impact of Armed Conflict on Children"**
—report to the General Assembly of the UN by Graça Machel
Relevant Passages: *"Specific recommendations on child soldiers:*

(a)...a global campaign should be launched... aimed at eradicating the use of children under the age of 18 years in the armed forces. The media, too, should be encouraged to expose the use of child soldiers and the need for demobilization;

(b) United Nations bodies, specialized agencies and international civil society actors should...encourage the immediate demobilization of child soldiers...

(c) All peace agreements should include specific measures to demobilize and reintegrate child soldiers into society...

(d) States should...rais[e] the age of recruitment and participation in the armed forces to 18 years."

20 Feb. 1997   **Resolution by the General Assembly on Children and Armed Conflict and the Rights of the Child**
Relevant Passage: *"Calls upon States and other parties to armed conflict to recognize the particular vulnerability of refugee and internally displaced children to recruitment into the armed forces."*

Also recommends that the secretary general appoint a special representative for the impact of armed conflict on children.

27 Apr. 1997   **Cape Town Symposium.**
Document produced: "Principles and Best Practices on the Recruitment of Children into the Armed Forces and on

Demobilization and Social Reintegration of Child Soldiers in Africa"
Relevant Passages: *"A minimum age of 18 years should be established for any person participating in hostilities and for recruitment in all forms into any armed force or armed group."*

"Those persons responsible for illegally recruiting children should be brought to justice."

"A permanent International Criminal Court should be established with jurisdiction covering, inter alia, the illegal recruitment of children."

19 Aug. 1997   **The secretary general of the UN appoints a special representative for children and armed conflict, Olara Otunnu.**

12 Mar. 1998   **Report by the special representative to the secretary general for Children and Armed Conflict on the Rights of the Child to the Commission on Human Rights/Council**

May 1998   **A group of leading international NGOs form The Coalition to Stop the Use of Child Soldiers.**

29 June 1998   **The issue of children and armed conflict is, for the first time, formally placed on the agenda of the Security Council, which holds an open debate and issues a President Statement on the issue.**
Relevant Passages: *"The Security Council strongly condemns the targeting of children in armed conflicts, including their humiliation, brutalization, sexual abuse, abduction and forced displacement, as well as their recruitment and use in hostilities in violation of international law, and calls upon all parties concerned to put an end to such activities."*

"The Security Council calls upon all parties concerned to comply strictly with their obligations under international law, in particular their obligations under the Geneva Conventions

of 1949, the Additional Protocols of 1977 and the United Nations Convention on the Rights of the Child of 1989."

17 July 1998   **Rome Statute—statute of the International Criminal Court (ICC)**
The ICC is established not as an organ of the UN but as an independent organization with an independent budget.
Note: The statute does not come into force until 1 July 2002.
Relevant Passage: *"Conscripting or enlisting children under the age of 15 years into the national armed forces or using them to participate actively in hostilities [is a war crime]."*

12 Oct. 1998   **Protection of children affected by armed conflict: Report of the special representative of the secretary general for Children and Armed Conflict to the General Assembly of the United Nations**

9 Dec. 1998   **Resolution by the General Assembly on Children and Armed Conflict and the Rights of the Child**

29 Nov. 1999   **African Charter on the Rights and Welfare of the Child**
Relevant Passages: *"For the purposes of this Charter, a child means every human being below the age of 18 years."*

"States Parties to the present Charter shall take all necessary measures to ensure that no child shall take a direct part in hostilities and refrain, in particular, from recruiting any child."

17 June 1999   **International Labour Organization (ILO) Convention 182 concerning the Prohibition and Immediate Action for the Elimination of the Worst Forms of Child Labour**
Relevant Passages: *"The term 'child' shall apply to all persons under the age of 18."*

"Child soldiering is one of the worst forms of child labour."

[Note from Human Rights Watch: *"In June of 1999, the use of child soldiers was recognized as a child labor issue when the International Labor Conference included a prohibition on the forced recruitment of children for use in armed conflict in a new convention on the worst forms of child labor. Trade unions and a broad group of governments, including Canada, Denmark, France, Italy, Mexico, Norway, Spain, Uruguay, and all African states, advocated for a broad prohibition on any participation in armed conflict by children under the age of eighteen. However, the United States, backed by the United Kingdom and the Netherlands, mounted an aggressive—and ultimately successful—lobbying campaign for a much narrower prohibition on the 'forced or compulsory recruitment of children or use in armed conflicts.'"*]

7 July 1999   **Lomé Peace Accord signed in Sierra Leone (contains specific article on child combatants)**
Relevant Passage: *"The Government shall accord particular attention to the issue of child soldiers. It shall, accordingly, mobilize resources, both within the country and from the International Community, and especially through the Office of the UN Special Representative for Children in Armed Conflict, UNICEF and other agencies, to address the special needs of these children in the existing disarmament, demobilization and reintegration processes."*

25 Aug. 1999   **Resolution 1261 of the Security Council on Children and Armed Conflict**
Relevant Passages: *Expresses "grave concern at the harmful and widespread impact of armed conflict on children and the long-term consequences this has for durable peace, security and development."*

"Recognizes the deleterious impact of the proliferation of arms, in particular small arms, on the security of civilians, including refugees and other vulnerable populations, particularly children."

1 Oct. 1999   **Protection of children affected by armed conflict: Report of the special representative of the secretary general for Children and Armed Conflict to the General Assembly of the United Nations**

17 Dec. 1999   Resolution by the General Assembly on Children and
Armed Conflict and the Rights of the Child

Sept. 2000   "From Words to Action"
—final report of The International Conference on
War-Affected Children, Winnipeg
Relevant Passages: *"It is necessary to urge the universal
ratification of ILO Convention N0.182 and the Optional
Protocol to the CRC without reservations, as well as the setting
of 18 as a minimum age for all forms of military recruitment."*

*"Ensure a blanket amnesty for children involved in armed
conflict. Recognize their role as perpetrators of violence through
testimony in truth and reconciliation commissions and at
community level but do not criminalize them."*

*"Governments must work to eradicate the supply and use of
small arms, light weapons, grenades, and ammunition in
conflict areas where crimes against humanity, obvious in most
cases through the abuse of children, are prevalent."*

*"Special emphasis needs to be placed on the demobilization
and reintegration of girl soldiers."*

*"The production and purchase of arms toys for children should
be stopped in order to build a culture of peace (the manufacturers
of these toys of destruction should be targeted)."*

9 Feb. 2000   Report by the special representative to the secretary general
for Children and Armed Conflict on the Rights of the
Child to the Commission on Human Rights/Council

23 Mar. 2000   African, Caribbean and Pacific States and the European
Community Joint Assembly adopt resolution against the
use of child soldiers

25 May 2000   General Assembly adopts the Optional Protocol to the
Convention on the Rights of the Child on the Involvement
of Children in Armed Conflict

Note: The optional protocol does not come into force until
12 Feb. 2002.
Relevant Passage: *"Ensure that children below the age of 18
years do not take part in hostilities."*

19 July 2000   **First report of the secretary general to the Security
Council of the United Nations on Children and
Armed Conflict**

11 Aug. 2000   **Resolution 1314 by the Security Council on Children and
Armed Conflict**
Relevant Passage: *"Notes that the deliberate targeting of
civilian populations or other protected persons, including
children, and the committing of systematic, flagrant and
widespread violations of international humanitarian and
human rights law, including that relating to children, in
situations of armed conflict may constitute a threat to
international peace and security, and in this regard reaffirms
its readiness to consider such situations and, where necessary
to adopt appropriate steps."*

3 Oct. 2000   **Protection of children affected by armed conflict:
Report of the special representative of the secretary general
for Children and Armed Conflict to the General Assembly
of the United Nations**

4 Dec. 2000   **Resolution by the General Assembly on Children and
Armed Conflict and the Rights of the Child**

26 Jan. 2001   **Special Session of the General Assembly for follow-up to
the World Summit for Children—"The Machel Review
1996–2000: A Critical Analysis of Progress Made and
Obstacles Encountered in Increasing Protection for
War-Affected Children"**
Relevant Passages: *"In spite of landmark progress, the
recruitment of child soldiers continues. And there is even the
chilling possibility that in recent conflicts children have been
recruited much more deliberately, not just due to their availability
and relative cheapness, but because they are more easily*

indoctrinated into violence and thus more willing than
adults to carry out atrocities."

"The Security Council must lead the international community
with speed to embrace the recommendations in this review and
to prevail against impunity for crimes committed against
children. Children's protection should not have to be
negotiated. Those who wage, legitimise and support wars must
be condemned and held to account. Children must be
cherished, nurtured and spared the pernicious effects of war.
Children can't afford to wait."

7 Sept. 2001   **Report of the secretary general on Children and Armed**
Conflict to the Security Council of the United Nations

9 Oct. 2001   **Protection of children affected by armed conflict: Report of**
the special representative of the secretary general for
Children and Armed Conflict to the General Assembly
of the United Nations

20 Nov. 2001   **Resolution 1379 by the Security Council on Children and**
Armed Conflict
Relevant Passage: *"Requests the Secretary-General to attach to*
his report a list of parties to armed conflict that recruit or use
children in violation of the international obligations applicable
to them."

19 Dec. 2001   **Resolution by the General Assembly on Children and**
Armed Conflict and the Rights of the Child

16 Jan. 2002   **Establishment of the Special Court for Sierra Leone**
Mandate: *"To try those who bear the greatest responsibility for*
serious violations of international humanitarian law and
Sierra Leonean law committed in the territory of Sierra Leone
since 30 November 1996." See 20 June 2007: First
international conviction on charges related to child soldiers.

7 Feb. 2002 Report by the special representative to the secretary general
for Children and Armed Conflict on the Rights of the
Child to the Commission on Human Rights/Council

7 May 2002 Statement by the president of the Security Council on
Children and Armed Conflict

8–10 May 2002 UN Special Session on Children.
Outcome document: "A World Fit for Children"
Relevant Passages: *"Children must be protected from the
horrors of armed conflict."*

*"End the recruitment and use of children in armed conflict
contrary to international law, ensure their demobilization and
effective disarmament and implement effective measures for
their rehabilitation, physical and psychological recovery and
reintegration into society."*

*"Provide appropriate training and education in children's rights
and protection as well as in international humanitarian law
to all civilian, military and police personnel involved in
peacekeeping operations."*

*"Curb the illicit flow of small arms and light weapons and
protect children from landmines, unexploded ordnance and
other war materiel that victimize them, and provide assistance
to victimized children during and after armed conflict."*

24 Sept. 2002 Protection of children affected by armed conflict:
Report of the special representative of the secretary general
for Children and Armed Conflict to the General Assembly
of the United Nations

26 Nov. 2002 Report of the secretary general on Children and
Armed Conflict to the Security Council of the United Nations

2003 Publication: "A Guide to the Optional Protocol on the
Involvement of Children in Armed Conflict"
Note: Essential reading for all young people.

2003   Publication: "Children and Armed Conflict: International
                Standards for Action" (The Human Security Network,
                UN special representative of the secretary general for
                Children and Armed Conflict)

30 Jan. 2003   Resolution 1460 by the Security Council on Children and
                Armed Conflict
                Relevant Passage: *"Noting the fact that the conscription or
                enlistment of children under the age of 15 or using them to
                participate actively in hostilities in both international and
                non-international armed conflict is classified as a war crime
                by the Rome Statute of the International Criminal Court."*

19 Feb. 2003   Resolution by the General Assembly on Children and
                Armed Conflict and the Rights of the Child

3 Mar. 2003   Report by the special representative to the secretary general
                for Children and Armed Conflict on the Rights of the
                Child to the Commission on Human Rights/Council

7 Mar. 2003   The Special Court for Sierra Leone charges former
                president of Liberia Charles Taylor with recruiting child
                soldiers, among other crimes
                Relevant Passage: *This is the first former head of state to be
                indicted for war crimes.*

25 June 2003   Vienna Declaration and Programme of Action
                Relevant Passage: *"National and international mechanisms
                and programmes should be strengthened for the defense
                and protection of children, in particular . . . children in
                armed conflict."*

29 Aug. 2003   Protection of children affected by armed conflict:
                Report of the special representative of the secretary general
                for Children and Armed Conflict to the General Assembly
                of the United Nations

10 Nov. 2003   Report of the secretary general on Children and
                Armed Conflict to the Security Council of the United Nations

9 Mar. 2004   **Resolution by the General Assembly on Children and Armed Conflict and the Rights of the Child**

22 Apr. 2004   **Resolution 1539 by the Security Council on Children and Armed Conflict**
Relevant Passages: *Requests the Secretary-General to "urgently devise an action plan for a systematic and comprehensive monitoring and reporting mechanism that would create a process for providing timely, objective, accurate and reliable information on the recruitment and use of child soldiers and other violations committed against children affected by armed conflict."*

"Deeply concerned over the lack of overall progress on the ground, where parties to conflict continue to violate with impunity the relevant provisions of applicable international law relating to the rights and protection of children in armed conflict."

"Strongly condemns the recruitment and use of child soldiers by parties to armed conflict."

"Takes note with deep concern of the continued recruitment and use of children by parties mentioned in the Secretary-General's report in situations of armed conflict which are on its agenda, in violation of applicable international law relating to the rights and protection of children and, in this regard: (a) Calls upon these parties to prepare within three months concrete time-bound action plans to halt recruitment and use of children in violation of the international obligations applicable to them, in close collaboration with United Nations peacekeeping missions and United Nations country teams, consistent with their respective mandates."

3 June 2004   **Trials begin at the Special Court for Sierra Leone**
Relevant Passage: *For the first time, an international court affirms that the recruitment and use of child soldiers is under its jurisdiction and an internationally illegal war crime, rejecting a preliminary motion which claimed that the crime only entailed individual criminal responsibility.*

8 Oct. 2004   Protection of children affected by armed conflict:
Report of the special representative of the secretary general
for Children and Armed Conflict to the General Assembly
of the United Nations

9 Feb. 2005   Annual Report of the secretary general to the Security
Council of the United Nations, including report on
Children and Armed Conflict

15 Feb. 2005   Report by the special representative to the secretary general
for Children and Armed Conflict on the Rights of the
Child to the Commission on Human Rights/Council

23 Feb. 2005   Statement by the president of the Security Council on
Children and Armed Conflict

8 July 2005   The ICC issues a warrant for the arrest of Joseph Kony,
leader of the Lord's Resistance Army, and other
commanders of the LRA on charges of war crimes,
including the forcible recruitment and use of child soldiers
in hostilities.

July 2005   The Security Council establishes The Security Council
Working Group on Children and Armed Conflict (CAAC).
Relevant Passages: *Examines country reports and negotiates
with or takes serious action against those who practise the war
crime of child soldier recruitment and employment.*

See Terms of Reference under 3 May 2006.

See also Addresses by the Working Group to specific
individuals and armed groups, e.g., 20 July 2007.

26 July 2005   Resolution 1612 by the Security Council on Children and
Armed Conflict
Relevant Passages: *"Gravely concerned by the documented links
between the use of child soldiers in violation of applicable
international law and the illicit trafficking of small arms and
light weapons and stressing the need for all States to take
measures to prevent and to put an end to such trafficking."*

> *"Requests the Secretary-General to implement without delay,*
> *the [monitoring and reporting mechanism on children and*
> *armed conflict]."*

31 July 2005   Olara Otunnu's term as special representative expires.

7 Sept. 2005   Protection of children affected by armed conflict:
                 Report of the special representative of the secretary general
                 for Children and Armed Conflict to the General Assembly
                 of the United Nations

9 Dec. 2005   Resolution by the General Assembly on Children and
                 Armed Conflict and the Rights of the Child

2006   Graça Machel's 10-Year Strategic Review: "Children and
                 Conflict in a Changing World"; follow-up to the landmark
                 study, "The Impact of Armed Conflict on Children"
                 Recommendations include:

                 "End impunity for violations against children"

                 "Prioritize children's security"

                 "Integrate children's rights in peacemaking, peacebuilding and
                 preventive actions"

                 (See also 13 Aug. 2007, when the review is presented to the
                 General Assembly of the United Nations.)

7 Feb. 2006   Radhika Coomaraswamy is appointed to the position of
                 special representative for children and armed conflict to
                 the secretary general.

3 May 2006   Terms of reference of the Working Group of the Security
                 Council on Children and Armed Conflict
                 Relevant Passage: *"The Working Group will examine*
                 information on compliance and progress in ending the
                 recruitment and use of children and other violations being
                 committed against children in situations of armed conflict."

13 June 2006   Report of the secretary general on Children and
Armed Conflict in the Democratic Republic of the Congo

10 July 2006   Report on the activities of the Working Group of the
Security Council on Children and Armed Conflict since
the adoption of resolution 1612 on 26 July 2005

24 July 2006   Statement by the president of the Security Council on
Children and Armed Conflict

17 Aug. 2006   Report of the special representative of the secretary general
for Children and Armed Conflict to the General Assembly
of the United Nations

17 Aug. 2006   Report of the secretary general on Children and Armed
Conflict in the Sudan

8 Sept. 2006   Security Council Working Group Toolkit and
Conclusions on parties in the armed conflict of the
Democratic Republic of the Congo

25 Oct. 2006   Report of the secretary general on Children and Armed
Conflict in Côte d'Ivoire

26 Oct. 2006   Annual Report of the secretary general to the Security
Council of the United Nations, including report on
Children and Armed Conflict

27 Oct. 2006   Report of the secretary general on Children and Armed
Conflict in Burundi

9 Nov. 2006   Resolution by the General Assembly on Children and
Armed Conflict and the Rights of the Child

28 Nov. 2006   Statement by the president of the Security Council on
Children and Armed Conflict

1 Dec. 2006   Security Council Working Group on Children and
Armed Conflict: Conclusions on parties in the armed
conflict in the Sudan

20 Dec. 2006 **Report of the secretary general on Children and Armed Conflict in Nepal**

20 Dec. 2006 **Report of the secretary general on Children and Armed Conflict in Sri Lanka**

2007 **Outcome document from above conference: "The Paris Principles: Principles and Guidelines on Children Associated with Armed Forces or Armed Groups"** Relevant Passages: *"'Child' refers to any person less than 18 years of age."*

"Ending impunity for those responsible for unlawfully recruiting or using children in armed conflict, and the existence of mechanisms to hold such individuals to account can serve as a powerful deterrent against such violations."

"Children who are accused of crimes under international law allegedly committed while they were associated with armed forces or armed groups should be considered primarily as victims of offences against international law; not only as perpetrators."

"Children should not be prosecuted by an international court or tribunal."

"Alternatives to judicial proceedings should be sought for children at the national level."

"If national judicial proceedings take place, children are entitled to the highest standards of safeguards available according to international law and standards and every effort should be made to seek alternatives to placing the child in institutions."

"Where large numbers of people are facing criminal proceedings as a result of armed conflict, the processing of the cases of children and of mothers who have children with them in detention should take priority."

5 Feb. 2007   International Conference: Free Children from War

Fifty-eight governments gather in Paris to commit to
protecting children from unlawful recruitment or use by
armed forces or armed groups.
Relevant Passage: *"While progress is being made, it is also true
that today, in over 30 situations of concern around the globe,
children are being brutalized and callously used to advance the
agendas of adults. It has been estimated that over 2 million
children have been killed in situations of armed conflict;
another 6 million have been permanently disabled; and more
than a quarter of a million children continue to be exploited
as child soldiers. Thousands of girls are being subjected to
rape and other forms of sexual violence and exploitation, and
girls and boys are being abducted from their homes and
communities. Schools and hospitals, which should be safe
havens for children, are also increasingly becoming the targets
of attack by armed groups."* —Radhika Coomaraswamy

7 Feb. 2007   **Report to the Human Rights Council of the Office of the
special representative to the secretary general for Children
and Armed Conflict**

13 Feb. 2007   **Security Council Working Group Conclusions on Burundi**

13 Feb. 2007   **Security Council Working Group Conclusions on
Côte d'Ivoire**

7 May 2007   **Report of the secretary general on Children and
Armed Conflict in Uganda**

7 May 2007   **Report of the secretary general on Children and Armed
Conflict in Somalia**

15 June 2007   **Statement by the Chair of the Security Council Working
Group, addressed to the leadership of the Tamil Makkal
Viduthalai Puligal and its military wing, the Karuna Faction.**

15 June 2007   Statement by the Chair of the Security Council Working Group, addressed to the leadership of the Liberation Tigers of Tamil Eelam

15 June 2007   Security Council Working Group Conclusions on Sri Lanka

15 June 2007   Security Council Working Group Conclusions on Nepal

20 June 2007   **First judgments for the Special Court for Sierra Leone**
Relevant Passages: *Alex Tamba Brima and two other militia leaders of the Armed Forces Revolutionary Council are convicted on eleven charges including the conscripting or enlisting of children under the age of fifteen years into armed forces or groups, or using them to participate actively in hostilities.*

This is the first time an international court convicts on charges relating to child soldiers, and sets an important precedent.

28 June 2007   **Report of the secretary general on Children and Armed Conflict in the Democratic Republic of the Congo**

3 July 2007   **Report of the secretary general on Children and Armed Conflict in Chad**

10 July 2007   **Annual Report on the Activities of the Working Group of the Security Council on Children and Armed Conflict**

20 July 2007   **Statement by the Chair of the Security Council Working Group, addressed to all parties to the conflict in Somalia**

20 July 2007   **Statement by the Chair of the Security Council Working Group: Message to the head of the Lord's Resistance Army delegation to the Juba peace talks through a public statement to be transmitted by the Special Envoy for the areas affected by the Lord's Resistance Army**

20 July 2007   **Security Council Working Group Conclusions on Uganda**

20 July 2007   **Security Council Working Group Conclusions on Somalia**

13 Aug. 2007   **Report of the special representative of the Secretary General for Children and Armed Conflict to the General Assembly of the United Nations, including the Machel 10-Year Strategic Review**
Relevant Passages: *"Many conflicts last longer than the duration of childhood. The present report focuses on children, but at times analysis is extended to youth, defined by the General Assembly to be those aged 15 to 24. We should recognize the capacities and agency of children and youth, and avoid characterizing children and youth as vulnerable or as delinquents who pose a threat to security. Moreover, adults are responsible for environments of conflict and violence."*

"While at the normative level there has been significant progress in addressing the recruitment or use of child soldiers in the last decade, large numbers of boys and girls continue to serve as fighters, cooks, porters and messengers, and to be used for sexual purposes. Since 2002, the Secretary-General has listed parties that recruit or use children in situations of armed conflict in 18 countries. That estimate is at the lower end; in 2004 the Coalition to Stop the Use of Child Soldiers identified 43 countries where either illegal recruitment or use was indicated."

"Over the past several years, the international community has focused concerted attention on the scourge of child soldiering, and I have prioritized this issue to ensure that the strong momentum that now exists is maintained and begins to yield more concrete results in terms of the application of international standards to put an end to this practice. I have also given special priority to girls in conflict because their plight, circumstances and experiences are often the most desperate, and at the same time they are often the most marginalized and stigmatized because of the abuses that have been perpetrated against them."

" . . . deeply concerned by the extent of sexual violence in the eastern part of the country [DRC] and the climate of impunity that prevails for such crimes. I visited Panzi hospital and spoke with many girls who had been subjected to multiple rapes and humiliation."

"Widespread rape or other grave sexual violence continues to be committed in virtually every conflict situation and can take the form of sexual slavery, forced prostitution, sexual mutilation or other forms of brutality. In the Democratic Republic of the Congo, a climate of impunity has resulted in rampant sexual violence, with children representing an alarming 33 per cent of victims."

"Attacks against schools or hospitals, including the occupation, shelling or destruction of facilities, as well as harm to personnel, have risen dramatically in recent years. Such attacks not only directly harm the individuals involved but severely limit others' access to basic services."

"A number of other conflict-related issues not listed among the six grave violations have a significant impact on children's lives. Illegal detention has been highlighted as a violation requiring greater attention."

"Too often, reintegration efforts inappropriately single out children who in the past were recruited, thereby perpetuating stigma. Likewise, cash benefits for returning children can be seen as rewarding their involvement in violence. To the extent possible, reintegration efforts should benefit all affected children, rather than select groups. A useful approach in the Democratic Republic of the Congo and Sierra Leone has involved the provision of materials to schools accepting demobilized children, thus benefiting all students."

29 Aug. 2007   **Report of the secretary general on Children and Armed Conflict in the Sudan**

30 Aug. 2007   **Report of the Secretary General on Children and Armed Conflict in Côte d'Ivoire**

24 Sept. 2007   **Security Council Working Group—Conclusions on Chad**

1 Oct. 2007   **Address to the Ministerial Meeting on Children and Armed Conflict**

25 Oct. 2007   Security Council Working Group—Conclusions on the
                Democratic Republic of the Congo

16 Nov. 2007   Report of the secretary general on Children and
                Armed Conflict in Myanmar

28 Nov. 2007   Report of the secretary general on Children and
                Armed Conflict in Burundi

21 Dec. 2007   Annual Report of the secretary general to the Security
                Council of the United Nations including Report on
                Children and Armed Conflict

21 Dec. 2007   Report of the secretary general on Children and
                Armed Conflict in Sri Lanka

1 Feb. 2008   Conclusions of the Security Council Working Group on
                Children and Armed Conflict in Côte d'Ivoire

12 Feb. 2008   Statement by the president of the Security Council on
                Children and Armed Conflict

15 Feb. 2008   Conclusions of the Security Council Working Group on
                parties to the situation of armed conflict in Burundi

20 Feb. 2008   Conclusions of the Security Council Working Group on
                parties in the armed conflict in the Sudan

22 Feb. 2008   Resolution by the General Assembly on Children and
                Armed Conflict and the Rights of the Child

25 Mar. 2008   Conclusions of the Security Council Working Group on
                Children and Armed Conflict in Côte d'Ivoire—Corrigendum

18 Apr. 2008   Report of the secretary general on Children and
                Armed Conflict in Nepal

24 Apr. 2008   Report of the secretary general on Children and
                Armed Conflict in the Philippines

30 May 2008　　Report of the secretary general on Children and
　　　　　　　　Armed Conflict in Somalia

23 June 2008　　Additional Report of the secretary general on Children
　　　　　　　　and Armed Conflict in Uganda

27 June 2008　　Report to the Human Rights Council of the Office of the
　　　　　　　　special representative to the secretary general for Children
　　　　　　　　and Armed Conflict

11 July 2008　　Annual Report on the Activities of the Security Council
　　　　　　　　Working Group on Children and Armed Conflict

17 July 2008　　The Security Council holds an open debate on children
　　　　　　　　and armed conflict.
　　　　　　　　Relevant Passages: *Adopts a presidential statement*
　　　　　　　　"condemning equally the six gravest violations against children
　　　　　　　　in conflict:

　　　　　　　　1. Killing or maiming

　　　　　　　　2. Recruitment or use of child soldiers

　　　　　　　　3. Rape and other forms of sexual violence

　　　　　　　　4. Abduction

　　　　　　　　5. Attacks against schools or hospitals

　　　　　　　　6. Denial of humanitarian access."

17 July 2008　　Statement by the president of the Security Council on
　　　　　　　　Children and Armed Conflict

25 July 2008　　Conclusions of the Security Council Working Group on
　　　　　　　　Children and Armed Conflict in Myanmar

6 Aug. 2008　　Report of the special representative of the secretary general
　　　　　　　　for Children and Armed Conflict to the General Assembly
　　　　　　　　of the United Nations

7 Aug. 2008   Report of the secretary general on Children and
Armed Conflict in Chad

3 Oct. 2008   Conclusions of the Security Council Working Group on
Children and Armed Conflict in the Philippines

21 Oct. 2008   Conclusions of the Security Council Working Group on
Children and Armed Conflict in Sri Lanka

10 Nov. 2008   Report of the secretary general on Children and
Armed Conflict in the Democratic Republic of the Congo

10 Nov. 2008   Report of the secretary general on Children and
Armed Conflict in Afghanistan

5 Dec. 2008   Conclusions of the Security Council Working Group on
Children and Armed Conflict in Nepal

5 Dec. 2008   Conclusions of the Security Council Working Group on
Children and Armed Conflict in Uganda

5 Dec. 2008   Conclusions of the Security Council Working Group on
Children and Armed Conflict in Somalia

5 Dec. 2008   Conclusions of the Security Council Working Group on
Children and Armed Conflict in Chad

26 Jan. 2009   The ICC begins the trial of Thomas Lubanga Dyilo on
charges of enlisting and conscripting children under the
age of fifteen as soldiers and using them to participate
actively in combat between Sept. 2002 and Aug. 2003.

3 Feb. 2009   Report of the secretary general on Children and
Armed Conflict in the Central African Republic

10 Feb. 2009   Report of the secretary general on Children and
Armed Conflict in the Sudan

13 Mar. 2009   Resolution by the General Assembly on Children and
Armed Conflict and the Rights of the Child

26 Mar. 2009   Annual Report of the secretary general to the Security
Council of the United Nations, including Report on
Children and Armed Conflict

29 Apr. 2009   Statement by the president of the Security Council on
Children and Armed Conflict

1 June 2009   Report of the secretary general on Children and
Armed Conflict in Myanmar

25 June 2009   Report of the secretary general on Children and
Armed Conflict in Sri Lanka

13 July 2009   Conclusions of the Security Council Working Group on
Children and Armed Conflict in the Democratic Republic
of the Congo

13 July 2009   Conclusions of the Security Council Working Group
on Children and Armed Conflict in the Central
African Republic

13 July 2009   Conclusions of the Security Council Working Group on
Children and Armed Conflict in Afghanistan

22 July 2009   Annual Report on the Activities of the Security Council
Working Group on Children and Armed Conflict

30 July 2009   Report to the Human Rights Council of the Office of the
special representative of the secretary general for Children
and Armed Conflict

4 Aug. 2009   Resolution 1882 of the Security Council on Children and
Armed Conflict
Relevant Passages: *"Deeply concerned over the lack of progress
on the ground in some situations of concern, where parties to
conflict continue to violate with impunity the relevant*

provisions of applicable international law relating to the rights
and protection of children in armed conflict."

"Recalling the responsibilities of States to end impunity and to
prosecute those responsible for genocide, crimes against
humanity, war crimes and other egregious crimes perpetrated
against children."

"Welcoming the fact that several individuals who are alleged to
have committed crimes against children in situations of armed
conflict have been brought to justice by national justice systems
and international justice mechanisms and mixed criminal
courts and tribunals."

"Strongly condemns all violations of applicable international
law involving the recruitment and use of children by parties to
armed conflict."

"Welcomes the efforts of the Department of Peacekeeping
Operations in mainstreaming child protection into
peacekeeping missions."

6 Aug. 2009   **Report of the special representative of the secretary general**
for Children and Armed Conflict to the General Assembly
of the United Nations

28 Aug. 2009   **Report of the secretary general on Children and Armed**
Conflict in Colombia

10 Sept. 2009   **Report of the secretary general on Children and Armed**
Conflict in Burundi

15 Sept. 2009   **Report of the secretary general on Children and**
Armed Conflict in Uganda

14 Oct. 2009   **Publication of the first Working Paper of the Office of the**
special representative for Children and Armed Conflict

28 Oct. 2009   Conclusions of the Security Council Working Group on
                Children and Armed Conflict in Myanmar

21 Dec. 2009   Conclusions of the Security Council Working Group on
                Children and Armed Conflict in Burundi

21 Dec. 2009   Conclusions of the Security Council Working Group
                on Children and Armed Conflict in the Sudan

21 Jan. 2010   Report of the secretary general on Children and
                Armed Conflict in the Philippines

3 Mar. 2010   General Assembly Resolution on Children and
                Armed Conflict and the Rights of the Child

13 Apr. 2010   Annual Report of the secretary general to the
                Security Council of the United Nations, including
                Report on Children and Armed Conflict

13 Apr. 2010   Report of the secretary general on Children and
                Armed Conflict in Nepal

2 June 2010   Security Council Cross-Cutting Report on Children
                and Armed Conflict
                Relevant Passage: "For over ten years the impact of war on
                children has been a significant thematic focus for the
                Security Council. There is now much greater awareness of the
                issue and some evidence that the inclusion of child protection
                principles in Council decisions in specific cases is having some
                impact. However, the Council still encounters some resistance
                from some governments. And the difficulty of applying effective
                pressure on non-state actors who recruit child soldiers is a
                continuing challenge."

RECOMMENDED READING

Abani, Chris. *Song for Night: A Novella*. Akashic Books, 2007.

Alfredson, Lisa S. *Creating Human Rights: How Noncitizens Made Sex Persecution Matter to the World*. University of Pennsylvania Press, 2008.

Bass, Gary J. *Freedom's Battle: The Origins of Humanitarian Intervention*. Knopf, 2008.

Beah, Ishmael. *A Long Way Gone: Memoirs of a Boy Soldier*. Douglas & McIntyre, 2007.

Blaker, Lisa French. *Heart of Darfur*. Hodder & Stoughton, 2008.

Boutwell, Jeffrey; Klare, Michael T. *Light Weapons and Civil Conflict: Controlling the Tools of Violence*. Rowman & Littlefield Publishers, 1999.

Boyden, Jo; de Berry, Joanna ed. *Children and Youth on the Front Line: Ethnography, Armed Conflict and Displacement*. Berghahn Books, 2004.

Brett, Rachel; Specht, Irma. *Young Soldiers: Why They Choose to Fight*. Lynne Rienner Publishers, 2004.

Briggs, Jimmie. *Innocents Lost: When Child Soldiers Go to War*. Basic Books, 2005.

Cameron, Sara (in co-operation with UNICEF). *Out of War: True Stories from the Front Lines of the Children's Movement for Peace in Colombia*. Scholastic, 2001.

The Commission for Africa. *Our Common Interest: An Argument*. Penguin Books, 2005.

Cook, Kathy. *Stolen Angels: The Kidnapped Girls of Uganda*. Penguin Canada, 2007.

Cooper, Robert. *The Breaking of Nations: Order and Chaos in the 21st Century*. Atlantic Monthly Press, 2004.

Coulter, Chris. *Bush Wives and Girl Soldiers: Women's Lives through War and Peace in Sierra Leone*. Cornell University Press, 2009.

Dallaire, Roméo. *Shake Hands with the Devil: The Failure of Humanity in Rwanda*. Random House Canada, 2003.

de Saint-Exupéry, Antoine. *Le Petit Prince*. Gallimard, 1946.

de Temmerman, Els. *Aboke Girls: Children Abducted in Northern Uganda*. Fountain Publishers, 1995.

Denov, Myriam. *Child Soldiers: Sierra Leone's Revolutionary United Front*. Cambridge University Press, 2010.

Dongala, Emmanuel. *Johnny Mad Dog*. Farrar, Strauss & Giroux, 2005.

Douglas, I; Gleichmann, C. Odenwald, M.; Steenken, K.; Wilkinson, A. *Disarmament, Demobilisation and Reintegration: A practical field and classroom guide*. German Technical Co-operation; The Norwegian Defence International Centre; Pearson Peacekeeping Centre/Centre Pearson pour le maintien de la paix; Swedish National Defence College, 2004.

Eggers, Dave. *What Is the What*. Vintage Canada, 2007.

Filipovic, Zlata. *Zlata's Diary: A Child's Life in Wartime Sarajevo*. Penguin UK, 1995.

Franck, Frederick; Roze, Janis; Connolly, Richard ed *What Does It Mean to Be Human? Reverence for Life Reaffirmed by Responses from Around the World*. St. Martin's Press, 2000.

Gates, Scott; Reich, Simon ed. *Child Soldiers in the Age of Fractured States*. University of Pittsburgh Press, 2009.

Gould, Terry. *Murder Without Borders: Dying for the Story in the World's Most Dangerous Places*. Random House Canada, 2009.

Gow, Melanie; Vandergrift, Kathy; Wanduragala, Randini. *The Right to Peace: Children and Armed Conflict (Working paper No. 2)*. World Vision International, 2000.

Honwana, Alcinda. *Child Soldiers in Africa*. University of Pennsylvania Press, 2006.

Ignatieff, Michael. *The Warrior's Honour: Ethnic War and the Modern Conscience*. Viking Canada, 1998.

Iweala, Uzodinma. *Beasts of No Nation*. Harper Perennial, 2005.

Jal, Emmanuel. *War Child: A Child Soldier's Story*. St. Martin's Press, 2009.

Kahn, Leora ed.; Moreno-Ocampo, Luis. *Child Soldiers*. powerHouse Books, 2008.

Kamara, Mariatu. *The Bite of the Mango*. Annick Press, 2008.

Kapuściński, Ryszard. *The Other*. Verso Books, 2008.

Keane, Fergal. *Season of Blood: A Rwandan Journey*. Penguin UK, 1997.

Keitetsi, China. *Child Soldier*. Souvenir, 2004.

Kuper, Jenny. *Military Training and Children in Armed Conflict: Law, Policy and Practice*. Martinus Nijhoff Publishers, 2005.

Kuperman, Alan J. *The Limits of Humanitarian Intervention: Genocide in Rwanda*. Brookings Institution Press, 2001.

Lebeau, Suzanne. *Le bruit des os qui craquent*. éditions Théâtrales, 2009.

London, Charles. *One Day the Soldiers Came: Voices of Children in War*. HarperCollins, 2007.

Louyot, Alain. *Les enfants soldats*. Perrin, 2007.

Machel, Graça. *The Impact of War on Children*. Palgrave Macmillan, 2001.

Mandela, Nelson. *Long Walk to Freedom: The Autobiography of Nelson Mandela*. Back Bay, 1995.

McDonnell, Faith J.H.; Akallo, Grace. *Girl Soldier: A Story of Hope for Northern Uganda's Children*. Chosen, 2007.

McKay, Sharon. *War Brothers*. Puffin Canada, 2008.

McKay, Susan; Mazurana, Dyan. *Where are the Girls? Girls in Fighting Forces in Northern Uganda, Sierra Leone and Mozambique: Their Lives During and After War*. Rights and Democracy, 2004.

McMahan, Jeff. *Killing in War*. Oxford University Press, 2009.

McRae, Rob; Hubert, Don ed. *Human Security and the New Diplomacy: Protecting People, Promoting Peace*. McGill-Queen's University Press, 2001.

Meharg, Sarah Jane ed. *Helping Hands and Loaded Arms: Navigating the Military and Humanitarian Space*. McGill-Queen's University Press, 2010.

Mensah, Dr. David. *Kwabena Kwabena: An African Boy's Journey of Faith*. Essence Publishing, 1998.

Novak, David. *In Defense of Religious Liberty*. Intercollegiate Studies Institute, 2009.

Pearson, Glen. *A Land of Designs: The Saga of Darfur and Human Intentions*. Self-published, 2009.

Ramcharan, Dr. Bertrand. *The Quest for Protection: A Human Rights Journey at the United Nations*. The Human Rights Observatory, 2009.

Rosen, David M. *Armies of the Young: Child Soldiers in War and Terrorism*. Rutgers University Press, 2005.

Shephard, Michelle. *Guantanamo's Child: The Untold Story of Omar Khadr*. John Wiley & Sons, 2008.

Singer, P.W. *Children at War*. Pantheon, 2005.

Stratton, Allan. *Chanda's Wars*. HarperCollins Canada, 2008.

Walters, Eric; Bradbury, Adrian. *When Elephants Fight: The Lives of Children in Conflict in Afghanistan, Bosnia, Sri Lanka, Sudan and Uganda*. Orca Book Publishers, 2008.

Wessells, Michael. *Child Soldiers: From Violence to Protection*. Harvard University Press, 2007.

Westley, Frances; Zimmerman, Brenda; Patton, Michael. *Getting to Maybe: How the World Is Changed*. Random House Canada, 2006.

Zartman, I. William; Rasmussen, J. Lewis, ed. *Peacemaking in International Conflict: Methods and Techniques*. United States Institute of Peace Press, 1996.

RECOMMENDED WEBSITES

Amnesty International—Children and Human Rights
http://www.amnesty.org/en/children

Child Soldier Relief
http://childsoldierrelief.org/

Child Soldiers Initiative (CSI)
http://childsoldiersinitiative.org/

Child's Rights information Network
http://www.crin.org/

Coalition to Stop the Use of Child Soldiers
http://www.child-soldiers.org/home

Human Rights Watch—Child Soldiers
http://www.hrw.org/en/topic/children039s-rights/child-soldiers

International Labour Organization (ILO)—International Programme
    on the Elimination of Child Labour (IPEC)
http://www.ilo.org/ipec/areas/Armedconflict/lang—en/index.htm

Network of Young People Affected by War
http://www.nypaw.org/

Office of the Special Representative of the Secretary-General for
    Children and Armed Conflict
http://www.un.org/children/conflict/english/index.html

Save the Children
http://www.savethechildren.org

UN Child Soldiers World Map
http://www.un.org/children/conflict/_media/worldmap/worldmap.html

UNICEF—Children in Conflcit and Emergencies
http:www.unicef.org/protection/index_armedconflict.html

War Child International Network
http://www.warchild.org/

Watchlist on Children and Armed Conflict
http://www.watchlist.org/

ACKNOWLEDGEMENTS

Seventy-five years ago, Antoine de Saint-Exupéry crashed his plane in the Sahara desert, where he was stranded for days, suffering from unimaginable thirst, hunger, heat and hallucinations. It was ten years before he told his story, and when he did, he told it through the soul of the child he once was, about the child that is in all of us. *Le Petit Prince* was published in the midst of the Second World War. A book of sweet innocence, for an era of harsh experience.

That natural human transformation from innocence to experience often comes too fast, too soon, too cruelly. Such is the transformation from child to child soldier.

Since my return from Rwanda, the horrors that I witnessed have not left me. I carry them with me always, though I tried my best to release some of the demons in my account of that time, *Shake Hands with the Devil*. But there was one horror that I was not ready to release, one horror so terrible it was unimaginable, inconceivable, even though it was also a constant, tangible reality. A horror that exists to this day, around the globe, and which must simply be eradicated: the use of children as soldiers.

For their support to me in producing this book, I am grateful to the following:

Antoine de Saint-Exupéry, for creating a fictional child who exemplified the true meaning of childhood, reminding his readers that there are important things that only the young can understand, that only the young can express, and that only the young can accomplish.

My family: my wife, my children, and my first grandchild — in hopes that this new child never experiences, but always remembers, the plight of child soldiers.

Anne Collins of Random House Canada, my editor, my champion, my friend, for her encouragement and patience, plus her dedication to this project and the urgency of this cause.

My research team: Brent Beardsley, for his deep knowledge and strength; Jessica Humphreys, for her enduring empathy and gift for writing; Tanya Zayed, for her expertise and dedication to this book, to children affected by war and the Child Soldiers Initiative.

For leading by brave example: Ishmael Beah.

For sharing their personal stories, insights, expertise and support: BGen Greg Mitchell (Ret'd), David Hyman, Imran Ahmad, Col Joseph Culligan (Ret'd), Linda Dale, Scott Davies, Dickson Eyoh, Caroline Fahmy, Nigel Fisher, Dr. Phil Lancaster, Marion Laurence, Sandra Melone, Maria Minna, Michael Montgomery, Jacqueline O'Neil, Ajmal Pashtoonyar, Diana Rivington, Michael Shipler, Sarah Spencer, Zeph Gahamanyi, Leo Kabalisa, Ruth Kambali, Muhammad Kayihura, Franko Ntazinda, Solange Umwali and John Ruku-Rwabyoma.

Also for providing invaluable stories, insights, and expertise, the following organizations: the Canadian Forces (Col. Jake Bell); Dalhousie University Centre for Foreign Policy Studies (Shelly Whitman); Halifax Regional Police Department (Sgt. Penny Hart); Invisible Children; McGill University — Harvard Humanitarian Initiative (Dr Kirsten Johnson); The Network of Young People Affected by War (NYPAW); The Pearson Peacekeeping Centre (Ken Nette, Ann Livingstone); Public Inc. (Adrian Bradbury); University of Victoria School of Child and Youth Care (Sibylle Artz and Marie Hoskins); University of Winnipeg — Global College (Tom Faulkner); and Search for Common Ground.

And for their contributions, support, and thousand kindnesses: Victor Amissi Sulubika, Kimberly Davis, Helga Holland, David Humphreys, David Hyman, Alana Kapell, Hélène Ladouceur,

Casimir and Imogene Legrand, Findley Shepherd-Humphreys and Brock Shepherd, Alison Syme, my agent, Bruce Westwood, and the staff of Westwood Creative Artists, and the team at Random House Canada, especially the book's designer, Scott Richardson; the insightful artist, Ben Weeks, who illustrated the world of my fictional child soldier; copy editor Stacey Cameron; my publicist, Scott Sellers, managing editor Deirdre Molina; and production head Carla Kean.

INDEX

abduction, 15, 114, 115, 127, 129, 132, 146, 163, 164, 227
Accra (Ghana), 168, 217, 221, 223, 227
Achodo, Charles, 173
Acholi people, 135, 146
activism, 234–63
adoption, post-conflict, 158
adult leaders, 14, 15, 24, 25, 26–27, 29, 36, 39, 123–24, 131, 132, 135, 214, 225, 234, 236, 241, 262–63
Afghanistan, 126, 222n, 230, 252, 287, 288
Africa, 3, 12, 30, 104, 105–9, 222, 229
African Charter on the Rights and Welfare of the Child, 269
African National Congress (ANC), 244, 234
African National Congress Youth League, 244
"Africa's Forever Wars" (Gettleman), 115
age of majority, 158, 160
AIDS. *See* HIV/AIDS
Akallo, Grace, 144, 170
al-Bashir, Omar, 252–53
alcohol, 39, 118, 151, 178
ammunition, 121
Anglophone/Francophone conflict, 22–23
Angola, 229
Annan, Kofi, 169
apartheid, 163, 244–45
Aristotle, 242–43
Armed Forces of the DRC, 125
arms control, 120–21, 162
Army for the Liberation of Rwanda (ALIR), 148–49

Art of War (Sun Tzu), 143
Arusha Peace Agreement, 32, 38
Arusha (Tanzania), 242
Asia, 104
Athens, 13
Auma, Alice, 135
Aung San Suu Kyi, 246
Australia, 261
Axworthy, Lloyd, 7–8, 231

Balkan wars, 106
bandit groups, 111, 114, 115–16, 127–28, 129, 155
Bangladesh, 246
Bass, Gary J., 236, 251
Beah, Ishmael, 115, 132, 137, 156, 168, 222
Belgium, 35, 108
belonging, sense of, 25, 26, 114, 117, 128, 132, 145 (*See also* youth, disenfranchised)
Berlin Wall, 108
Betancourt, T.S., 128–29
bikes for guns, 161
birth certificates, 163
Bisesèro (Rwanda), 44–45
Bite of the Mango, The (Kamara), 140–41
Black, David, 228–29
blood diamonds, 3
border control, 115, 209, 229, 250, 259–60
Bosnia, 251
Botswana, 229
boy soldiers, 36, 37, 40–41, 42, 43, 63, 75, 78, 88, 129, 133, 156–67, 175

LGEN THE HON. ROMÉO DALLAIRE (Ret'd) served thirty-seven years with the Canadian Armed Forces and now sits in the Canadian Senate. His Governor General's Literary Award-winning book, *Shake Hands with the Devil*, exposed the failures of the international community to stop the worst genocide in the twentieth century. It has been turned into an Emmy Award-winning documentary as well as a feature film; it has also been entered into evidence in war crimes tribunals trying the perpetrators of the Rwandan genocide. Dallaire has received numerous honours and awards, including Officer of the Order of Canada in 2002, Grand Officer of the National Order of Québec in 2005, the Aegis Award for Genocide Prevention from the Aegis Trust (United Kingdom) and the United Nations Association in Canada's Pearson Peace Medal in 2005. As a champion of human rights, his activities include work on genocide prevention, the non-proliferation of nuclear weapons and the Child Soldiers Initiative, which seeks to develop a conceptual base for the elimination of the use of child soldiers.

www.romeodallaire.com
www.childsoldiersinitiative.com